# MASTERING THE ART OF 3D CONSTRUCTION MODELING

*The CD is an **interactive** index linked to **SketchUp** models, downloads, and **138** short videos*

The book **Mastering the Art of 3D Construction Modeling** and its accompanying compact disk are part of a series of books on construction graphics and visual communications. All in a graphic narrative style.

Copyright 2011 for the book and the CD by Dennis Fukai. All rights reserved.
**Printed in the United States of America.**

No part of this book or the accompanying drawings or compact disk can be reproduced in any way shape or form without the written permission of Insitebuilders, the publisher, except in a classroom, critical articles, or reviews. For information, contact **Barbara Fukai**, Insitebuilders, 16708 SW 132nd Lane, Archer FL 32618.

ISBN 978-09762741-6-2

SketchUp is a registered trademark of @Last Software, Inc. U.S. Patent 6,628,279. Made in the USA, Copyright 2004 @Last Software All rights reserved. 821 Pearl Street, Boulder CO 80302

1st Printing: February 2011
by Alta Systems Inc, Gainesville FL 32653

a publication of

i n s i t e b u i l d e r s

16708 SW 132nd Lane
Archer FL 32618
(352) 870-7127

babs@insitebuilders.com

## ACKNOWLEDGEMENTS

Thanks to Mike Lucey, Gaieus (Csaba Poszarko), Coen Naninck, Rich O'Brien, TBD (Tavi Chis), and the other moderators and contributors that hold the SketchUp community together at **www.SketchUcation.com**. This book and construction modeling in general would not be possible without their efforts and the help and guidance of the hundreds of members on **SketchUcation** forums.

Ask a question at the **SketchUcation** Corner Bar or in one of the discussion areas of their forums and an answer will be posted in minutes by one of a skilled group of generous experts. The **SketchUcation** site also includes links to detailed articles in their **Daily CatchUp** newsletter, tips and tricks, tutorials, components, materials, and the indispensable Ruby scripts by the geniuses that power SketchUp well beyond the standard free and pro versions available from Google.

And of course thanks again to my wife, **Barbara Fukai**, the editor, coordinator, sales, marketing, and publisher who makes this book physically possible.

Dennis Fukai is a licensed architect and construction manager with more than forty years experience as a professional construction administrator, researcher, and university professor.

He is a Fulbright Scholar and earned his PhD in architecture from the University of California, Berkeley. Dennis has been recognized internationally for his work in advanced construction modeling and graphic communications.

# CONTENTS
## MASTERING CONSTRUCTION

This book is an illustrated index of the step-by-step video **explanations** posted to the Insitebuilders video collection and **linked** from the book's CD. Look for the icons to find **embedded** links to videos and **downloads** that will help you master the art of construction modeling.

### 1. STARTUP
SketchUp install, menus, tools, model setup, modeling method.

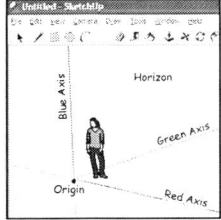

### 2. SITE SETUP
Site map, scale, model base, set workpoint and phase dummies.

### 3. SITE LAYOUT
Overview of drawings, site and setback layout from corners, visual scale.

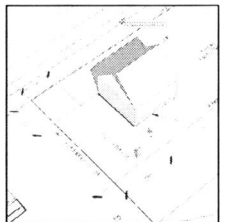

### 4. EXCAVATION
Set up batter boards, string lines, and lay down areas for the cut and fill.

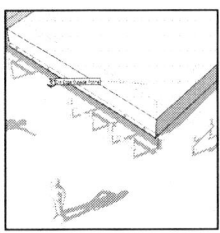

### 5. FOUNDATION
Forms for reinforced footing and concrete and masonry foundation walls.

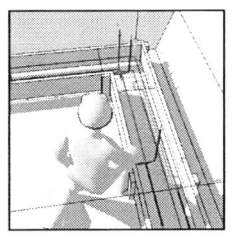

### 6. FLOOR FRAMING
Insert, scale, rotate and place, girders, joists, blocking, and subfloor.

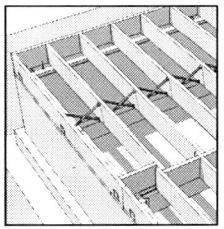

### 7. WALL FRAMING
Assemble studs, plates, sills, and headers for each wall in sequence.

### 8. ROOF FRAMING
Assemble headers, ridges, rafters, rakes, blocking and sheathing.

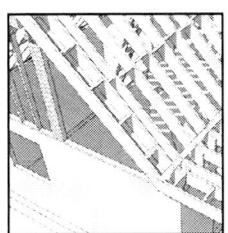

### RESOURCES*
Index of tips and tricks, buzzwords, and shortcuts in the book and videos.

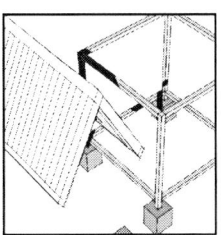

*The resource pages including the shortcut, buzzword, and tips and tricks indexes are in the back of the book

# 1. STARTUP  16 - 31

Download and install SketchUp, **review** menu and tools, and the built-in instructor. Set up Preferences, Model Info, Styles and **import** template and shortcuts. Use the three step modeling method to build **pieces** for the assembly.

### THE BASICS
01InstallSketchUp - Install SketchUp and startup
02ReviewMenus - Review the construction modeling menus
03ReviewTools - Review the construction modeling tools
04Instructor - Use the built-in Instructor and Help menus

### THE SETUP
05SetUpInterface - Set up the SketchUp Interface
06Preferences - Set up Preferences for the construction
07ModelInfo - Orient the jobsite with Model Info
08ModelSetUp - Stage the construction model

### THE MODELING METHOD
09Component2x4 – Build everything like a 2x4
10ComponentBlock –Build a typical concrete block
11FootingBlock - Assemble a block wall

..............................................................

### TIPS & TRICKS
01TypicalAssembly - Assemble with inferences, snaps, rotate
02SimplifyColors – Simplify colors and textures to focus on the construction
03HandlesHelp – Add handles to align and guide the assembly
04AlignHandles- Use component and group handles to align the pieces

05OutlinerOverview - Use the Outliner to organize your materials
06GuidelinesGuide - Use guidelines to lay out the construction
07HidingPieces - Hide pieces to edit the model
08ObjectInferences - Object inferences speed assembly
09ScenesSpeed – Use Scenes to speed construction modeling

### LINKS AND FILES ON THE CD
Chapter 1 - StartUp Checklist
Google SketchUp download page
SketchUp Reference Card
The completed model (for deconstruction)
Insitebuilders Template and Shortcuts file

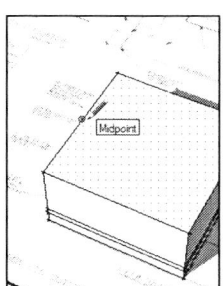

## 2. SITE SETUP  32 - 43

Import the 2D drawing and **resize** it to the real-world. Use the drawing to build the model base and **phase** dummies. Size the dummies to match the model base and assign to Layers. Control **visibility** with Layers and Hide/Unhide.

### IMPORT AND RESIZE
01ScaleDrawing - Scale the 2D drawing to the real-world

### EXTRUDE INTO 3D
02Extrude3D - Extrude the model base into 3D

### PHASE DUMMIES
03DummyLayers - Build a series of phase dummies and add layers

### USE LAYERS
04LayersAssigned - Assign the dummies to separate layers

### SETUP SEQUENCES
05SequenceDummies - Use the layers to sequence the phases

### RESIZE THE SITE PLAN
06ResizeAll - Resize the model base for the sitework
07SetWorkpoint - Lay out a workpoint to start the construction

..............................................................

### TIPS & TRICKS
01EraserTool - The Eraser tool deletes, hides, and smoothes
02FaceStyles - Change Face Styles during construction

03GoogleMap - Use Google Maps, aerials, and Google Earth in 3D
04PrintSend - Print a map or send a link location via email
05EmbedMaps - Embed the map on a website or a html email
06Screenshots - Use screenshots to capture images

07ScaleStar - Use the Scale tool to make a star
08LineScale - Scale a line with a temporary line

### LINKS AND FILES ON THE CD
Chapter 2 - Site Setup Checklist
2D drawings for the construction
150 Insitebuilders Components Library
Google Maps and Google Earth

*The printed pages are a **visual** index of the video **explanations** on the book's CD*

## 3. SITE LAYOUT    44 - 57

Review the drawing and crop the model base. Move the workpoint to the **origin** and set up Scenes to move around. Use **guidelines** to mark property and setback lines and cut the model base, locate site features, and **add** components.

**THE 2D DRAWING**
01DrawingOverview - Overview of the construction drawing

**SITE AND WORKPOINT**
02ResetWorkPoint - ReSet the workpoint to the origin

**SCENES AND VIEWPOINTS**
03SetUpScenes - Set up Scenes as saved viewpoints

**STAKE OUT THE CORNERS**
04MarkCorners - Stake out the corners of the jobsite

**LAY OUT CONSTRUCTION**
05GuidelineLayouts - Layout lines to guide the construction

**POPULATE THE JOBSITE**
06VisualScale - Give the jobsite a visual scale

• • • • • • • • • • • • • • • • • • • • • • • • • • • • • • • • • • • • • • • • • • • • • • • • • • • • • • • • • • • • • • •

**TIPS & TRICKS**
01Import&Crop- Import and crop an image in the model
02ImageStretch- Stretch an imported image to fit the site
03StayOrganized - Use the Outliner to name and organize the pieces
04ToggleOrbit - Use the Shift key to toggle between Orbit and Pan

05CheckPlumb&Level - Regularly check for plumb and level
06Dock&Undock - Dock and undock toolbars to customize your workspace
07ComponentLibrary - Build a custom component library
08GoogleWarehouse - Avoid the bloated models in the Google Warehouse

**LINKS AND FILES ON THE CD**
Chapter 3 - Site Layout Checklist
Plat map and satellite aerials
@Last Software Component Library

*Group and name pieces **immediately** to keep the construction model **organized***

## 4. EXCAVATION  58 - 69

Check the workpoint before placing the batter boards and string lines to **lay out** the location and depth of the excavation. Then use the excavation to shape a **massing** model for the backfill and rotate into place as a stockpile in the **background**.

### CHECK WORKPOINT
01WorkpointCheck - Use Tape Measure to check dimensions

### BATTER BOARDS
02PlaceBatterBoards - Lay out and position the batter boards

### STRING LINES
03StretchStringlines - Set up the string lines to guide the work

### EXCAVATE AND BACKFILL
04Excavate&Backfill - Excavate the foundation and stockpile the backfill

..................................................................

### TIPS & TRICKS
01OutlineExcavation - Review the Outliner to organize the excavation phase
02LayerControls - Review visibility controls to hide pieces of the model
03ZoomField - Change the field of view for the Zoom tool
04ZoomPrevious - Zoom Previous to go back to recent viewpoints

05InsideOutFlip - Reverse scaling and mirror flips to copy or edit assemblies
06MoveLock - Left, right, and up arrow keys lock moves and lines to an axis
07TypicalInferences - Use SketchUp inferences to speed the construction
08EquipmentOperation - Use handles as pivots to operate equipment

### LINKS AND FILES ON THE CD
Chapter 4 - Excavation Checklist
PickPic: Screen Capture
FastStone: Free image editor
Phase Dummies Model (site utilization and to deconstruct)

# 5. FOUNDATION    70 - 83

Make **simple** components for the pieces of the assembly and set up work areas to add visual scale for the footing formwork and **reinforcing**.* The rebar and J-bar in the forms visually **tie** the footing to the foundation walls.

### MAKE COMPONENTS
01MakeAnchorBolt - Make a three part anchor bolt with a washer and nut
02EmbedBlockDummy - Embed a component dummy in a concrete block
03BendJbar - Use Follow-me tool to bend rebar around a wireframe handle
04MakeStake - Scale a 2x4 to a point to shape a wooden stake

### WORK AREAS AND SCENES (AGAIN)
05LaydownWorkAreas - Set up work areas to scale and stage screenshots
06SetUpScenes - Reset the Scenes and viewpoints for the foundation work

### FOOTING FORMWORK
07PlaceFormwork - Build the formwork from scaled components
08PlaceRebar - Use guidelines to position the rebar in the forms
09AddJbar - Place J-bar components and array and rotate-copy

### PLACING CONCRETE
10PlaceConcrete - Place concrete into the forms and hide the rebar

### CONCRETE FOUNDATION WALL
11BuildConcreteWall - Snap lines to footing to extrude the concrete wall

### MASONRY FOUNDATION WALL
12BuildMasonryWall - Assemble the block to build the masonry wall

• • • • • • • • • • • • • • • • • • • • • • • • • • • • • • • • • • • • • • • • • • • • • • • • • • • • • •

### TIPS & TRICKS
01CopyArrays - Make quickly spaced copies in two ways
02MaintainComponents - Save and update component changes to your library
03FoundationOrganized - Organize the foundation pieces in the Outliner
04DividedAssemblies - Divide assemblies with the line and protractor

05OffsetMove - In tight spaces, move objects using offset references
06Scale2Fit - Add a component and scale to resize and fit
07HideSplice - Hide edges to form a seamless splice
08PumperOperation - Stage equipment and personnel for screenshots

Chapter 5 - Foundation Checklist

*Simplify components by minimizing edges and surfaces, eliminating color, and reducing file size

## 6. FLOOR FRAMING          84 - 93

Start by setting up the foundation **dummy** for the sill plates and anchor bolts. Add, scale, and copy the girder components to **support** the floor joists. Scale and array the rim and floor joists and finish with a **staggered** subfloor.

### FOUNDATION DUMMY
01FoundationDummy - Simplify the foundation with the modified phase dummy

### SILL PLATES AND ANCHORS
02Sills&Anchors - Add, scale, and rotate the sill components for the framing

### SETTING THE GIRDER
03SetGirder - Add the girder component and scale and copy to fit

### PLACE THE FLOOR JOISTS
04PlaceJoists - Scale and array the floor joists over the sills and girders

### STAGGERED SUBFLOOR
05StaggerSubFloor - Laydown sheathing in a staggered pattern for subfloor

### DETAIL THE FRAMING
06DetailConnectors - Add standard connectors from a component library
07MoistureProtection - Stage the moisture protection as a 3D detail

•••••••••••••••••••••••••••••••••••••••••••••••••••••••••••••••••

### TIPS & TRICKS
01RotateCopies - Make array and divided copies for fast modeling
02ReviewComponents - Add framing components and scale to fit

03PasteInPlace - Cut objects to a new file with Paste-In-Place for editing
04StayOrganized - Organize the pieces of the floor framing model

### LINKS AND FILES ON THE CD
Chapter 6 - Floor Framing Checklist
Insitebuilders Connectors file
Floor Framing Model (to deconstruct)

*Build pieces and components on **Layer0** then group and move to new layers as **necessary***

# 7. WALL FRAMING    94 - 113

Reshape the floor dummy and use the Tape Measure tool to lay out **guidelines** for the wall framing and rough openings. Use the Outliner to **organize** the nested assemblies. Select walls to copy, modify, and rename as new walls.

### FRAMING THE WALL
01FloorDummy - Shape the floor framing dummy as the base for wall framing
02BasicsWall01 - Build Wall01 as an overview of wall assembly process

### FRAMING AN OPENING
03OpeningWall02 - Build Wall02 with a header and sill at a rough opening

### ORGANIZE THE OUTLINER
04OutlinerWall03 - Assemble and organize Wall03 using the Outliner
05NestedWall04 - Use nested groups to organize each wall assembly
06TwistWall05 - Lay out and build Wall05 at an angle and rotate into position
07ReviewWall06 - Quick review of the wall layout and assembly process

### FAST COPIES AND FLIPS
08CopyWall07 - Copy and modify a completed wall and rename as a new wall
09ReviewWall08 - Review layout and framing of a window wall
10RotateWall09 - Rotate or flip copy a wall and rename as a new wall
11AlignWall10n11 - Use guidelines to align and position copies of walls
12ModifyWall12 - Copy an existing wall and modify plates, headers, and studs

### BUILD IN PLACE
13BuildWall13 - Install a two part wall and span the opening with a header

### INTERLOCKING TOP PLATES
14WallTopPlates - Add a top plate and copy, scale, and rotate to fit the walls

• • • • • • • • • • • • • • • • • • • • • • • • • • • • • • • • • • • • • • • • • • • • • • • • • • • • • • • • • • • • • • •

### TIPS & TRICKS
01WallTypeComponent - Add and modify walls from a library of wall types
02NestedGroups - Access and modify nested groups within groups

### LINKS AND FILES ON THE CD
Chapter 7 - Wall Framing Checklist
Insitebuilders Shortcut Index

## 8. ROOF FRAMING  114 - 131

Set up a wall dummy, then add headers at the **bearing** and entry walls. Lay out a template and use it to shape the gable walls, position rafters, and set the **height** of the ridge. Flip and **array-copy** the rafters on the ridge and **add** blocking and nailers.

### RAFTER SUPPORT
01DummyWall - Quickly reshape the dummy for the wall framing
02GableClerestory - Lay out and assemble the gable clerestory wall
03GableWall - Lay out and assemble the studs in the gable wall
04HeaderSupports - Set up headers at the bearing and entry walls
05RidgeBeam - Lay out the height of the ridge beam and set in place

### RAFTER AND BLOCKING
06ShapeRafters - Lay out and trim the rafters and array-copy along the ridge
07EastRake - Add rake rafters and fascia to the east side of the roof
08RidgeBlocking - Add ridge blocking and outlooks to stiffen the frame
09WestRake - Add rakes and blocking to the west side of the roof
10BlockingNorth - Flip copy blocking and rakes to the north side of the roof

### SHEATHING
11AddSheathing - Add staggered sheathing to the roof rafters

### DUMMIES
12RoofDummy - Simplify the roof and framing as a roof dummy
13SectionCut - Cut a section to expose framing details and phasing

•••••••••••••••••••••••••••••••••••••••••••••••••••••••••••

### TIPS & TRICKS
01LockUnlock - Lock objects to keep them in place while editing
02GuideAsRails - Use guidelines to move and edit objects in space
03DoubleClickEdit - Double-click in the Outliner to edit a piece or group

04NestedOutliner - Use the Outliner again to organize and nest the pieces
05SetUpSequence - Set up a Scene animation for the phases
06ExportIllustrations - Export views and animations as separate files
07FastFabrication - Use Group or Make Unique to edit a single component

### LINKS AND FILES ON THE CD
Chapter 8 - Roof Framing Checklist
Insitebuilders Buzzword Index
Roof Framing Model

## SHORTIES

These quick and simple videos explain the printed pages of the book with demonstrations that can be paused and played again (and again).

Quick tips and things to keep in mind as you work through the pages of the book and build your own construction models.

Downloads and links to models, programs, files, examples, references, and checklists found on the book's CD.*

• • • • • • • • • • • • • • • • • • • • • • • • • • • • • • • • • • • • • • • • • • • • • • • • • • • • • • • • • • • • • • •

If you have any problems viewing the videos or the models on the book's CD, please email or call and we will be happy to help.

**Barbara Fukai**
babs@insitebuilders.com, (352) 870-7127 Cell
16708 SW 132nd Lane, Archer FL 32618

## www.insitebuilders.com

*Models can be viewed with Google SketchUp, see www.SketchUp.com for the free version

# CONSTRUCTION DRAWING

*Construction drawing: See the book's CD for a printable PDF version of this drawing.*

2DDrawing

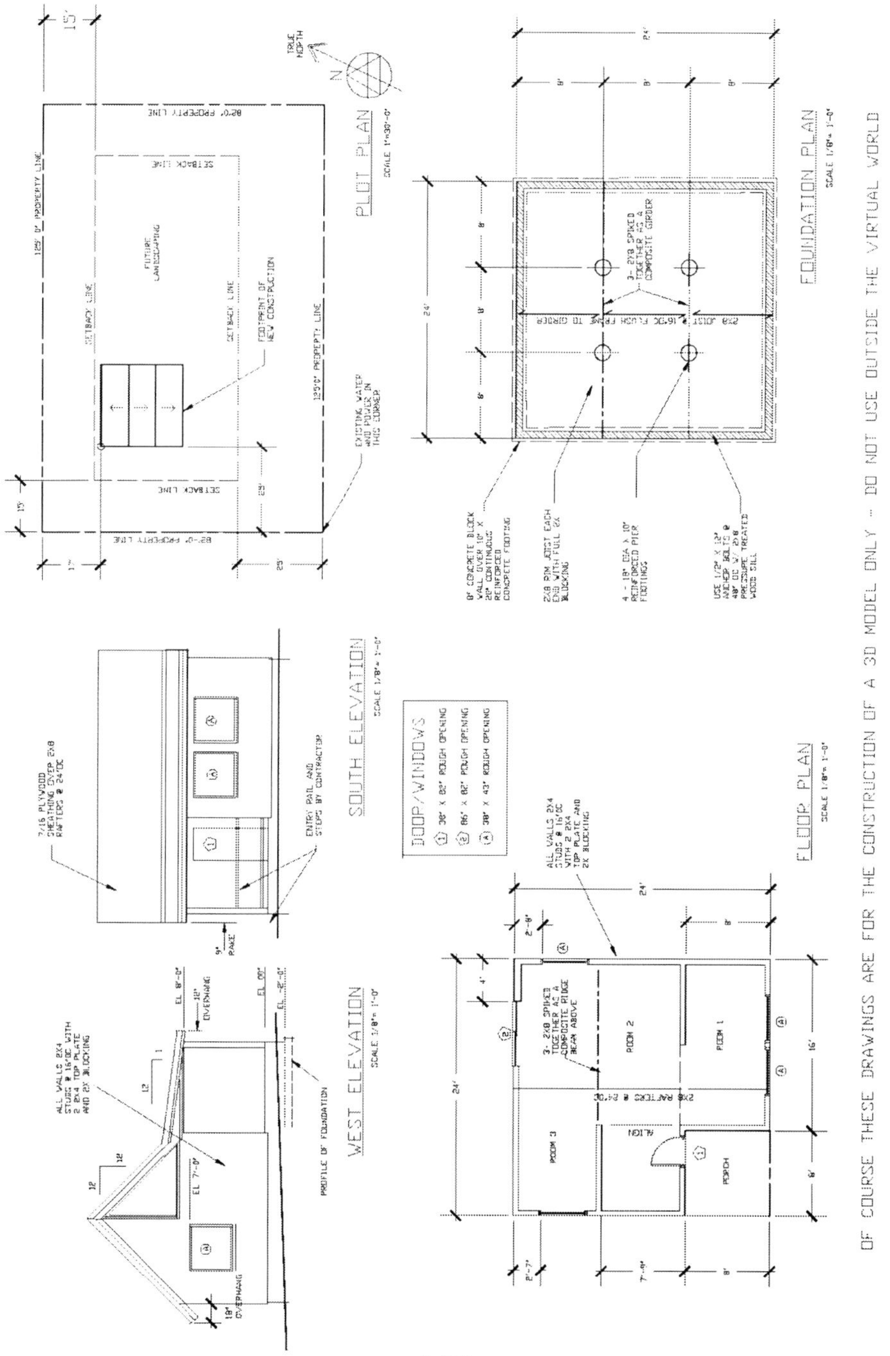

# CHAPTER 1. STARTUP

Visit the Google website to download the latest FREE version of SketchUp.

## INSTALL SKETCHUP

1. Go to www.sketchup.com
2. Click the download button
3. Save to your desktop
4. Open the installer
5. Follow the picks
6. Reboot and open SketchUp

Download and install the latest FREE version of SketchUp*

Go to  www.sketchup.com

## RESOURCE LINKS FROM THE CD

Virtual construction, just like **real-world** construction, is nothing more than using the right tools, a little practice, and knowing some simple tips and tricks. Each of the videos in this book **explains** something to keep in mind while you're working on your own construction models.

See these resources for even more tips, tricks, and tutorials:

SketchUcation: Tutorials and Tips and Tricks

SketchUp Wiki postings
SketchUp Sage collection
SketchUp Fans tips and tricks

GoToSchool list of tips and tricks
Bonnie Roskes's website

SketchUpVideos
Aidan Chopra's books

SketchUp Quick Reference card for Windows and Mac

Remember, these pages are a **visual** index to the video **explanations** on the book's CD

*SketchUp improves gradually over the years, but the tools for construction modeling remain largely unchanged

## Overview of a simple 3D modeler

### THE BASICS
SketchUp opens the first time with a Welcome Window and **startup** links.

### TEMPLATES
Import the **Insitebuilders** Template file from the book's CD and modify it for your own models. Templates give you a head **start** setting up a model format you can use on all of your projects.

Take a look at the menus

# MENUS AND TOOLS

Menus are similar to other programs, but rarely used because of the shortcut keys and icons.*

ReviewMeus

**View Menu** controls the toolbars and details you see

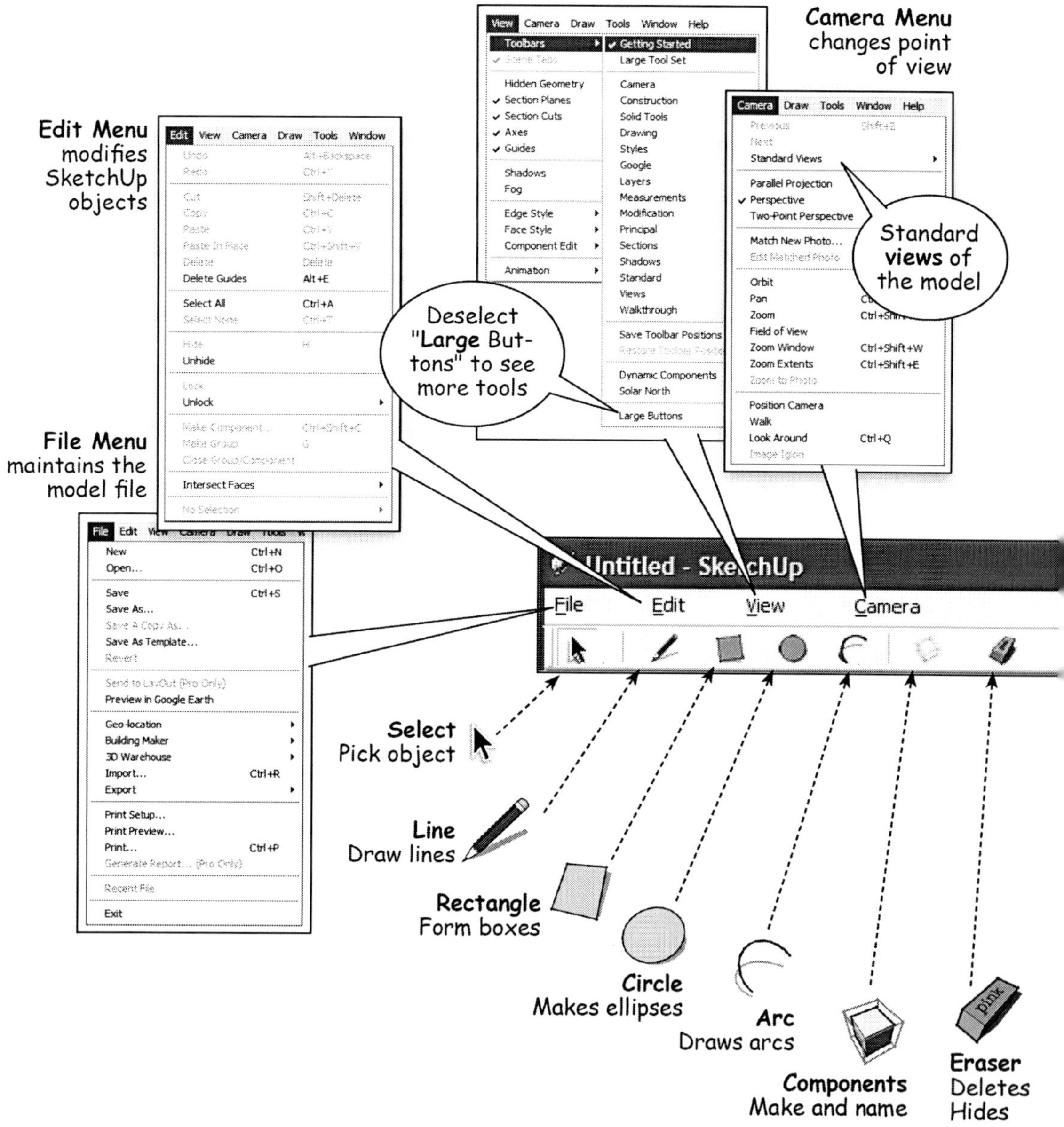

**Camera Menu** changes point of view

**Edit Menu** modifies SketchUp objects

Deselect "Large Buttons" to see more tools

Standard **views** of the model

**File Menu** maintains the model file

File  Edit  View  Camera

**Select** Pick object

**Line** Draw lines

**Rectangle** Form boxes

**Circle** Makes ellipses

**Arc** Draws arcs

**Components** Make and name

**Eraser** Deletes Hides

*Shortcut keys speed construction and minimize the time it takes to pull down menus and click on icons

ReviewTools

Take a look at the tools

## TOOLS
SketchUp **opens** with the basic tools found on the **Getting Started Toolbar**

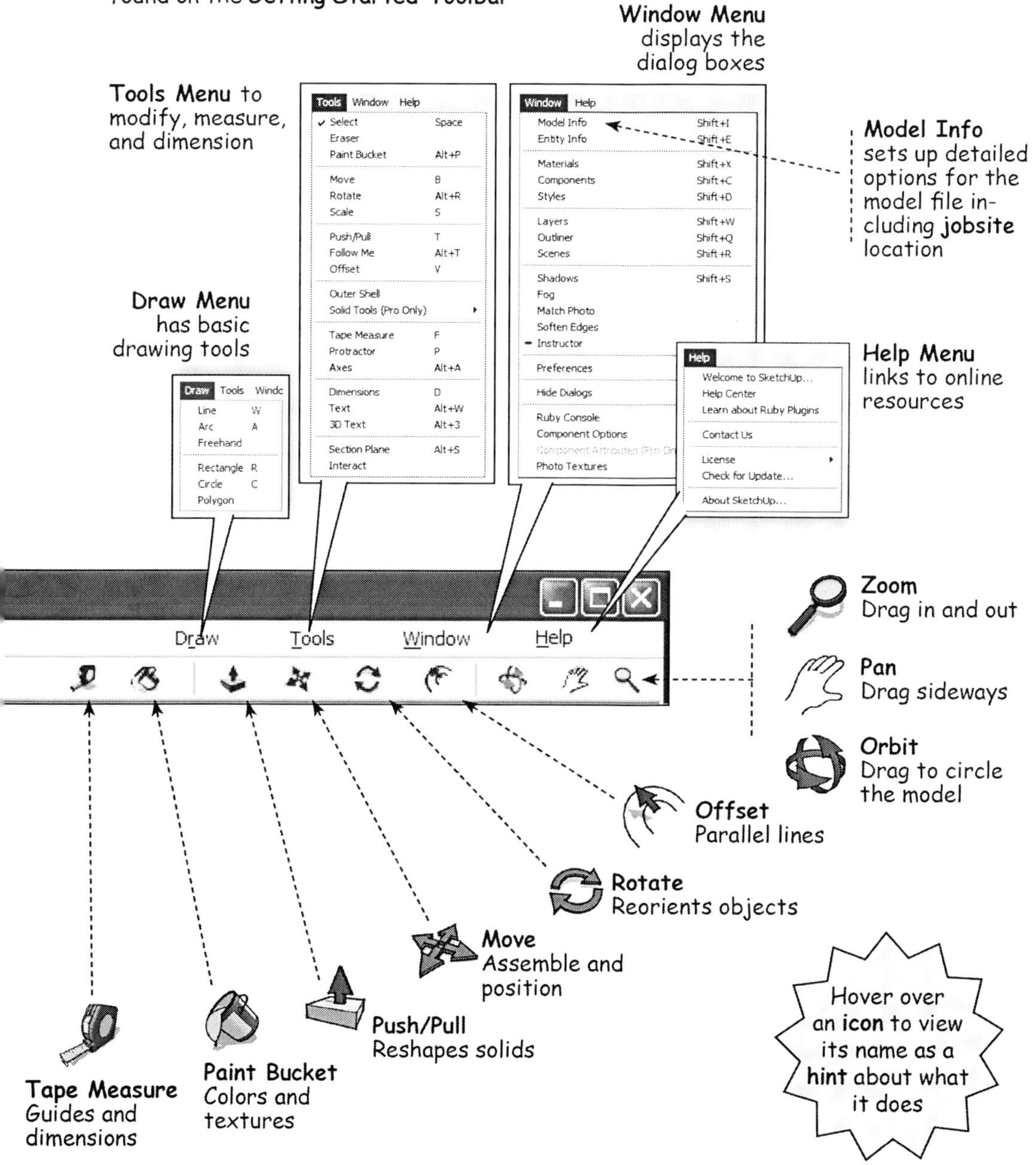

**Tools Menu** to modify, measure, and dimension

**Window Menu** displays the dialog boxes

**Model Info** sets up detailed options for the model file including **jobsite** location

**Draw Menu** has basic drawing tools

**Help Menu** links to online resources

**Zoom** Drag in and out

**Pan** Drag sideways

**Orbit** Drag to circle the model

**Offset** Parallel lines

**Rotate** Reorients objects

**Move** Assemble and position

**Push/Pull** Reshapes solids

**Paint Bucket** Colors and textures

**Tape Measure** Guides and dimensions

Hover over an **icon** to view its name as a **hint** about what it does

19

## Basic startup interface

Instructor

SetUpInterface

### SKETCHUP STARTS

Startup window **opens** with the Getting Started toolbar and a scale figure to **orient** you to the 3D space.

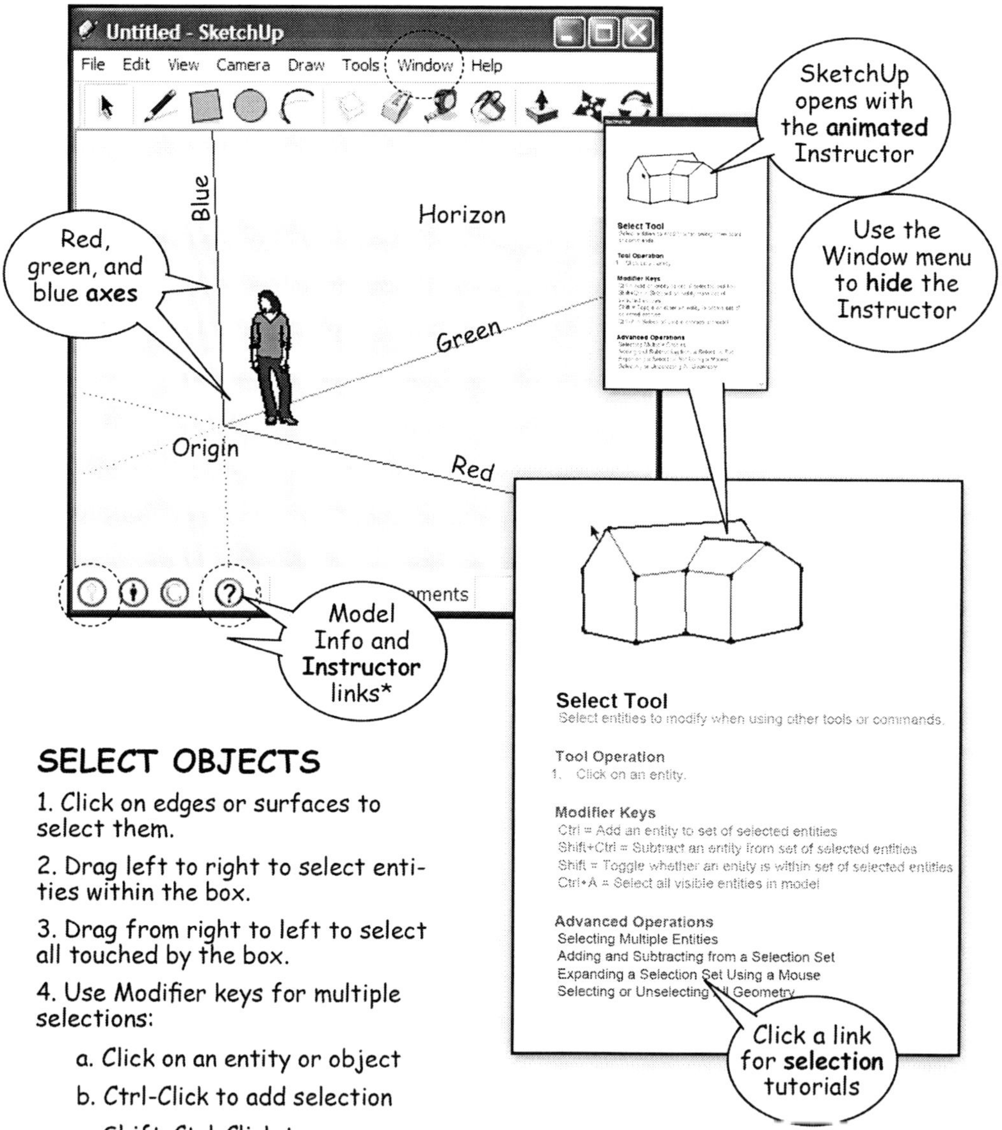

- Red, green, and blue **axes**
- SketchUp opens with the **animated** Instructor
- Use the Window menu to **hide** the Instructor
- Model Info and **Instructor** links*
- Click a link for **selection** tutorials

### SELECT OBJECTS

1. Click on edges or surfaces to select them.

2. Drag left to right to select entities within the box.

3. Drag from right to left to select all touched by the box.

4. Use Modifier keys for multiple selections:

    a. Click on an entity or object

    b. Ctrl-Click to add selection

    c. Shift-Ctrl-Click to remove

    d. Shift-Click to add or remove

    e. Ctrl-A to select all objects

*Click the "?" at the bottom left of the SketchUp window to open the Instructor for any tool, see also Help

9Tips&Tricks

Videos linked from the book's CD

## TIPS AND TRICKS*
For PC users, the three button mouse is an essential tool for zooming and panning for fast construction modeling.

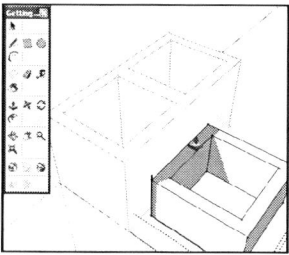
**01TypicalAssembly:** move, rotate and assemble objects with snaps and inferences

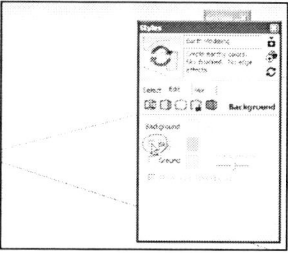
**02SimplifyColors:** avoid colors and textures to reduce file size and focus on the message

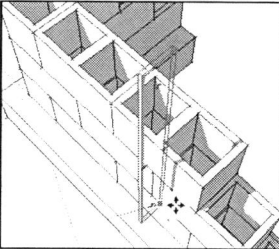
**03HandlesHelp:** use handles and wireframes to align and guide the assemblies

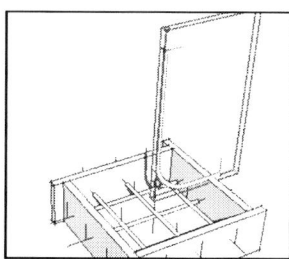
**04AlignHandles:** use component and group handles to align pieces in the assemblies

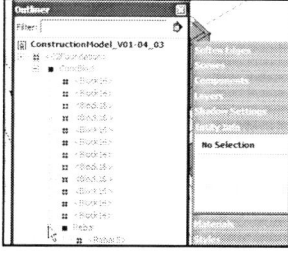
**05OutlinerOverview:** the Outliner is the key to organizing materials and pieces in the assembly

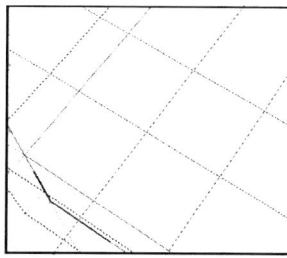
**06GuidelinesGuide:** use guidelines as construction lines to lay out the assemblies

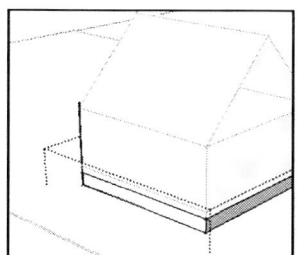
**07HidingPieces:** Hide and unhide pieces as you edit pieces and work on model details

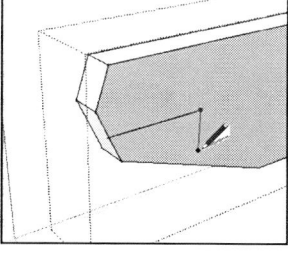
**08ObjectInferences:** inferences speed assembly by anticipating placement alternatives

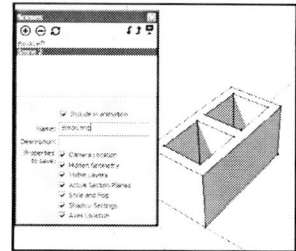
**09ScenesSpeed:** use Scenes to move around the model and speed the construction

*See the complete list of tips and tricks, buzzwords, and shortcuts at the back of the book and on the CD

Set up Preferences for the construction

Preferences

## SET PREFERENCES
Use the Windows Menu to open the **Preference** dialog box.  There are 10 **options** available to set up, but **only 4** are important at startup.

**Applications** links to an Image Editor

**Compatibility** sets groups and component visibility

**Drawing** changes behavior of Line tool

**Files** sets location of model resources

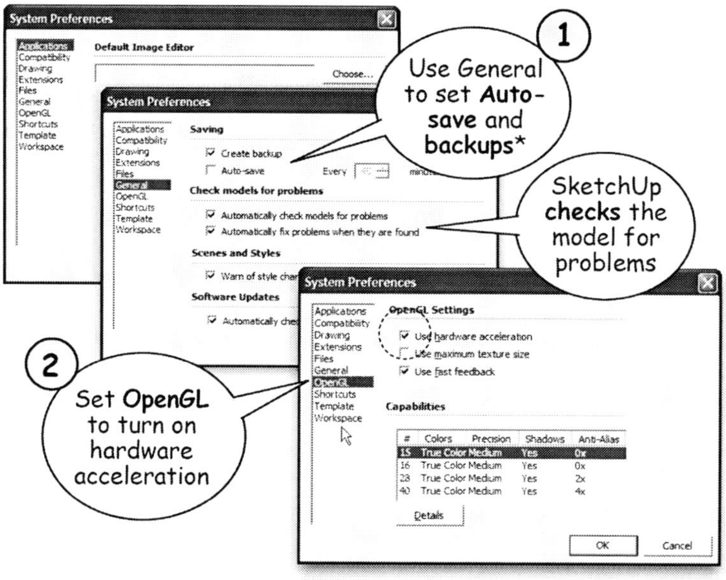

① Use General to set **Auto-save** and **backups***

SketchUp **checks** the model for problems

② Set **OpenGL** to turn on hardware acceleration

**Filter** searches for particular commands

**Shortcuts** are the key to fast modeling

③ Select a command then **key-in** a shortcut and click "+" to add it to SketchUp

InsiteShortcuts

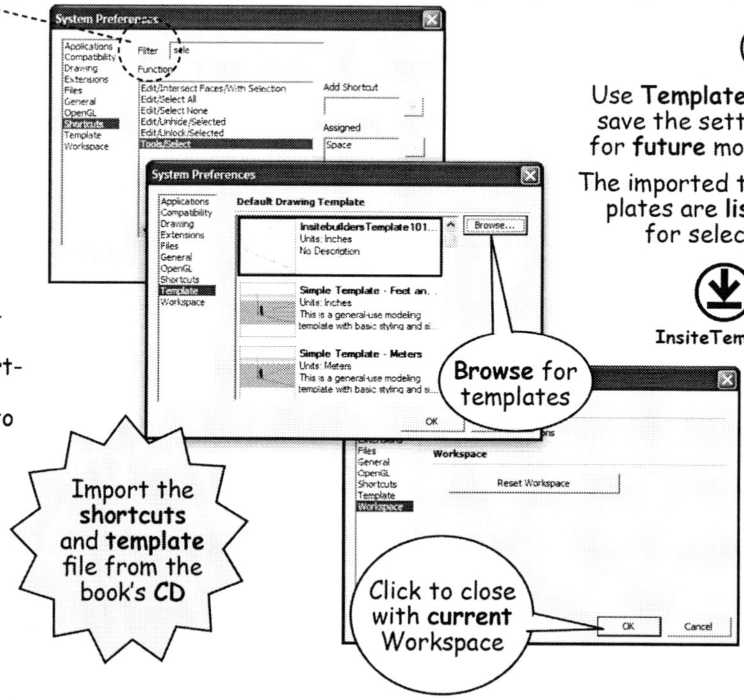

Import the **shortcuts** and **template** file from the book's **CD**

④ Use **Templates** to save the settings for **future** models

The imported templates are **listed** for selection

InsiteTemplate

Browse for templates

Click to close with **current** Workspace

*Use manual saves or longer Auto Save times as the file size increases to minimize delays waiting for saves

## Set up the jobsite with Model Info

# MODEL INFO

Select Model Info from the **Windows** menu. A dialog box opens with 10 options that can be set **anytime** after construction begins, **2** are important at this time.

**Animation** sets transition and timing for Scenes

**Components** changes editing visibility and axes

**File** information about this model

**(1) Geo-location** orients the jobsite to the earth**

**Rendering** enables material textures

**Statistics** lists an inventory of model elements

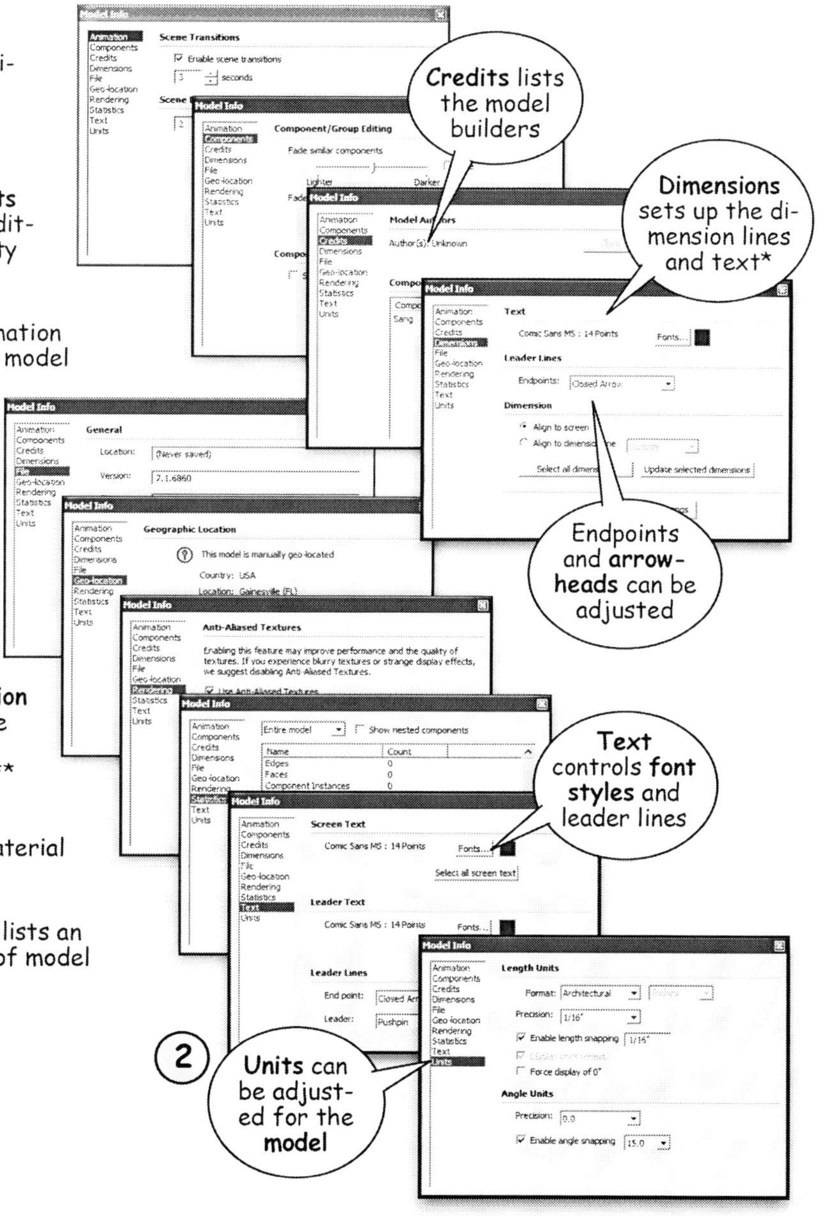

**Credits** lists the model builders

**Dimensions** sets up the dimension lines and text*

Endpoints and **arrowheads** can be adjusted

**Text** controls **font styles** and leader lines

**(2) Units** can be adjusted for the **model**

*Select and preview font styles for dimensions and detail notes for model annotations and text boxes

**Location is important to accurately project shade and shadow and visualize solar patterns during construction

Clear the jobsite of distractions

## STYLES DIALOG BOX
Use the Windows Menu to **open** the Styles dialog box. Pick the Edit tab and **check** the settings for the 5 different display icons.

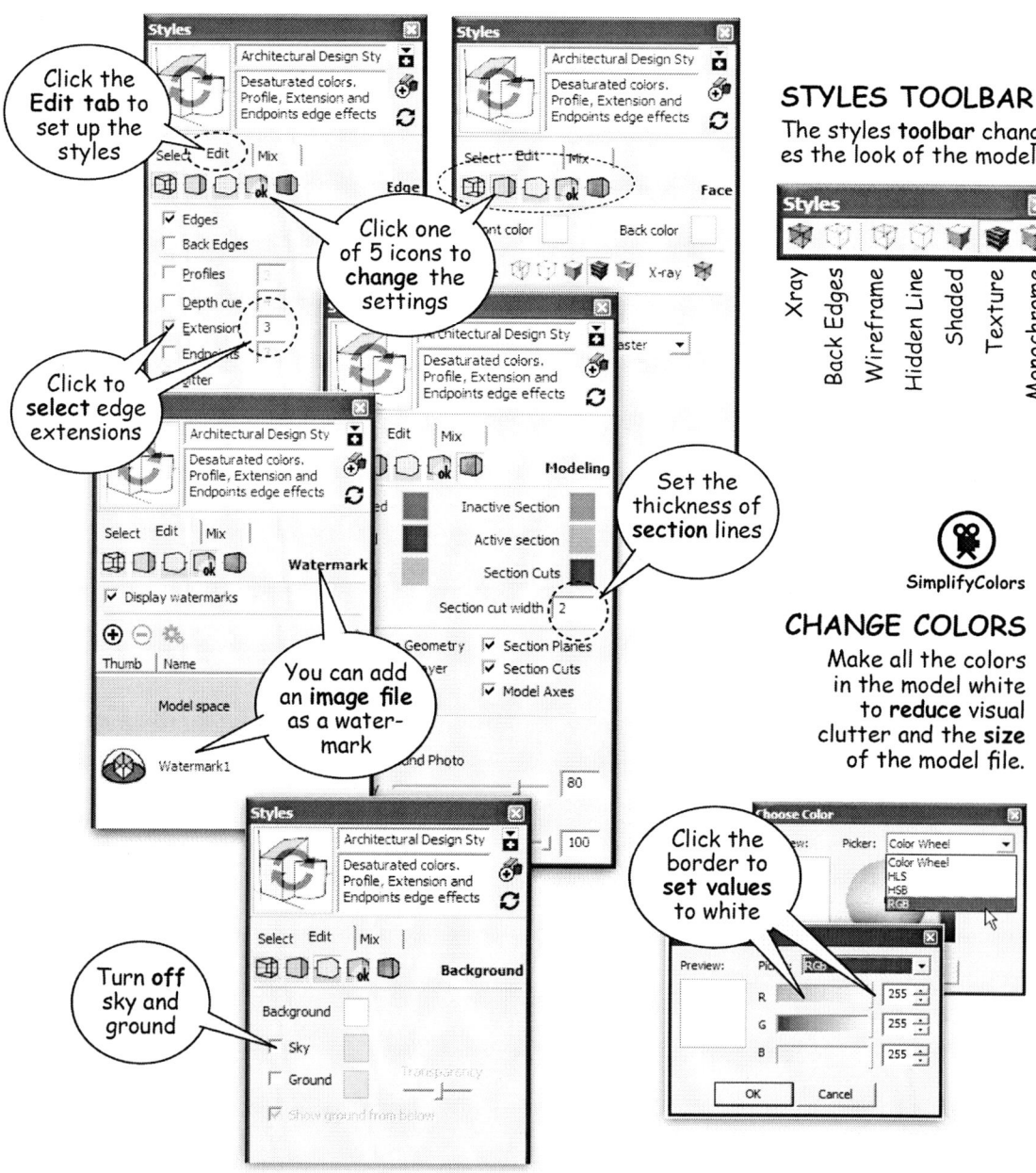

ModelSetUp

Finalize the model file for construction

## SET UP THE MODEL FOR CONSTRUCTION
Use the Window Menu to **open** the Materials, Layers, and Shadows dialog boxes, set up the Toolbars, and Save As a **working** template for **future** construction

Select Colors from the **pull down** menu

Use **white** and one or **two** grays in a model

Use Small Thumbnails to see **more** options

Click the title bar to **minimize** or drag to move

Click the **X** to close

Set time, date, and **shadow** density

Shade **without** shadow

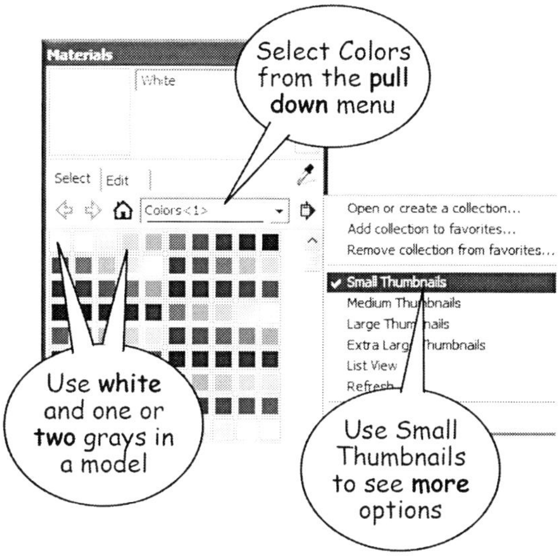

## TOOLBAR RESHAPING
Select any toolbar from the View Menu.
Drag the handle to undock and reposition.

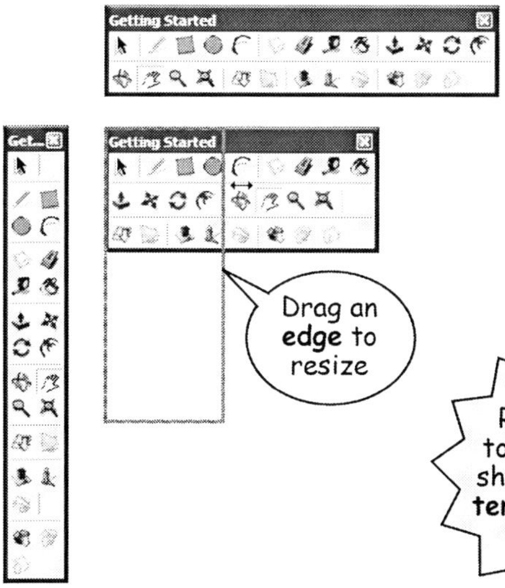

Drag an **edge** to resize

Name the template

## SAVE AS A TEMPLATE
When everything is set up, save the file as a template

Click to **save** the template for **future** models*

Remember to **install** the shortcuts and **template** from the CD

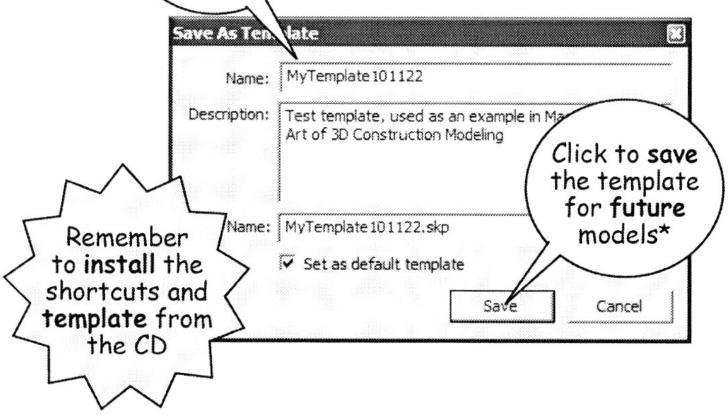

*Once the model is set up, use the File Menu to Save the file as a template for future construction models

# Fabricate the pieces for assembly

Component2x4

## THREE STEP MODELING METHOD
Every **piece** of a construction model is made using the **same** 3 steps:

**1** Drag out a 2D profile

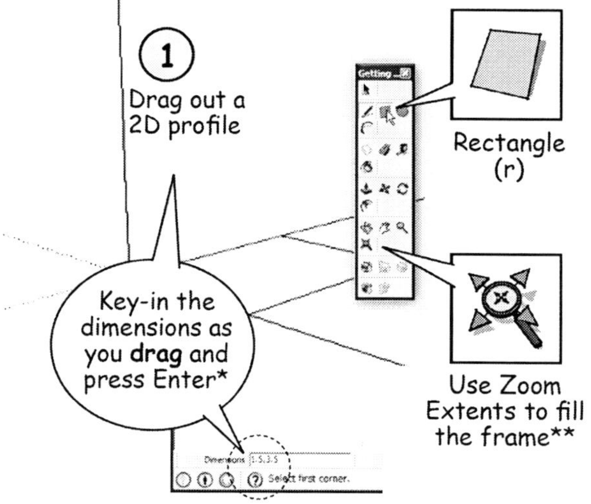

Rectangle (r)

Key-in the dimensions as you **drag** and press Enter*

Use Zoom Extents to fill the frame**

**2** Drag the surface **into 3D** with Push/Pull (t)

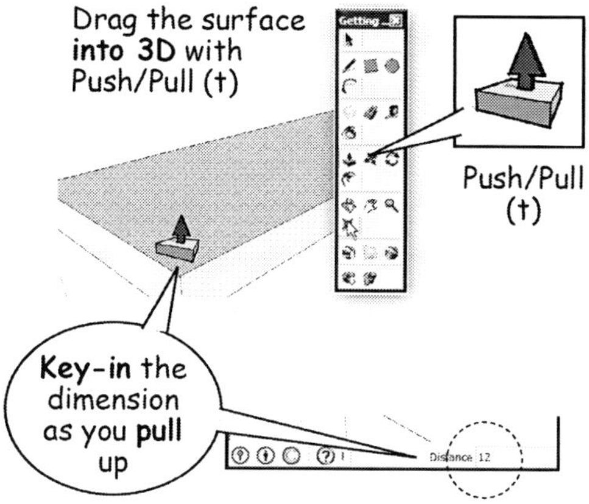

Push/Pull (t)

**Key-in** the dimension as you **pull** up

**3** Group and name the object to make it a "**piece**" ready for assembly

a. **Triple**-click to select edges and surfaces

b. **Right-click** to Group (g) or Make Component (Ctrl-Shift-c)

c. **Name** the group or component and it's ready for assembly

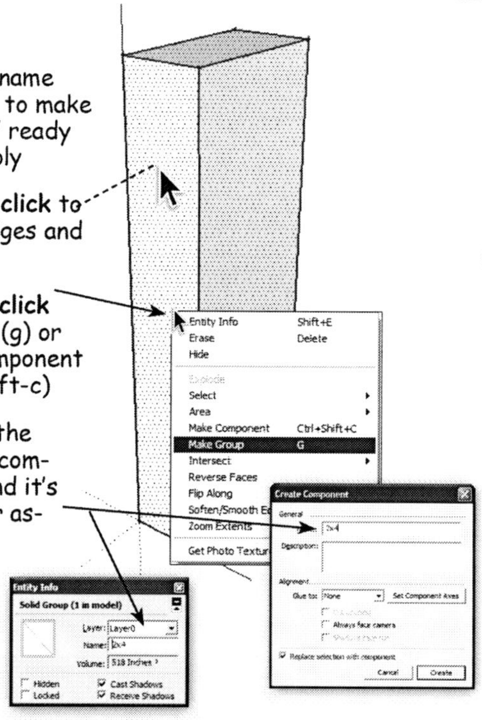

## EDIT OBJECTS

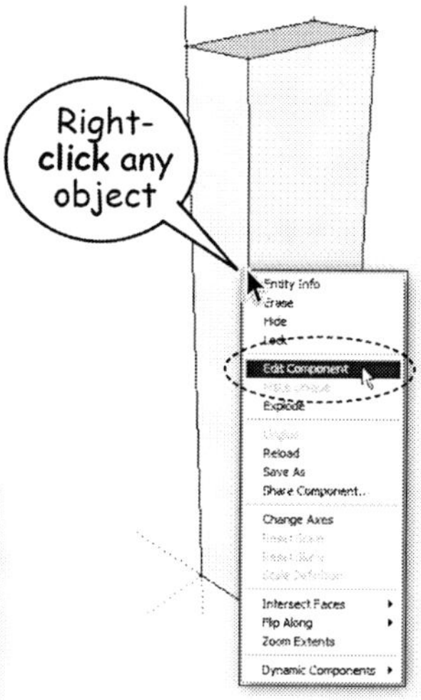

**Right-click** any object

*Enter width and height separated by a comma, with inches as plain numbers and feet with an apostrophe

**Zoom Extents to see the entire model or Zoom Window to bring objects closer for editing or assembly

 ComponentBlock

# Scenes and shortcuts for faster modeling

## SCENES ARE VIEWPOINTS
Use Scenes to set up key **viewpoints** to work and move around the model quickly

ScenesSpeed

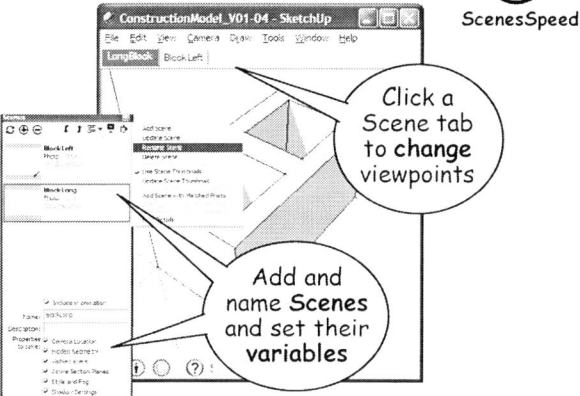

Click a Scene tab to **change** viewpoints

Add and name **Scenes** and set their **variables**

## SHORTCUTS & CTRL KEY*

 ShortcutsIndex

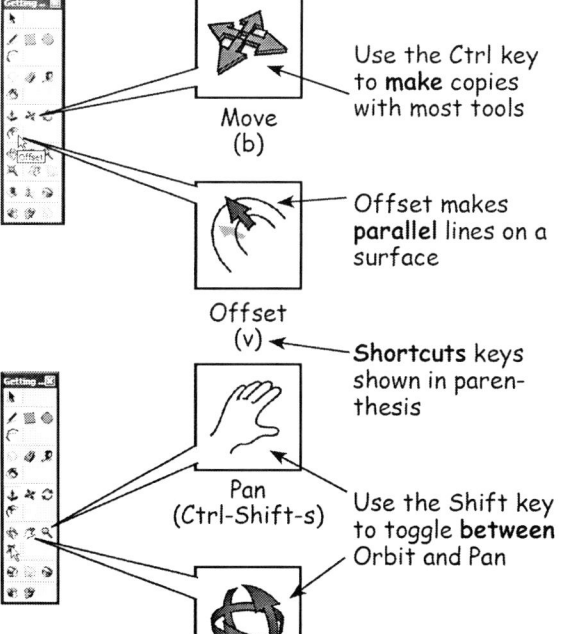

Move (b) — Use the Ctrl key to **make** copies with most tools

Offset (v) — Offset makes **parallel** lines on a surface

**Shortcuts** keys shown in parenthesis

Pan (Ctrl-Shift-s) — Use the Shift key to toggle **between** Orbit and Pan

Orbit (Ctrl-Shift-q)

## REVIEW THE METHOD
Use the same **3 steps** to build every piece of the assembly

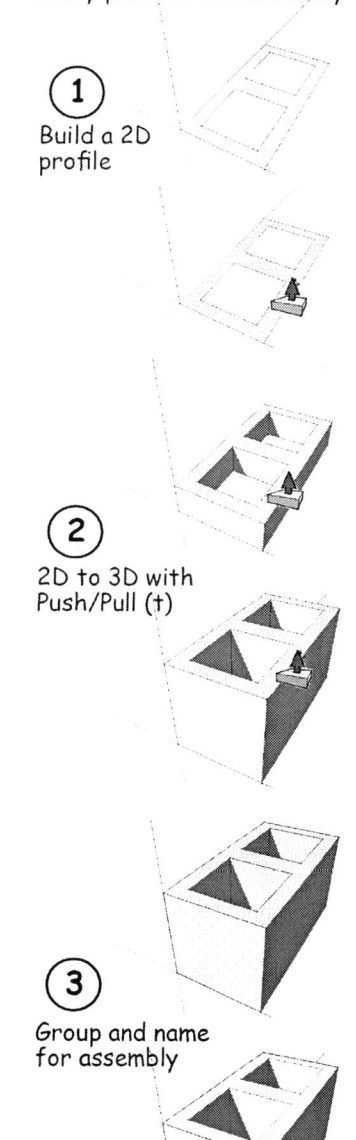

① Build a 2D profile

② 2D to 3D with Push/Pull (†)

③ Group and name for assembly

*For more on shortcuts, see the Preferences tutorial and the Shortcuts Index at the back of the book

Assemble pieces by snapping them together

 Typical Assembly   Object Inferences

# INFERENCES AND SNAPS
Snaps, rotations, and **inferences** make it easy to put the pieces of a building **together** in phases or as subassemblies of the **total** construction.

### 2D TO 3D
Double-click to edit **2D** groups or components to bring them into **3D**

Make the half block using the **3 step** method

Push/Pull to 3D

### OBJECT INFERENCE
Touch an edge or point on an adjacent object to **match** its height

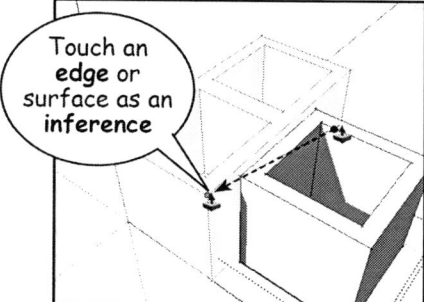

Touch an **edge** or surface as an **inference**

### CONSTRAINT
Hold the Shift key down to **constrain** along any inference axis

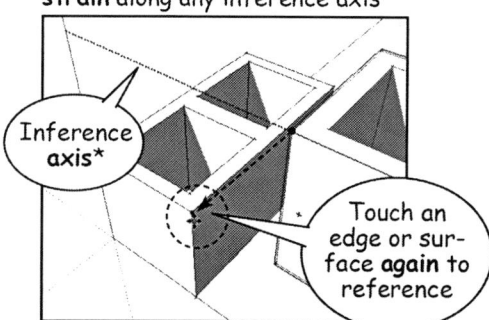

Inference axis*

Touch an edge or surface **again** to reference

### INFERENCE SNAP
Use inferences to snap objects **together** at corners and midpoints

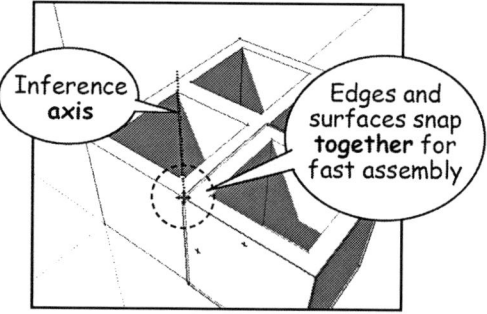

Inference **axis**

Edges and surfaces snap **together** for fast assembly

### SHIFT ROTATION
The Shift key **locks** the plane of rotation to set the axis of rotation

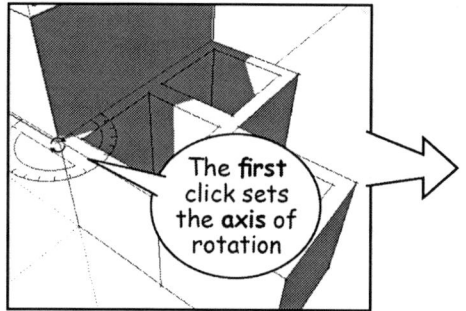

The **first** click sets the **axis** of rotation

### ROTATION ARM
Key-in degrees of rotation or click a **reference** point to set position

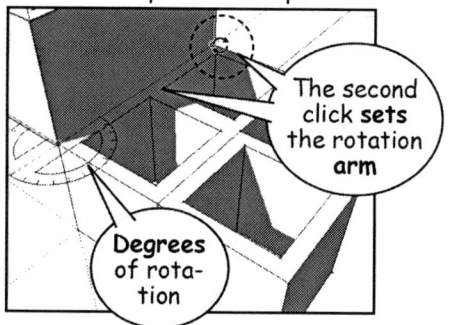

The second click **sets** the rotation **arm**

**Degrees** of rotation

*Inference axes match the SketchUp axes or a new axis parallel to a referenced edge or guideline

 FootingBlock  HandlesHelp

Use Move and Rotate Copy

## ASSEMBLING THE PIECES

Construction begins when individual pieces or clusters of objects are moved or rotated into position and snapped together for fast assembly

- Rebar placed using relative **geometry** of the block
- Select corner with the **Move** tool and click **again** to position
- Select multiple objects for **repetitive** assembly
- Form the footing using the **3 step** modeling **method**
- Use Push/Pull to **shape** the footing from a **2D** rectangle
- Add a **handle** and wireframe to position **small** components
- Toggle the **Ctrl key** with the Move or Rotate tool to leave a copy

GuidelineGuides

AlignHandles

29

# CHAPTER 1 CHECKLISTS - STARTUP

StartUpChecklist

## A. THE BASICS
Download and **install** SketchUp, then take a quick look at the menus, getting started tools, and **short video** tutorials on the Instructor.

- [ ] Download the free version of SketchUp
- [ ] Install SketchUp and reboot
- [ ] Open the program to the Welcome Window
- [ ] Choose Template
- [ ] Deselect "Always shown... "
- [ ] Click Start using SketchUp
- [ ] Review the Menus and tools
- [ ] Explore Help and the Instructor

## B. THE SETUP
Set up Preferences, Model Info, Styles and Save As a template or **import** the **template** and **shortcuts** from the book's CD for your first model.

- [ ] Set Auto Save timer
- [ ] Select hardware acceleration
- [ ] Geo-location set to the jobsite
- [ ] Turn Profiles off
- [ ] Set extensions to 3 pixels
- [ ] Reset all colors to white
- [ ] Deselect sky and ground
- [ ] Set Section cut width to 2 pixels
- [ ] Use Small Thumbnails in the Materials box
- [ ] Set date and time in Shadows Dialog box

## C. THE MODELING METHOD

Use the **three step** modeling method to build groups and components as pieces for the assembly using **inferences** and object **snaps**.

- ☐ Lay out the object in 2D
- ☐ Push/Pull the object into 3D
- ☐ Group and name the object as a piece
- ☐ Groups and components must be named
- ☐ Shortcuts are faster than menus & toolbars
- ☐ Add and update Scenes for fast modeling
- ☐ Right-click for a context menu to edit
- ☐ Ctrl key toggles copies
- ☐ Shift key toggles Orbit and Pan
- ☐ Assemble using inferences and snaps

## D. TIPS, TRICKS AND RESOURCES

Click on the **Instructor** icon for quick videos on selected tools, use shortcut keys for speed, and **Scenes** to quickly move around the model.

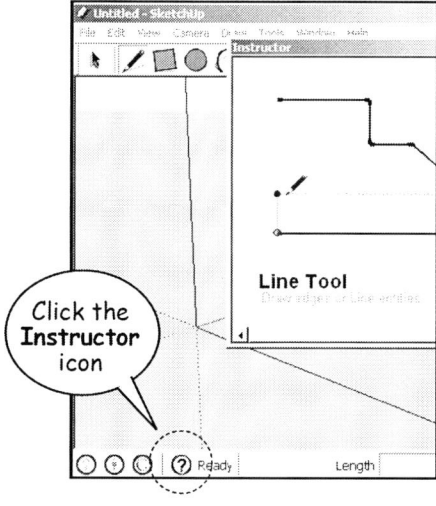

- ☐ Simple interface
- ☐ Basic assembly
- ☐ Add a footing
- ☐ Setting rebar
- ☐ The Outliner
- ☐ Guideline layouts
- ☐ Hide and Unhide
- ☐ Segment spacing

- ☐ SketchUp Reference card
- ☐ Insitebuilders Template file
- ☐ Insitebuilders Shortcut file
- ☐ The completed model

# CHAPTER 2. SITE SETUP

Use the two-dimensional **drawings** from the book's CD to **set up** the model base for the construction.*

**2dDrawings**

- Resized phase dummy on **scaled** site plan
- **Import** and **scale** the 2D drawing to start construction**
- Dummies **represent** construction phases

**PHASE DUMMIES**

Modeled **over** the scaled foundation plan

- ROOF FRAMING
- WALL FRAMING
- FLOOR FRAMING
- FOUNDATION

Push/Pull the **base** down from plan **edges**

- Work-point
- Door and window schedule
- North

**ELEVATIONS**

**SITE PLAN**

**FLOOR PLAN**

**FOUNDATION PLAN**

**CONSTRUCTION DRAWINGS**

*See Chapter 3 for an overview of the construction drawing and details of the scope of the model

**Import and scale the foundation plan to match the foundation plan and scale again to match the site plan

Preview these tips and tricks

## TIPS AND TRICKS

SketchUp will fail, setting **Auto Save** helps, but it's much better to continually save **new** versions of the same model file to create a series of **backups**.

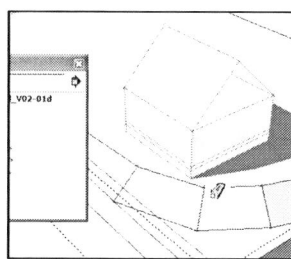

**01EraserTool:**
use this tool to delete, hide, and smooth pieces of the model assembly

**02FaceStyles:**
change Face Styles to xray, white out, or see back edges of the model

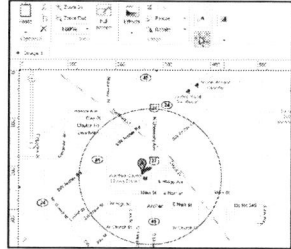

**03ScreenShots:**
capture images of the model to annotate and illustrate details*

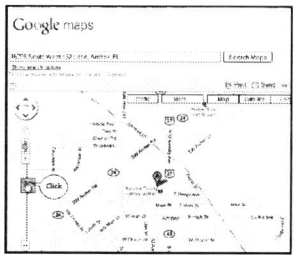

**04GoogleMaps:**
Use Google maps to capture vicinity maps and satellite views of the site

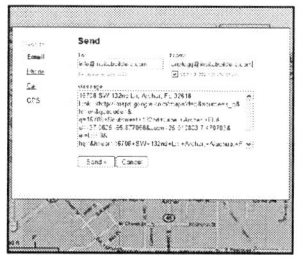

**05PrintSend:**
Print a map or send a link as an annotated vicinity map of the jobsite

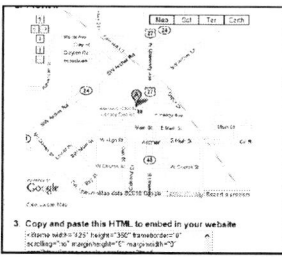

**06EmbedMaps:**
embed the map or aerial views on a web page or in an HTML email

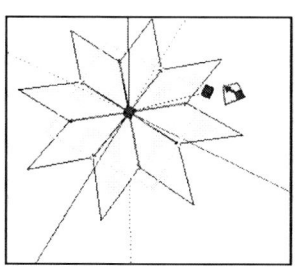

**07ScaleStar:**
demonstrates the use of the Scale tool to make a star with Ctrl Scale

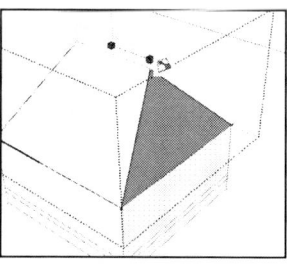

**08LineScale:**
Scale a line by grouping it with a parallel copy, then deleting the copy

Use shade and shadow to **simulate** solar exposure on the jobsite.

Turn-off shade and shadow to **reduce** calculations and **speed** construction as the model gets more **complex**

*See the CD for links to PickPic and Faststone, two open source screen capture and image editing programs

**33**

# Resize the foundation plan to the real world

ScaleDrawings

## IMPORT THE 2D DRAWING
SketchUp imports JPEG, PNG, TIFF, and bitmap file formats as **floating** two dimensional objects.* Double-click at the **origin** to drop the 2D drawing into 3D model space.

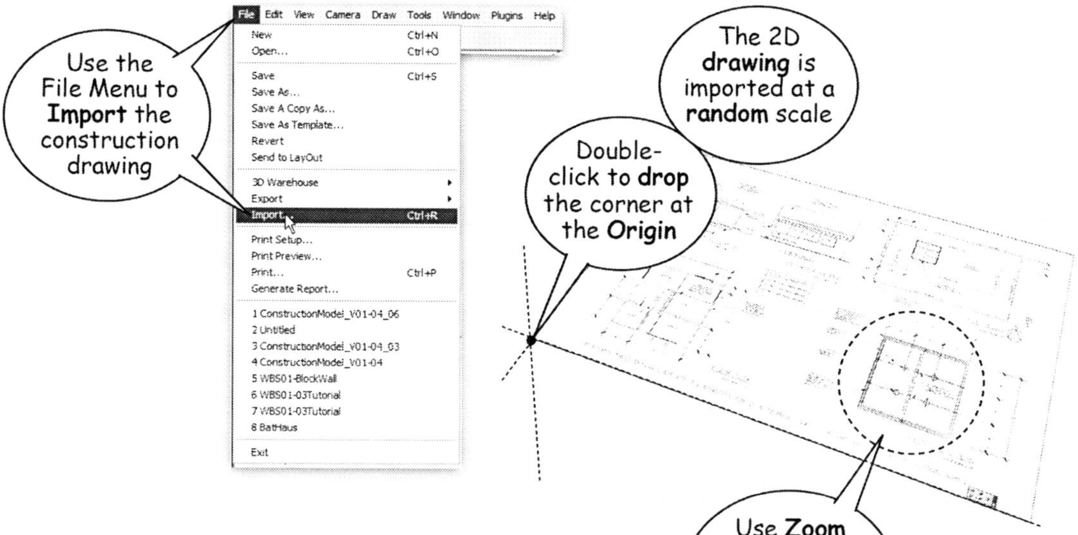

Use the File Menu to **Import** the construction drawing

The 2D **drawing** is imported at a **random** scale

Double-click to **drop** the corner at the **Origin**

Use **Zoom Window** (Ctrl-Shift-w) to zoom into the drawing

## SCALE THE 2D DRAWING
Use the Tape Measure tool to **resize** the imported drawing to **match** the scale of the real world

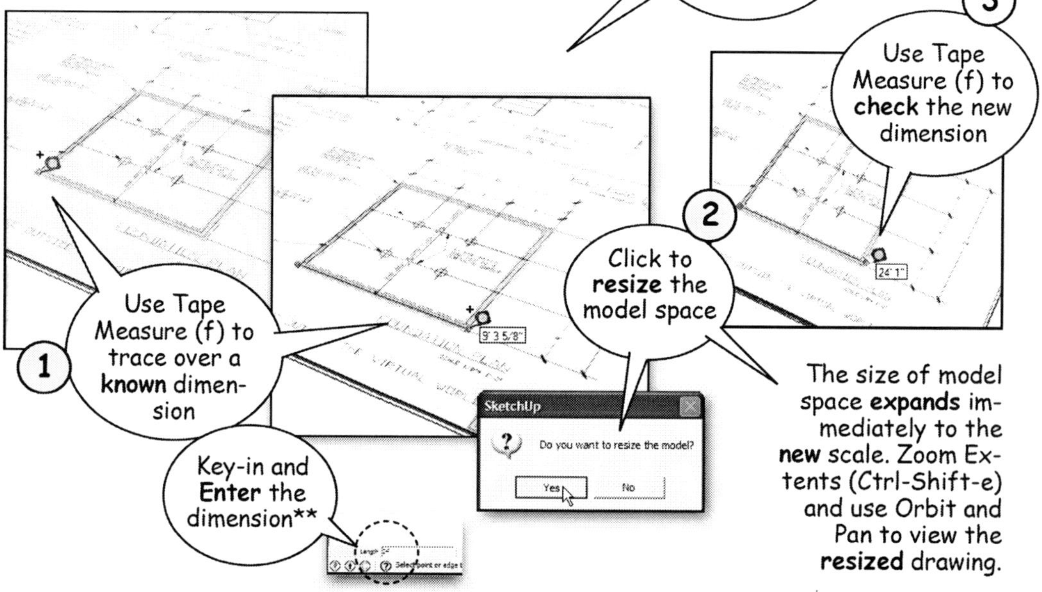

① Use Tape Measure (f) to trace over a **known** dimension

Key-in and **Enter** the dimension**

② Click to **resize** the model space

③ Use Tape Measure (f) to **check** the new dimension

The size of model space **expands** immediately to the **new** scale. Zoom Extents (Ctrl-Shift-e) and use Orbit and Pan to view the **resized** drawing.

*A bit map file is a digitally compressed image like a scan, digital photograph, or bitmap illustration

**Key-in the new dimension and press Enter at any time while the tool action remains active

Extrude3D

## Use the drawing to build a model base

### EXTRUDE THE MODEL BASE
Drag out a rectangle to trace the **edges** of the construction drawing to build the top **2D** surface of the model base, then Push/Pull the surface **down** to form the **3D** box.

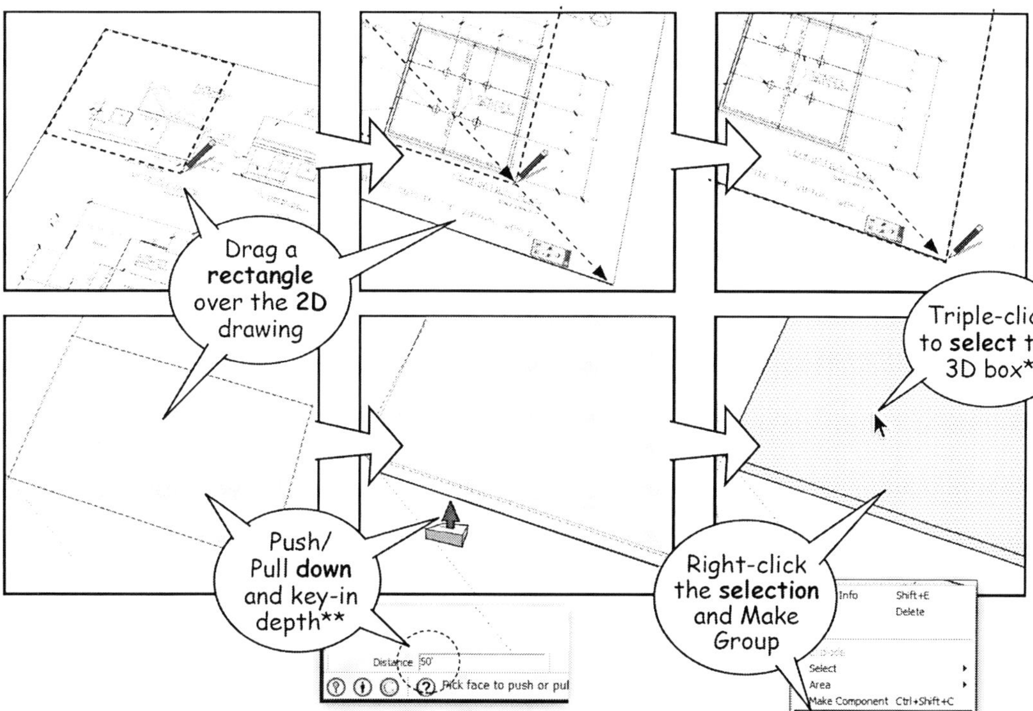

Drag a **rectangle** over the **2D** drawing

Triple-click to **select** the 3D box*

Push/Pull **down** and key-in depth**

Right-click the **selection** and Make Group

### EXPLODE THE IMPORTED DRAWING
Explode, group, and name the imported image so that it can be controlled as a separate object.

Click to **select** the drawing

Move the image **up** the blue axis **into** view

Right-click and **Explode** the drawing

Group and **name** the exploded drawing

Always **name** groups and components

*Double-click to select the surface and triple-click to select the 3D object, then group and name as a solid

**Pull the surface down deeper than the anticipated foundation, excavation, or other subsurface sitework

# Build the component phase dummies

DummyLayers

## SET UP DUMMIES

Dummies are built on the face of the 2D drawing to help **visualize** the **scope** of the work and plan the construction. They are reshaped **later** to match the framing and used to reduce the **level of detail** as the model gets more complex.

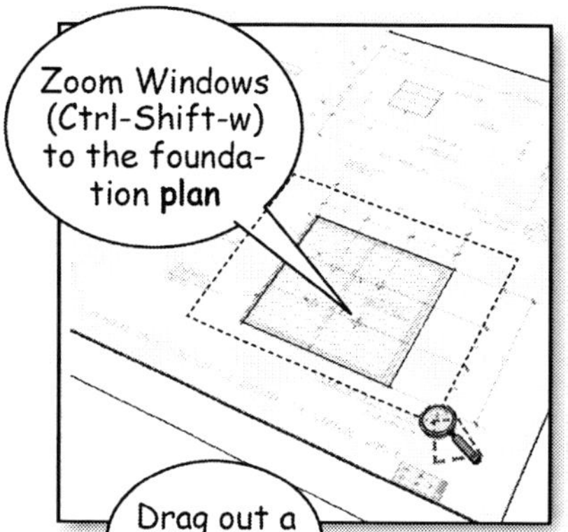

Use the **three step** fabrication method to build each of the dummies.

1. Draw the object profile in **2D**.
2. Push/Pull the surface into **3D**.
3. Group and name the object as a **piece** of an assembly.

*Zoom Windows (Ctrl-Shift-w) to the foundation **plan***

*Drag out a **rectangle*** — 1

*Push/Pull to **form** the foundation **dummy***

2 — *Triple-click to **select** the dummy*

*Right-click and **Make Component***

*Name the Component as a **piece** of the assembly* — 3

*Objects are **loose** edges and surfaces until **joined** as a Group or Component*

LayersAssigned

Place each dummy on a separate layer

## LAYERS SEPARATE
Use layers to **separate** large groups such as phases or **subassemblies** and **control** their visibility in the model.

Each **phase** of construction is represented by a **dummy**

### ROOF FRAMING
Ridge beam, rafters, blocking, outlooks, fascias and rakes.

### WALL FRAMING
Studs, plates, blocking, and headers and jambs at openings.

Each **dummy** is identified by a **different** name on the Outliner

### FLOOR FRAMING
Foundation sills, anchor bolts, floor girders, joists, and posts.

### FOUNDATION
Layout, excavation, footings, reinforcing, concrete, and block.

Each **dummy** is transferred to a **separate** layer*

Add a new **layer** for each **phase** of the construction

Click Layer to **select** new layer

### NOTE
Both the foundation drawing and dummies are at the scale of the real world.

FaceStyles

## QUICK ROOF SHAPE
The line **cuts** the rectangle's surface. Moving the line in any direction stretches and **reshapes** the surface.

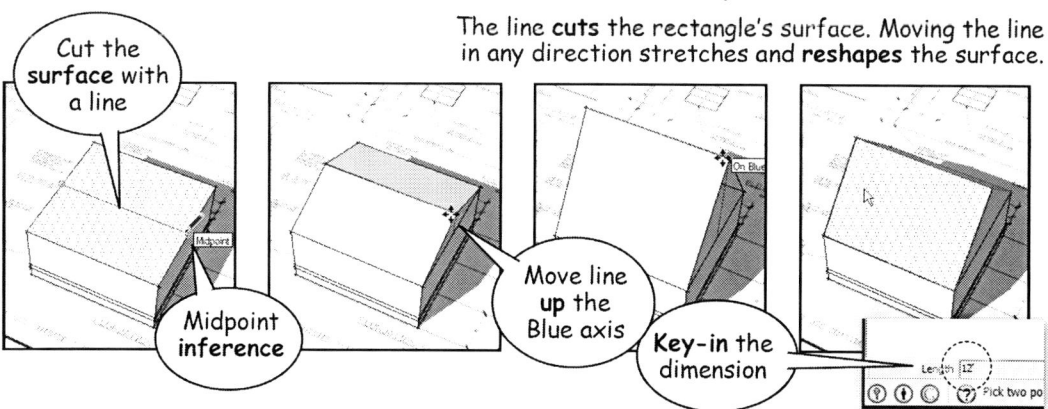

Cut the **surface** with a line

Midpoint inference

Move line **up** the Blue axis

**Key-in** the dimension

*Build pieces on Layer0, then transfer grouped assemblies or distinct objects to separate layers for display

**37**

# Visually control the sequence of dummies

SequenceDummies

## VISUALIZATION

The dummies are **sequenced** on separate layers to **control** visibility and animate the construction process.

When dummies are components they can be **saved** as separate files in a component reference library.

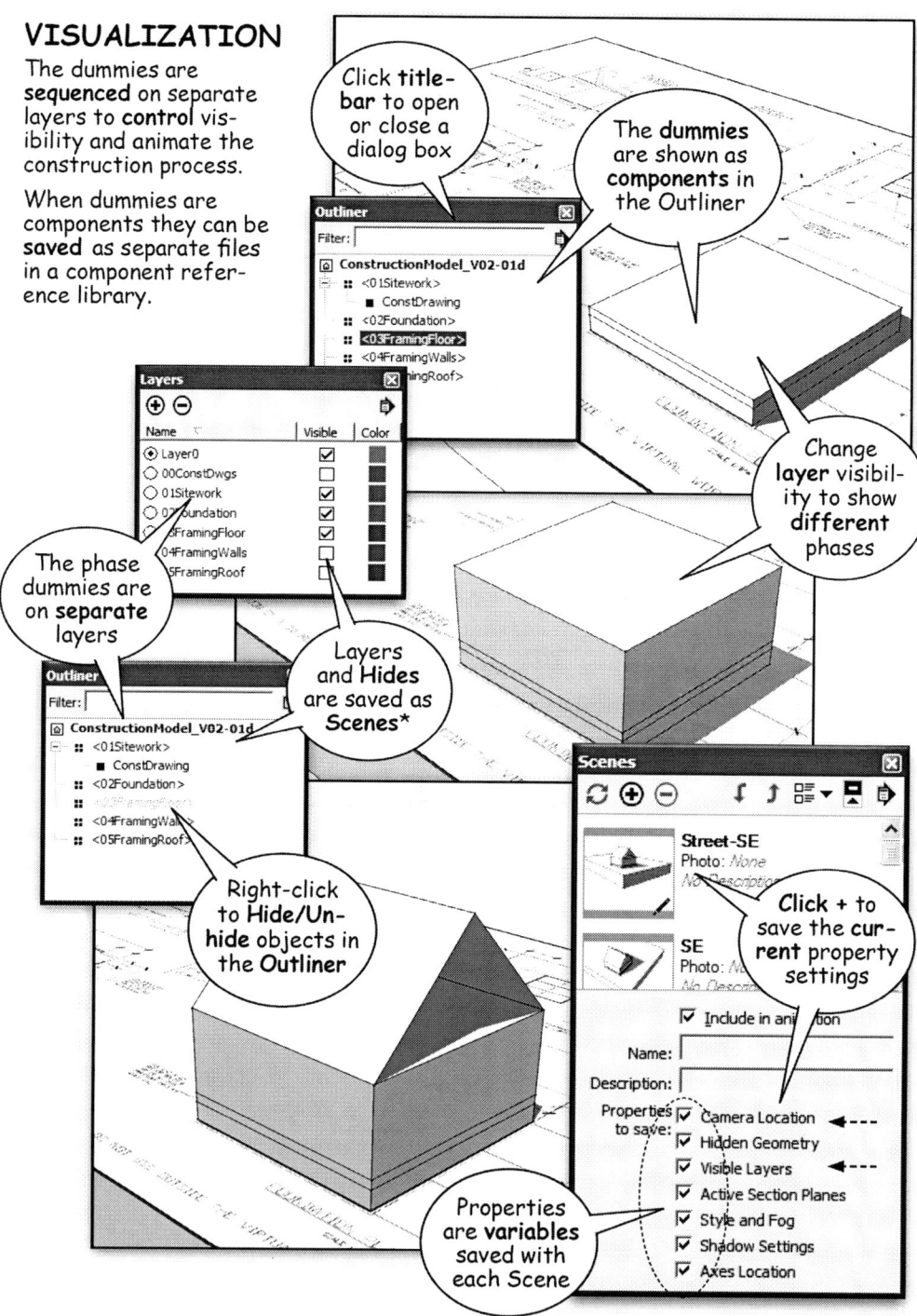

Click **title-bar** to open or close a dialog box

The **dummies** are shown as **components** in the Outliner

Change **layer** visibility to show **different** phases

The phase dummies are on **separate** layers

Layers and **Hides** are saved as **Scenes***

Right-click to **Hide/Unhide** objects in the **Outliner**

Click + to save the **current** property settings

Properties are **variables** saved with each Scene

*Layers control the visibility of nested objects--nested Hide/Unhide settings are ignored with layer changes.

38

ResizeAll

Resize the model base for the sitework

## RESIZE THE SITE PLAN

Once the phase dummies are **saved** as components, the 2D drawing and model base are resized to match the scale of the **site plan**. Important is the site plan is resized but the component dummies remain **unchanged**.

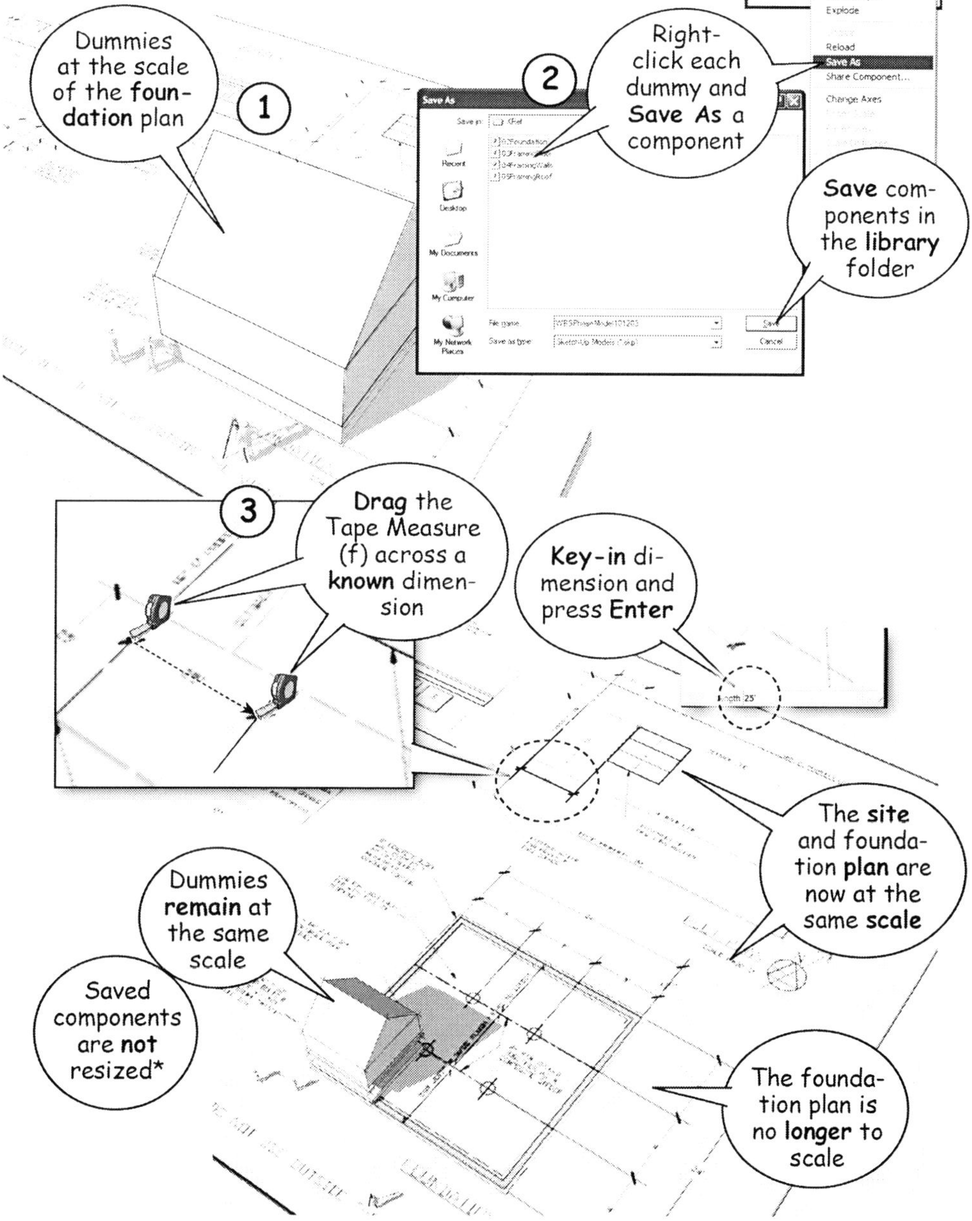

1. Dummies at the scale of the **foundation** plan

2. Right-click each dummy and **Save As** a component

   **Save** components in the **library** folder

3. **Drag** the Tape Measure (f) across a **known** dimension

   **Key-in** dimension and press **Enter**

   The **site** and foundation **plan** are now at the same **scale**

   Dummies **remain** at the same scale

   Saved components are **not** resized*

   The foundation plan is no **longer** to scale

*The component dummies were built to full scale on the foundation plan and now match the scale of the site plan

Lay out the setbacks and workpoint

## OVERVIEW OF THE SITE PLAN

The site plan will be the **basis** of the construction model. It was scaled to **full** size after the dummies were built on the foundation plan and **saved** to a library folder.

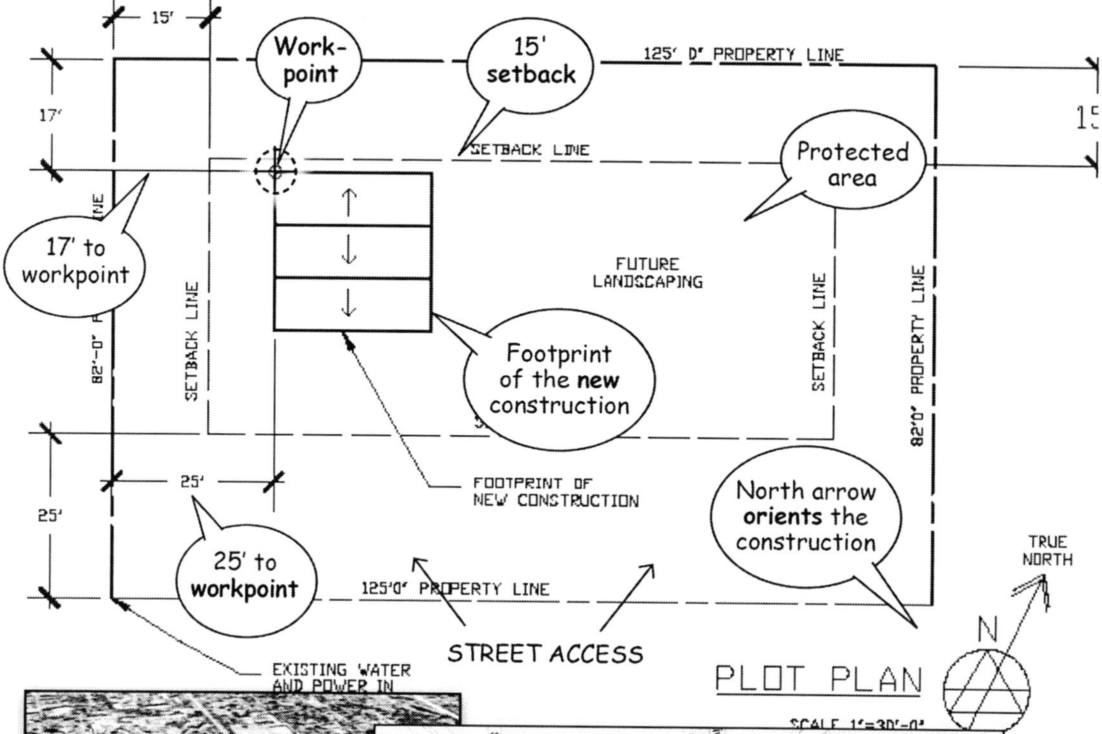

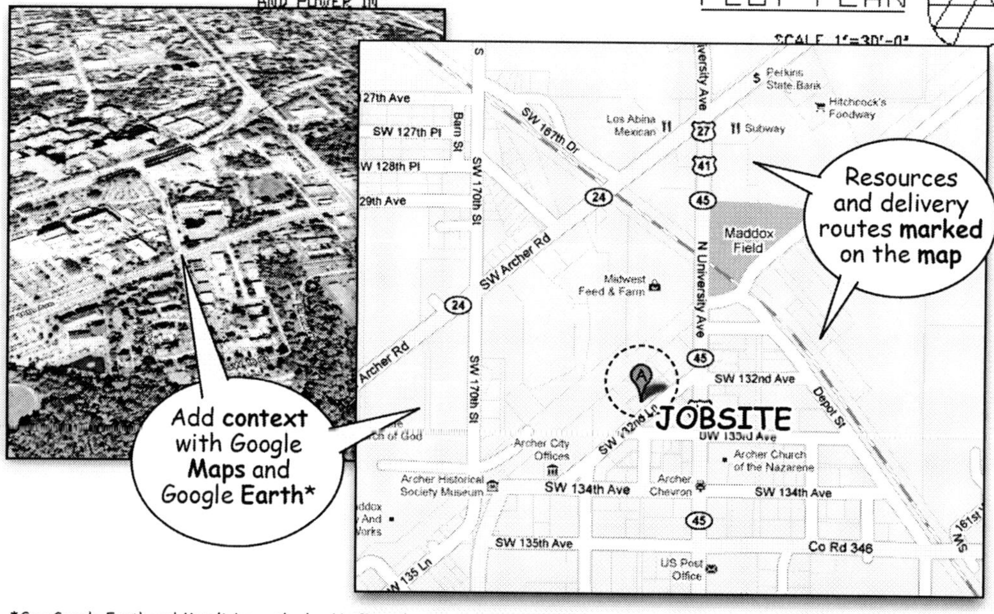

*See Google Earth and Map links on the book's CD and our companion book "A (Small) Home of Your Own"

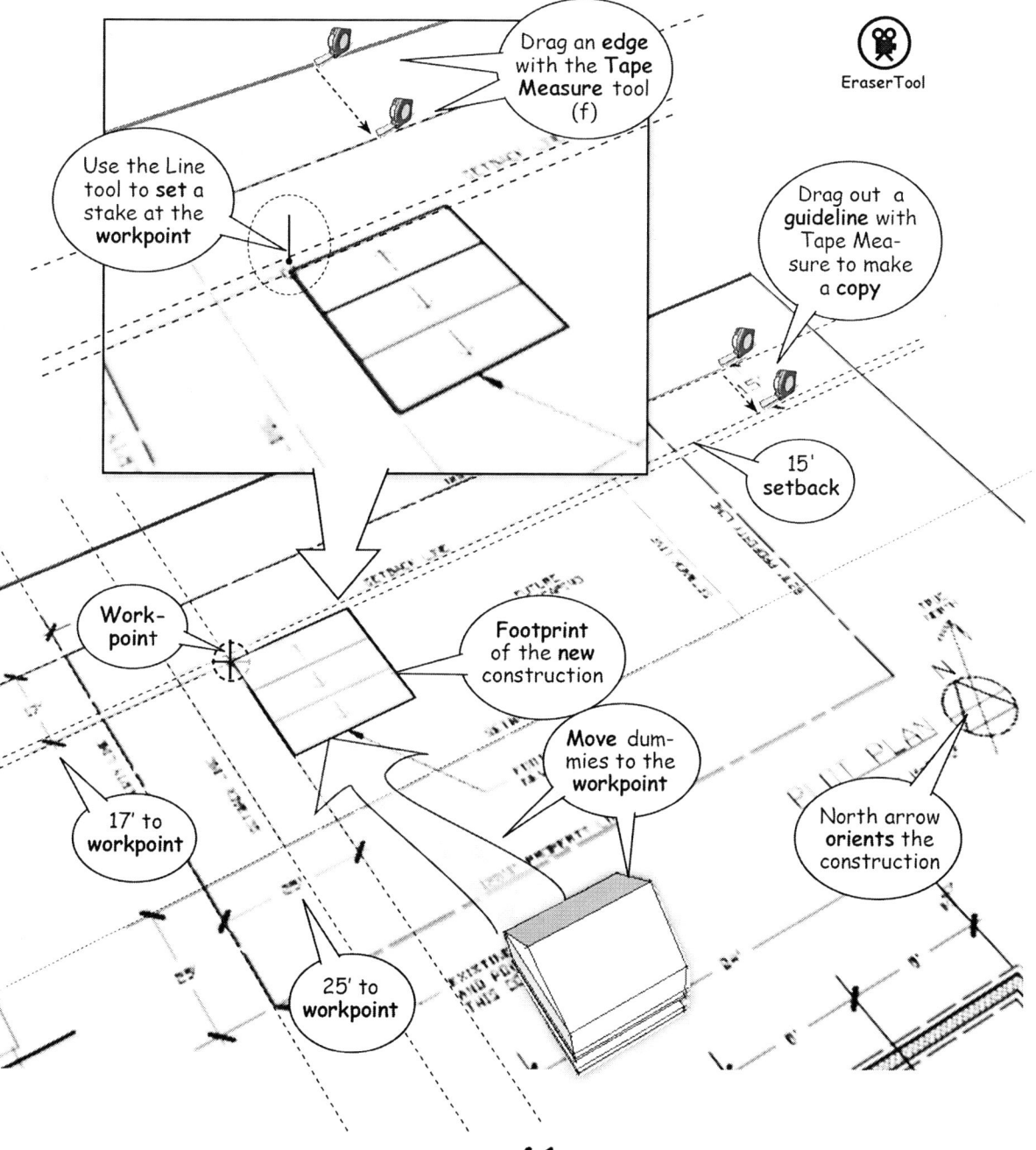

# CHAPTER 2 CHECKLISTS - SITE SETUP

SetUpChecklist

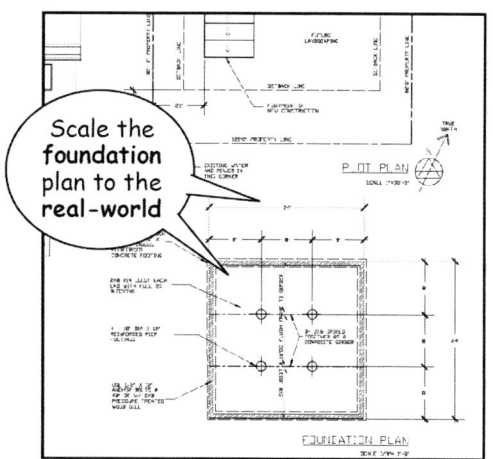
Scale the **foundation** plan to the **real-world**

## A. RESIZE DRAWING
Import a scan of the construction drawing into SketchUp and use the Tape Measure tool to resize model to the real-world.

- [ ] Open a SketchUp file
- [ ] Import the 2D drawing
- [ ] Double-click to the origin
- [ ] Zoom to a known dimension
- [ ] Tape Measure the dimension
- [ ] Click OK to resize the model

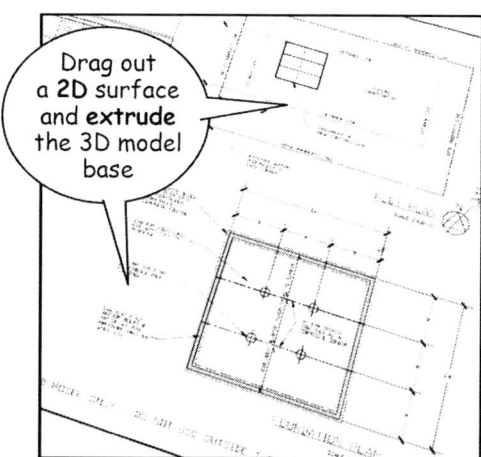
Drag out a **2D** surface and **extrude** the 3D model base

## B. EXTRUDE MODEL BASE
Drag out a rectangle on top of the drawing and extrude into 3D to form the model base.

- [ ] Drag out a rectangle
- [ ] Match the drawing edges
- [ ] Push/Pull underground 50'
- [ ] Triple-click the box to select
- [ ] Group and name the model base
- [ ] Explode & regroup the drawing

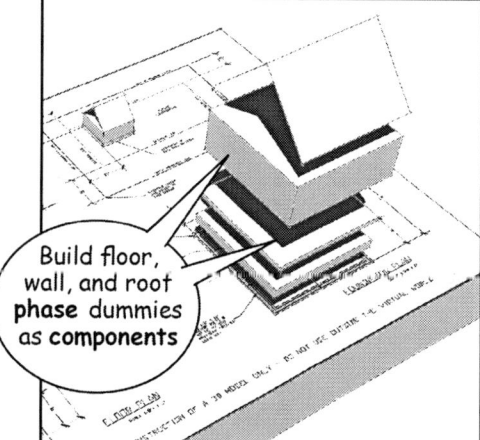
Build floor, wall, and roof **phase** dummies as **components**

## C. PHASE DUMMIES
Use modeling method to build and name the phase dummies as components for the foundation, floor, wall, and roof framing.*

- [ ] Zoom to the resized plan
- [ ] Drag a rectangle over the plan
- [ ] Match the scaled foundation
- [ ] Push/Pull the surface to 3D
- [ ] Triple-click to select the box
- [ ] Make Component and name
- [ ] Repeat, up to the roof

*See our companion book "How a House is Built" for details on the construction of a small house and its systems

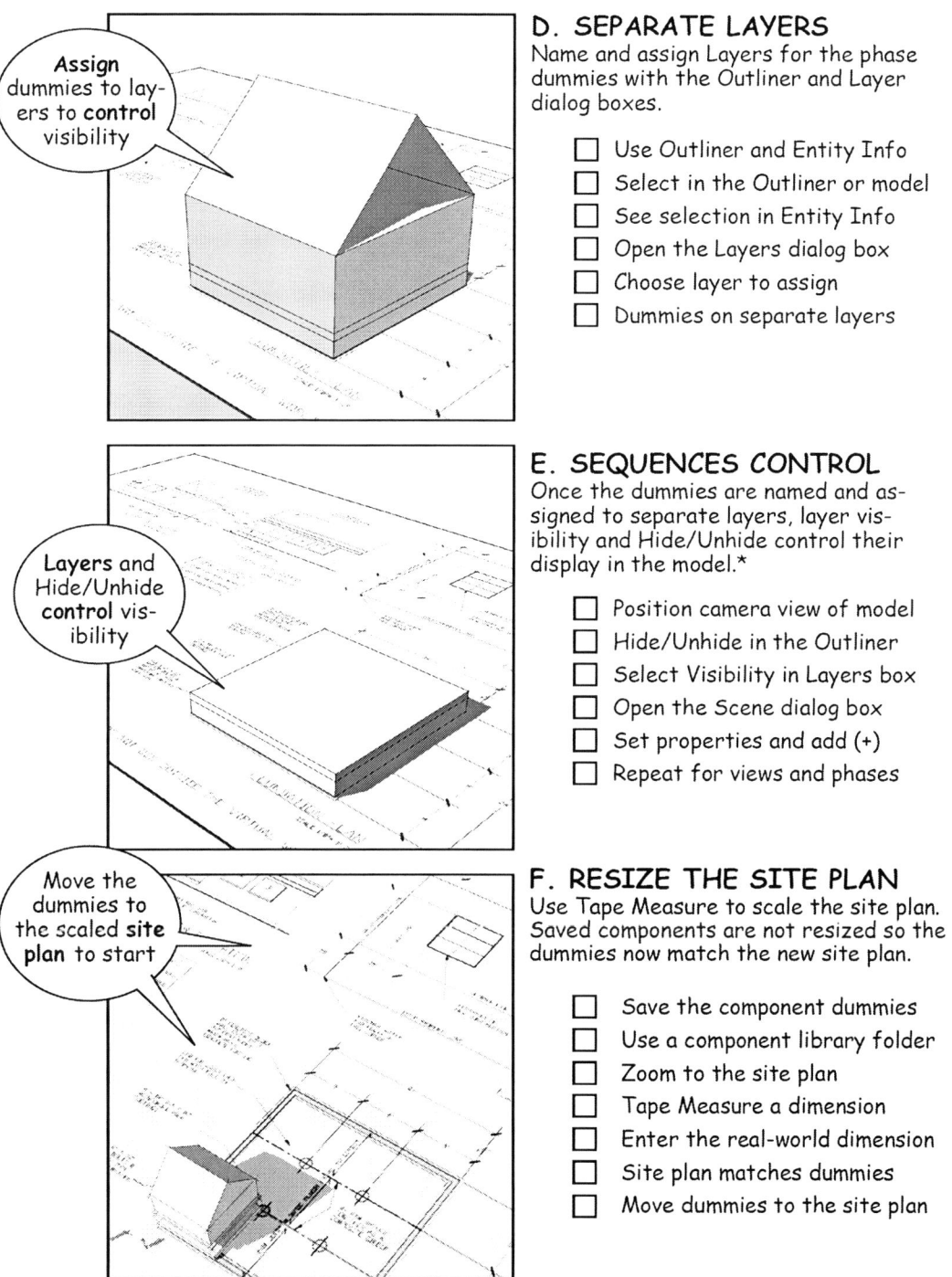

## D. SEPARATE LAYERS
Name and assign Layers for the phase dummies with the Outliner and Layer dialog boxes.

- [ ] Use Outliner and Entity Info
- [ ] Select in the Outliner or model
- [ ] See selection in Entity Info
- [ ] Open the Layers dialog box
- [ ] Choose layer to assign
- [ ] Dummies on separate layers

## E. SEQUENCES CONTROL
Once the dummies are named and assigned to separate layers, layer visibility and Hide/Unhide control their display in the model.*

- [ ] Position camera view of model
- [ ] Hide/Unhide in the Outliner
- [ ] Select Visibility in Layers box
- [ ] Open the Scene dialog box
- [ ] Set properties and add (+)
- [ ] Repeat for views and phases

## F. RESIZE THE SITE PLAN
Use Tape Measure to scale the site plan. Saved components are not resized so the dummies now match the new site plan.

- [ ] Save the component dummies
- [ ] Use a component library folder
- [ ] Zoom to the site plan
- [ ] Tape Measure a dimension
- [ ] Enter the real-world dimension
- [ ] Site plan matches dummies
- [ ] Move dummies to the site plan

*When Scenes are added the current layer visibility and first level Hide/Unhide settings are saved until updated

# CHAPTER 3. SITE LAYOUT

## SITE UTILIZATION PLAN

Just like the real world, **site utilization plans** (SUP) for construction modeling are used to help visualize the **scope** of the work and put together a management plan to complete the construction as **efficiently** as possible.

## MANAGEMENT PLAN

A management plan begins with careful preparation of a **jobsite** layout. This means thinking through **equipment** movement, identifying risks, and locating storage and lay down areas and work areas for **each phase** of the construction.

• • • • • • • • • • • • • • • • • • • • • • • • • • • • • • • • • • • • • • • • • • • • • • • • • • • • • • • • • • • • • • • • •

## DOWNLOADS FOR THIS CHAPTER

See the **book's CD** for **links** to these downloads:

2D Construction Drawings

Plat Map (from public records)

Satellite Image (from Google Earth)

Insitebuilders Component Library folders

*Orienting the site to a compass direction is necessary to orient the construction drawings to the jobsite

# Overview of the 2D construction drawing

## VISUALIZE THE CONSTRUCTION

Three-dimensional **tools** like SketchUp make it possible to think through the construction and the most **efficient** layout for the jobsite.

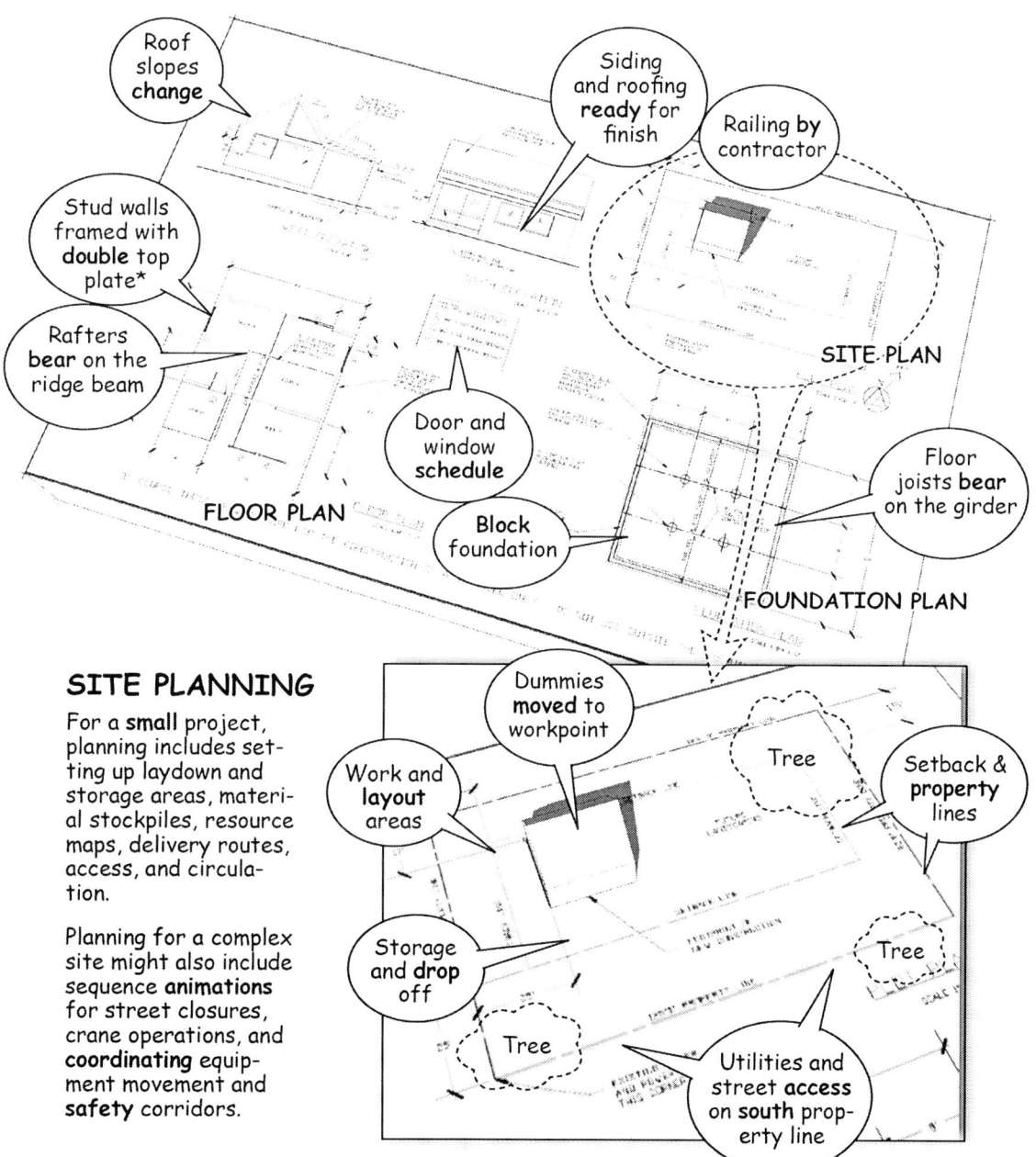

## SITE PLANNING

For a **small** project, planning includes setting up laydown and storage areas, material stockpiles, resource maps, delivery routes, access, and circulation.

Planning for a complex site might also include sequence **animations** for street closures, crane operations, and **coordinating** equipment movement and **safety** corridors.

*Standard platform framing with joists, open stud wall units, headers, and jambs at openings, and roof rafters

# Push/Pull the boundaries of the model base

ImportCrop

## PREPARE THE MODEL BASE
Crop the drawing to the **property** lines and Push/Pull the **base** to start site planning.

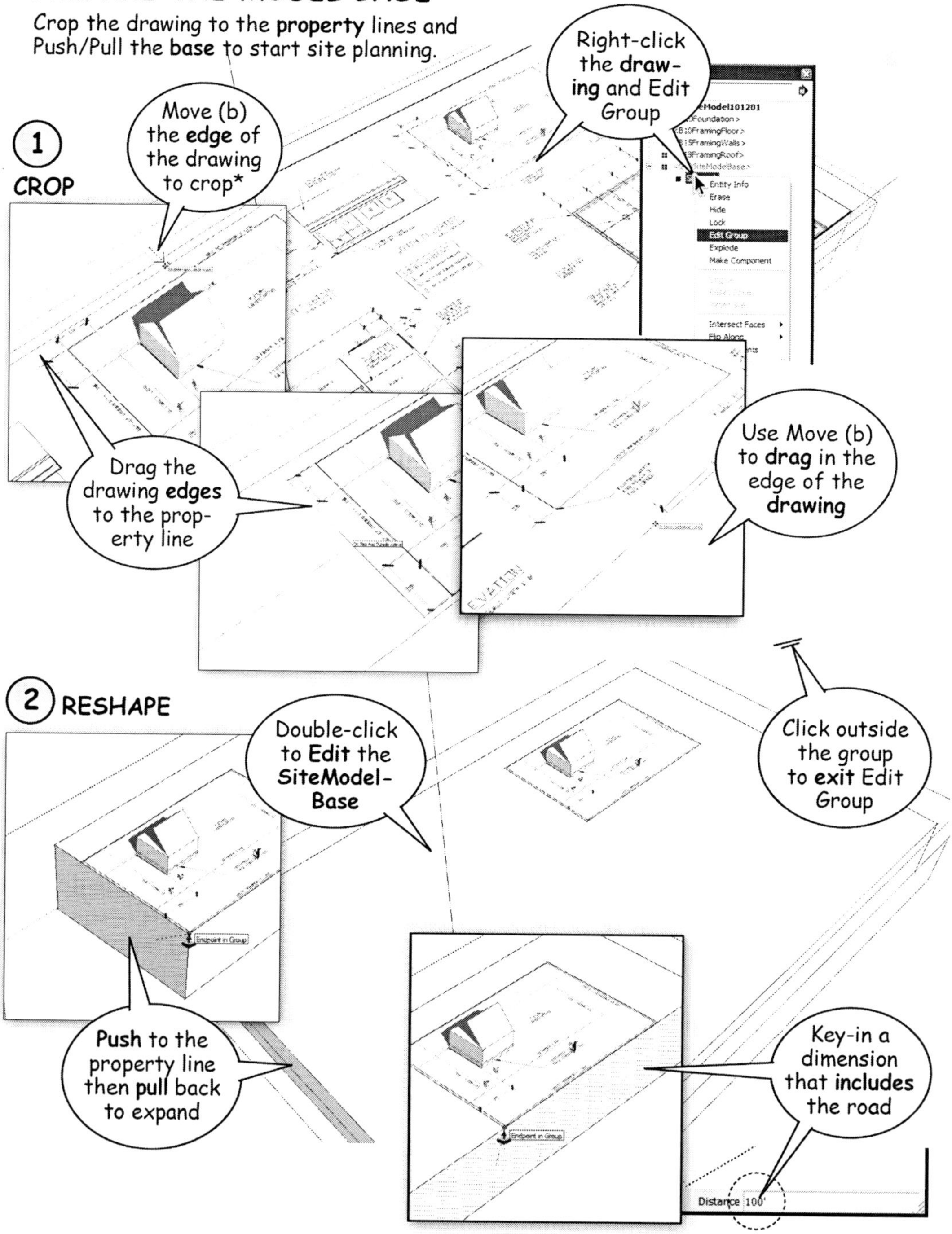

**① CROP**

- Move (b) the **edge** of the drawing to crop*
- Right-click the **drawing** and Edit Group
- Drag the drawing **edges** to the property line
- Use Move (b) to **drag** in the edge of the **drawing**

**② RESHAPE**

- Double-click to **Edit** the SiteModel-Base
- Click outside the group to **exit** Edit Group
- **Push** to the property line then **pull** back to expand
- Key-in a dimension that **includes** the road

*To keep the site plan from distorting, be certain to edit the drawing group in the sitework component

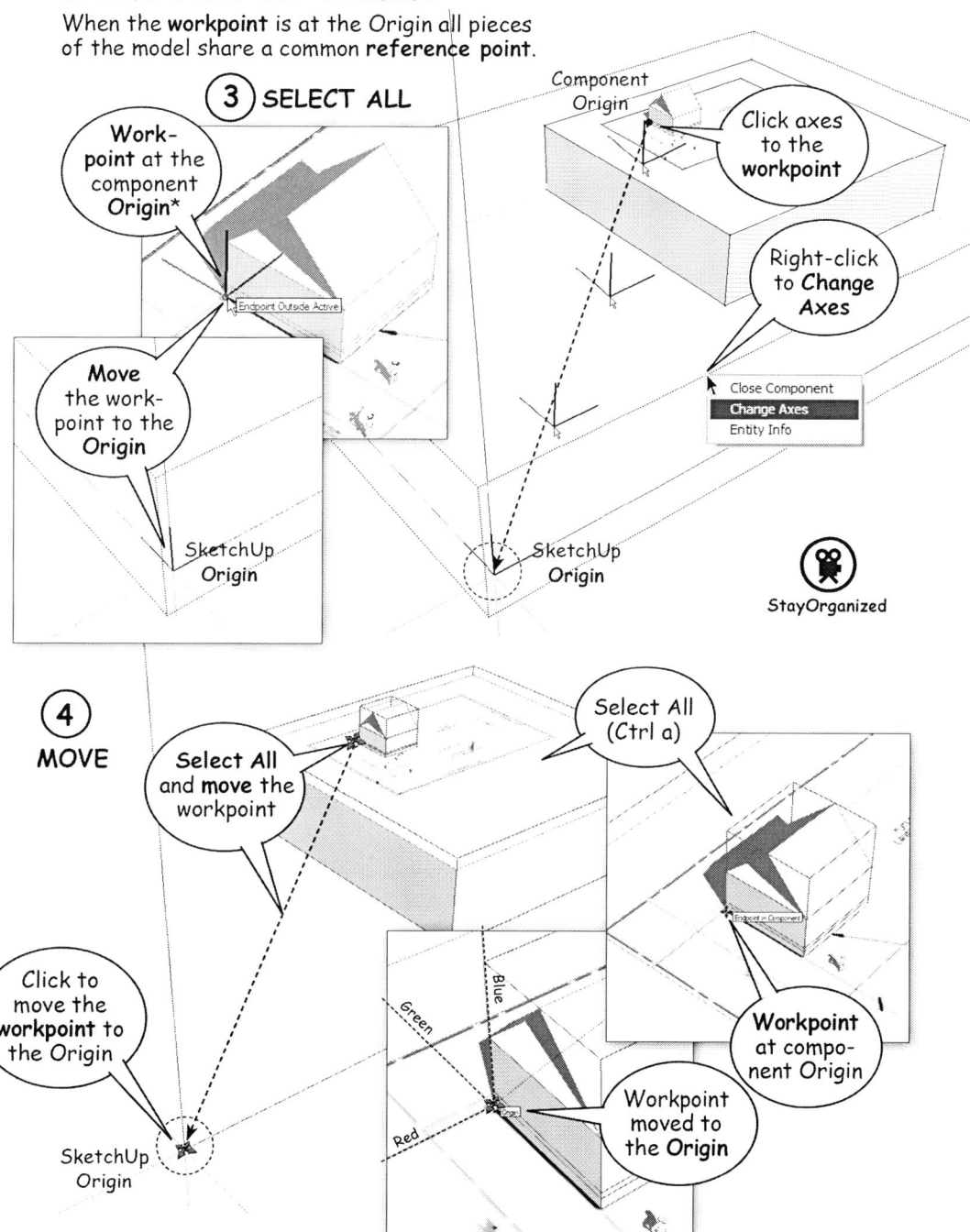

### Set the Scenes for the startup

## SAVED VIEWPOINTS

Scenes make it faster to **jump** to different points around the jobsite.

SetupScenes

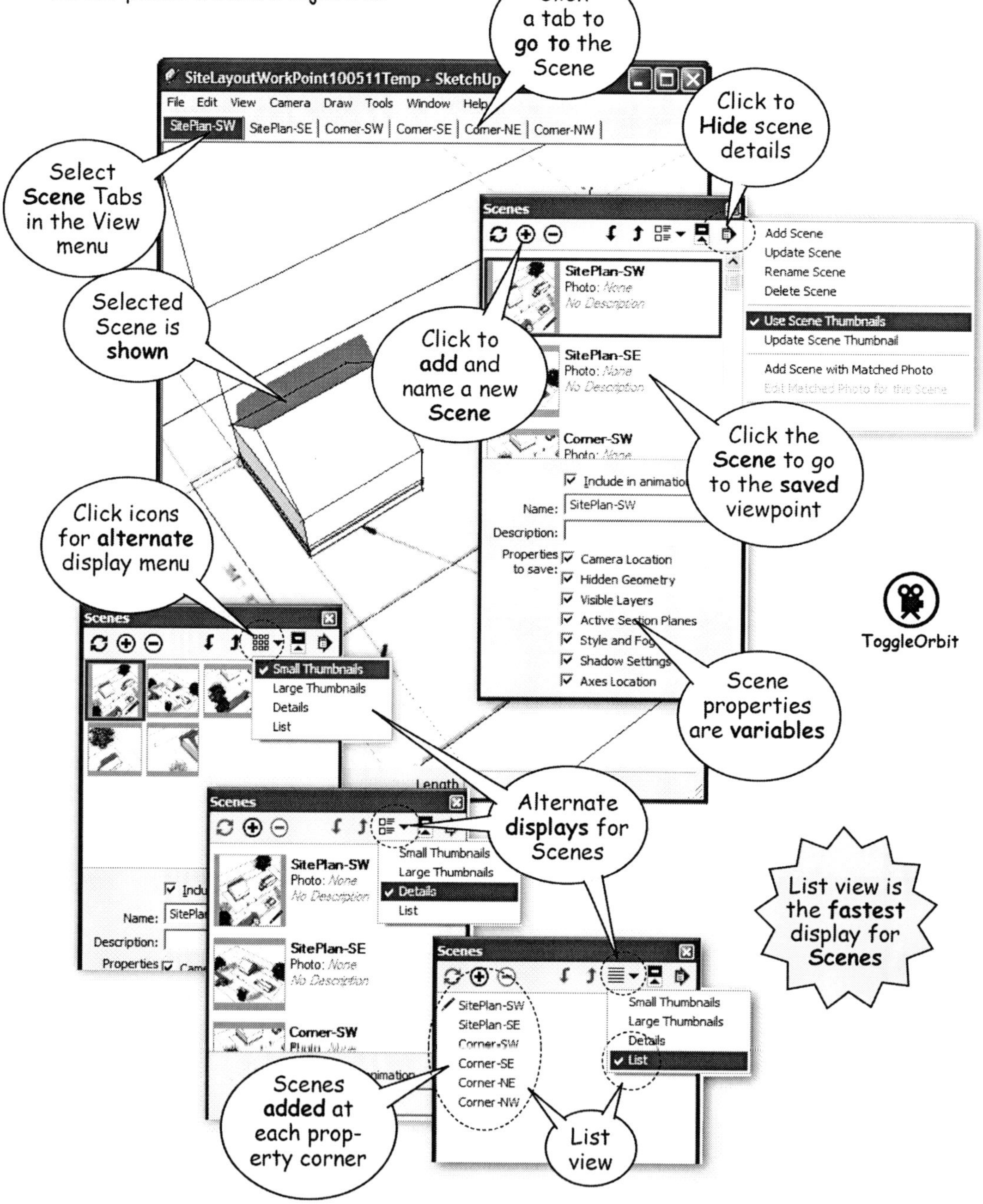

- Click a tab to **go to** the Scene
- Click to **Hide scene** details
- Select **Scene** Tabs in the View menu
- Selected Scene is **shown**
- Click to **add** and name a new **Scene**
- Click the **Scene** to go to the **saved viewpoint**
- Click icons for **alternate** display menu
- Scene properties are **variables**
- Alternate **displays for** Scenes
- Scenes **added** at each property corner
- **List view**

ToggleOrbit

List view is the **fastest** display for **Scenes**

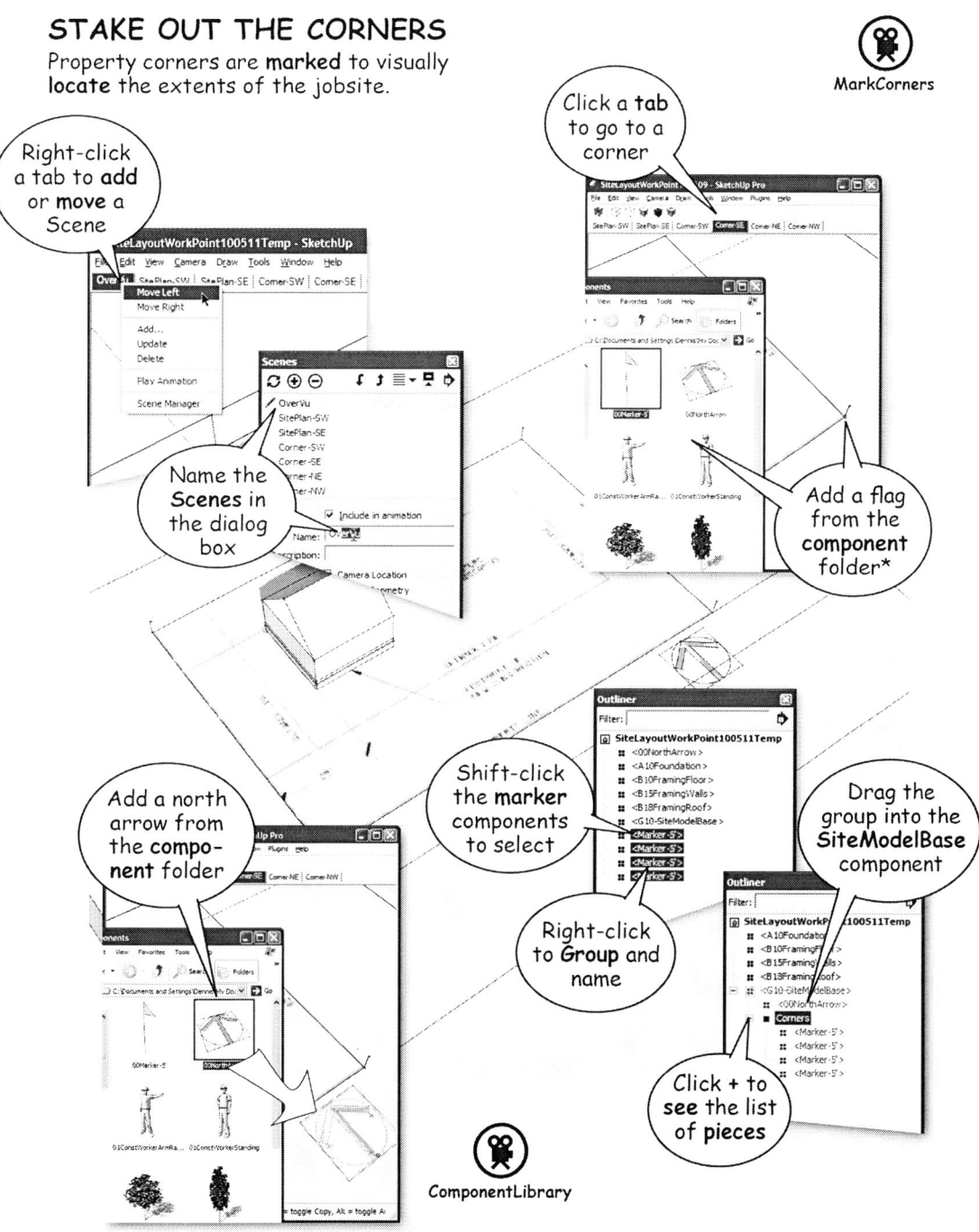

Set up the jobsite

# LAY OUT THE CONSTRUCTION
Clearly mark the **limits** of the jobsite to **locate** the extents of the construction.

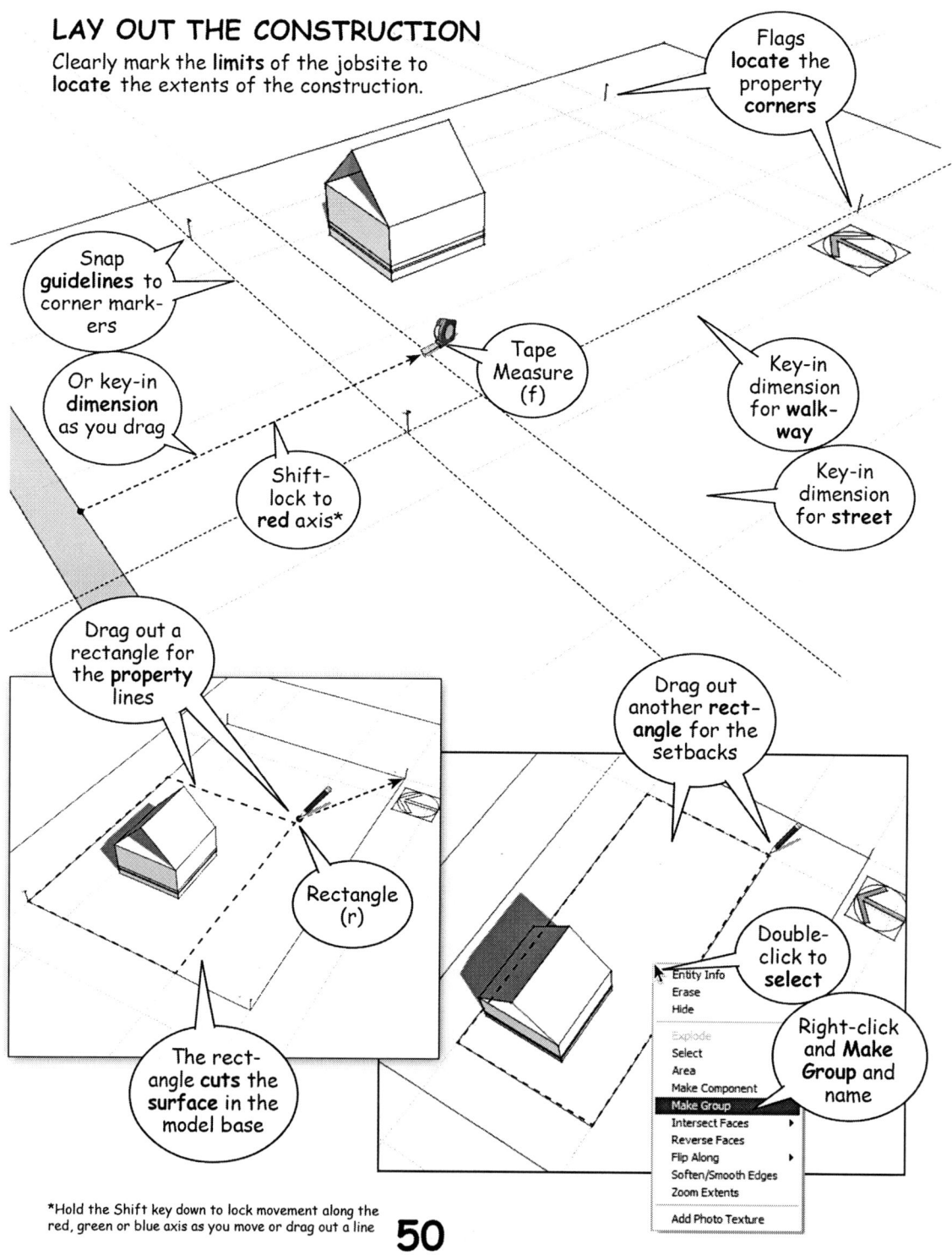

*Hold the Shift key down to lock movement along the red, green or blue axis as you move or drag out a line

# Orient the jobsite to public areas

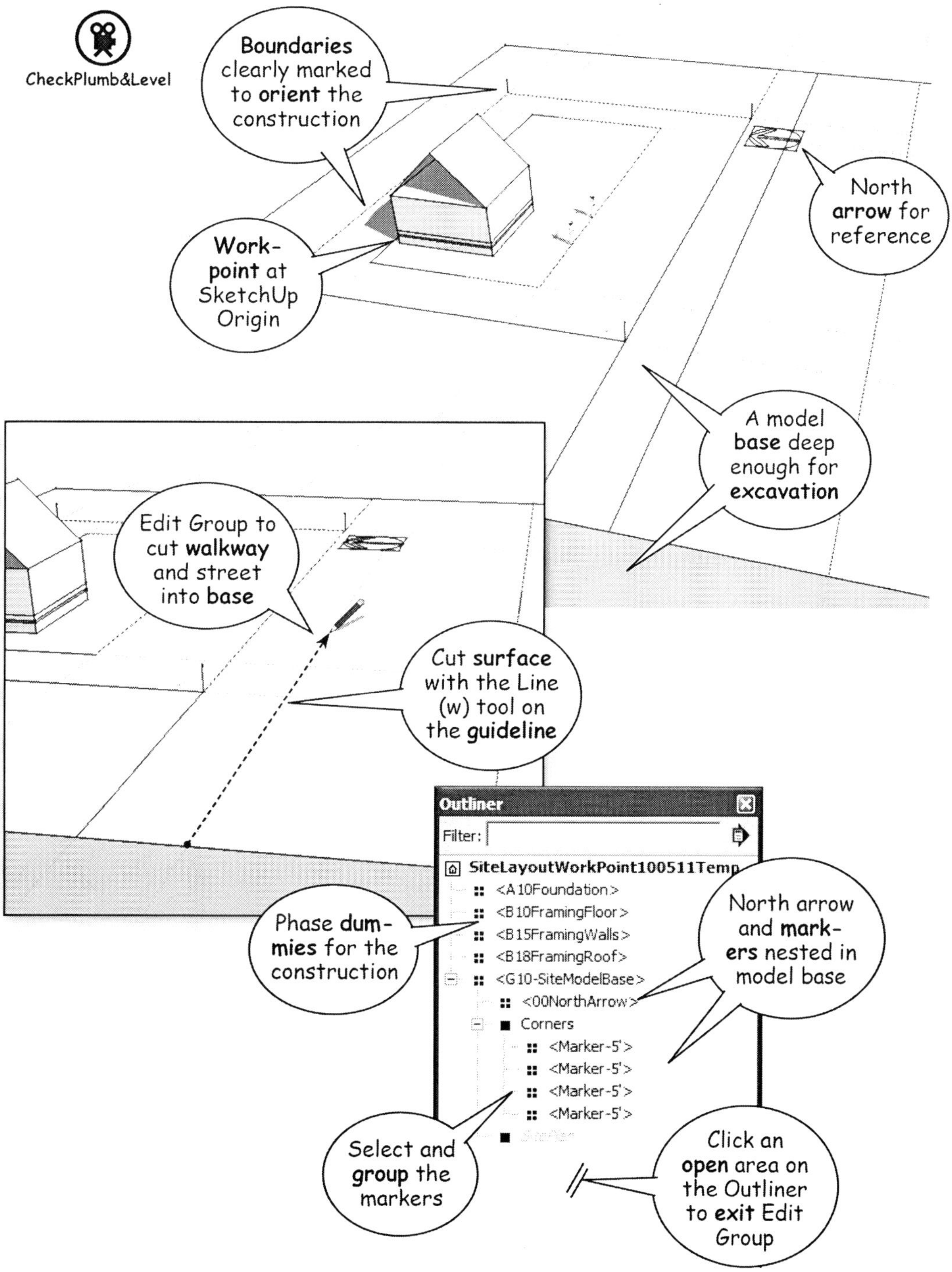

- **Boundaries** clearly marked to **orient** the construction
- **North arrow** for reference
- **Work-point** at SketchUp Origin
- A model **base** deep enough for **excavation**
- **Edit Group** to cut **walkway** and street into **base**
- Cut **surface** with the Line (w) tool on the **guideline**
- Phase **dummies** for the construction
- North arrow and **markers** nested in model base
- **Select** and **group** the markers
- Click an **open** area on the Outliner to **exit** Edit Group

Import images to setup visual scale

VisualScale

## POPULATE THE JOBSITE
Components give the jobsite a **visual** scale making it easier to **see** the construction as a simulation.

PlatMap   SatelliteAerial

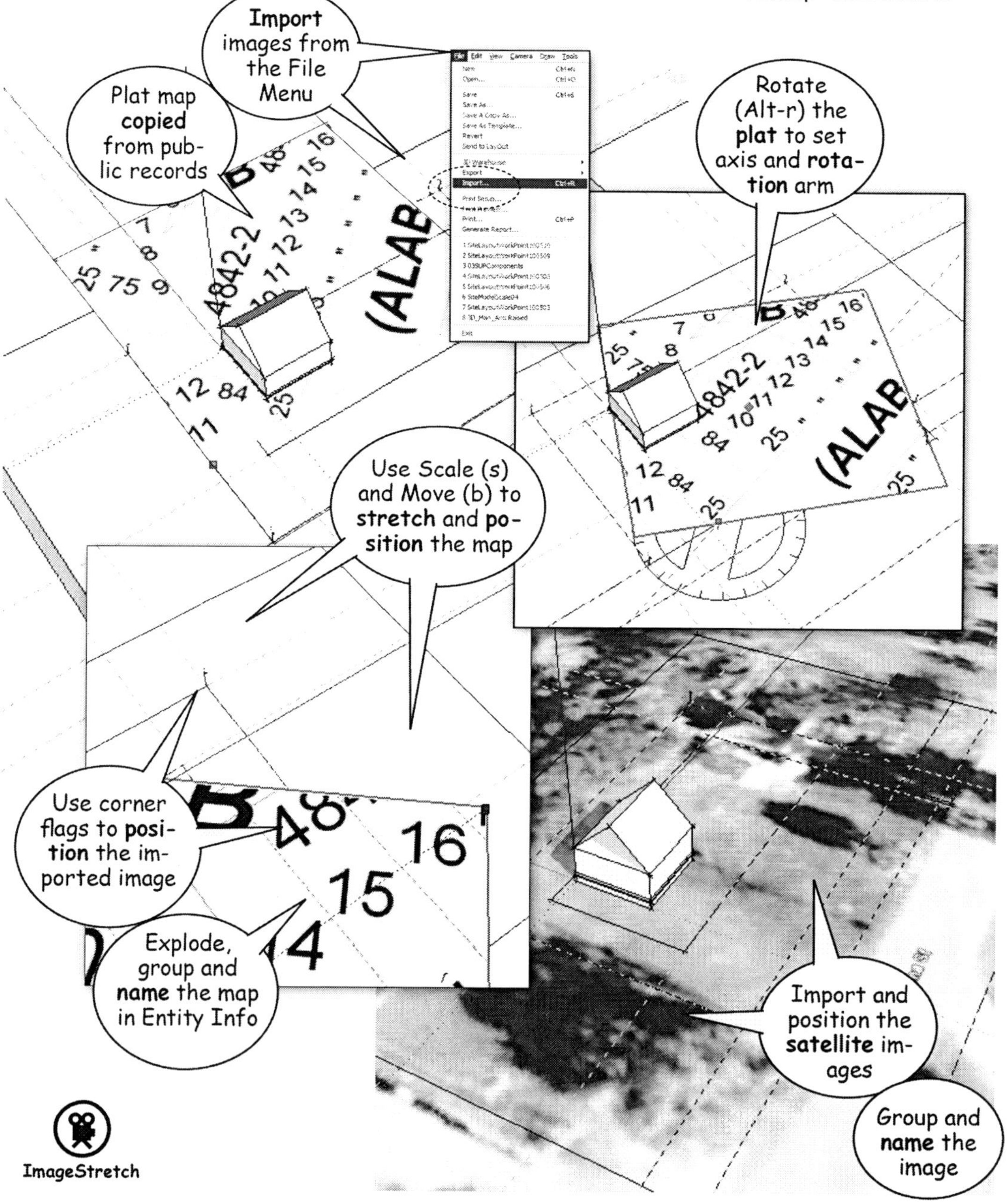

- **Import** images from the File Menu
- Plat map **copied** from public records
- Rotate (Alt-r) the **plat** to set axis and **rotation** arm
- Use Scale (s) and Move (b) to **stretch** and **position** the map
- Use corner flags to **position** the imported image
- Explode, group and **name** the map in Entity Info
- Import and position the **satellite** images
- Group and **name** the image

ImageStretch

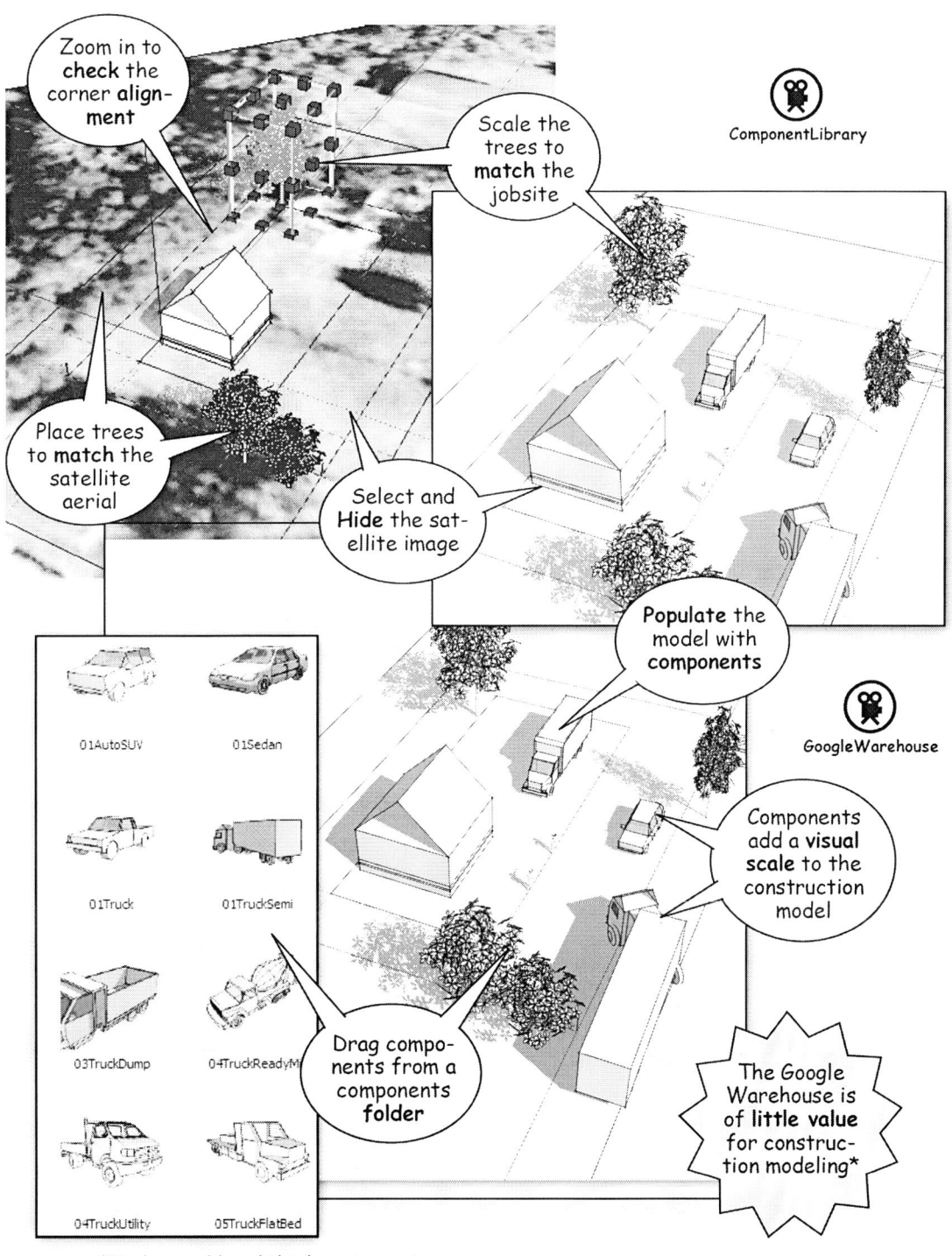

*Warehouse models are high-poly count conversions with details that make them difficult to use effectively

# Basic tips and tricks for setup

## TIPS AND TRICKS

The Outliner is faster and more **versatile** than Layers. You can **reorganize** pieces, double-click to **edit** objects or groups, and Hide/Unhide pieces and assemblies.

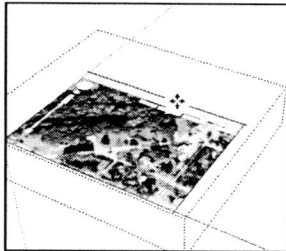

**01Import&Crop:** import an image and Explode and rename it to crop the edges to fit

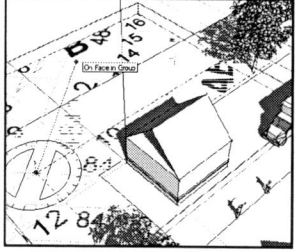

**02ImageStretch:** stretch the corners of an imported image to fit an object in model space

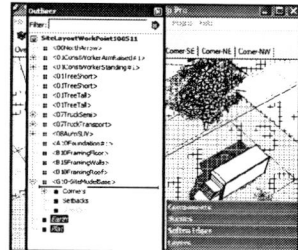

**03StayOrganized:** use the Outliner to name and organize the pieces of the assemblies

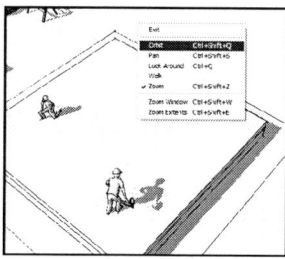

**04ToggleOrbit:** hold down the Shift key to toggle between Orbit and Pan

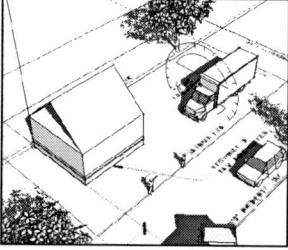

**05CheckPlumb&Level:** regularly check plumb and level using the Protractor or Circle tool

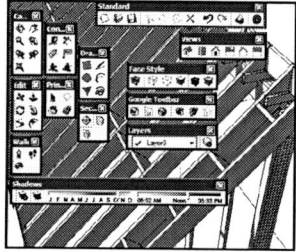

**06Dock&Undock:** reshape and dock and undock toolbars to organize your workspace

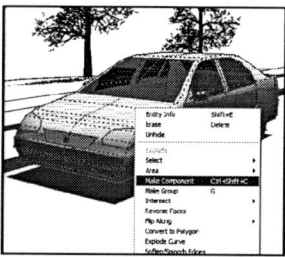

**07ComponentLibrary:** use the Insitebuilders Components Library to start your own collection

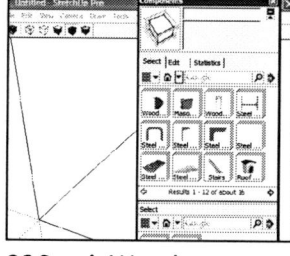

**08GoogleWarehouse:** avoid the bloated models found in the Google Warehouse

Check the size and quality of an **unknown** component by importing it into a **new** file and simplifying the colors and details **before** placing it in **your** construction models.

54

Constantly add to your component collection

## COMPONENT SOURCES

Components are three-dimensional objects that are quickly **added** to a construction model. They can be modified and **resaved** or saved again with a **different** name to setup a custom component library. The key is to keep the file sizes of these components as **small** as possible by avoiding colors, textures, and unnecessary details.

Start your own custom components folder with the **Insitebuilders** Components Library on the book's CD. These models have been **modified** and put together specifically to **speed** construction and add **visual** scale to your models.

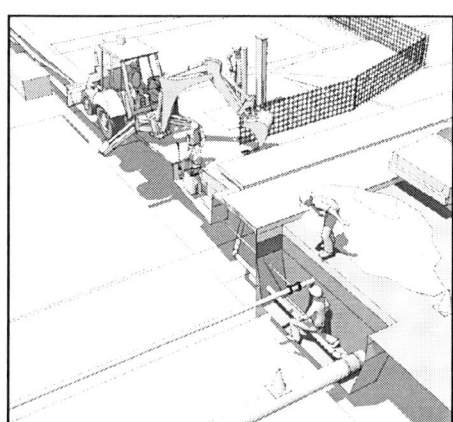

## THE @LAST COMPONENT LIBRARIES

Because early versions of SketchUp were much more compact, the **original** component libraries from @Last Software were much **simpler** and faster to use. These components are still available for **download** for both Mac and Windows. See the links from the **book's CD**.

| | | |
|---|---|---|
| Architecture | 723 items | 12.7mb |
| Construction | 797 items | 6mb |
| Film and Stage | 107 items | 3,4mb |
| Landscape | 583 items | 14.3mb |
| People | 166 items | 5.7mb |
| Symbols | 26 items | 1.9mb |
| Transportation | 48 items | 3mb |

# CHAPTER 3 CHECKLISTS - SITE LAYOUT

SiteChecklist

## A. VISUALIZE CONSTRUCTION
Review the content of the construction drawing and the scope of the work for each phase of the construction.

- [ ] Move dummies to the workpoint
- [ ] Review the drawing in phases
- [ ] Use the dummies to visualize
- [ ] Review site organization
- [ ] Plan layout and work areas
- [ ] Develop a management plan

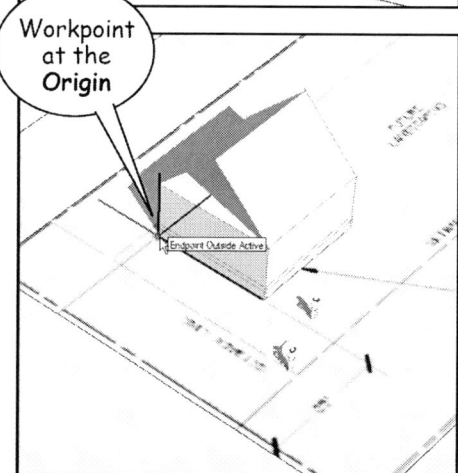

Workpoint at the **Origin**

## B. SITE & WORKPOINT
Crop the drawing and model base to prepare for construction, includes moving the workpoint to the Origin.

- [ ] Right-click to Edit Group
- [ ] Drag an edge to the property line
- [ ] Double or Right-click the model base
- [ ] Push/Pull the sides of the base
- [ ] Click outside the group to exit
- [ ] Select All at the Workpoint
- [ ] Move the workpoint to Origin

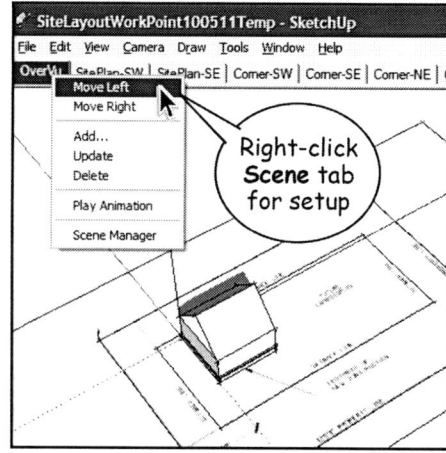

Right-click **Scene** tab for setup

## C. SCENES & VIEWPOINTS
Set up Scenes as saved viewpoints around the jobsite. Scenes make it easy to move around during construction.

- [ ] Use Zoom, Orbit, and Pan
- [ ] Position the point of view
- [ ] Click + to add a Scene
- [ ] Repeat for different views
- [ ] Use the View > Scene Tabs Menu
- [ ] Click any tab to change views

*Component folder in **Windows** Explorer\**

### D. STAKE CORNERS
Adjust Scenes by changing viewpoints and updating tabs to move around and set up property corners.

- ☐ Right-click Scene tabs to add
- ☐ Right-click to shift tab positions
- ☐ Use tabs to move around model
- ☐ Open a component folder
- ☐ Add a marker to each corner
- ☐ Add a north arrow to orient
- ☐ Name the grouped components

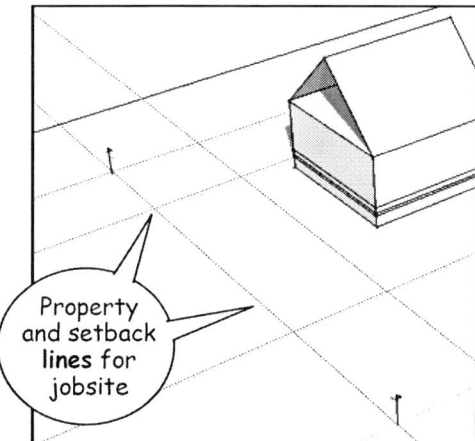

*Property and setback **lines** for jobsite*

### E. CONSTRUCTION LAYOUT
Drag out guidelines to mark property and setback lines. Use them as guidelines to cut the top surface of the model base.

- ☐ Right-click the base to Edit Group
- ☐ Use the Tape Measure tool
- ☐ Drag an edge to add a guideline
- ☐ Use the Rectangle and Line tool
- ☐ Add lines to corners and setbacks
- ☐ Cuts the surface of the model base

### F. POPULATE THE JOBSITE
Use public records and satellite maps to locate site features then add components from the component folder.*

- ☐ Import maps/aerials from the web
- ☐ Stretch and scale the maps
- ☐ Align image to corners & guidelines
- ☐ Add components from library
- ☐ Scale vegetation to match site
- ☐ Position components for the work

*Add components from either Windows or Macintosh folders by dragging them into the construction model

# CHAPTER 4. EXCAVATION

## START THE CONSTRUCTION

Keep in mind that a construction model is a **process model** and not a static representation of the pieces of the assembly. Design models are to be admired, **construction models** are built to go to **work**.

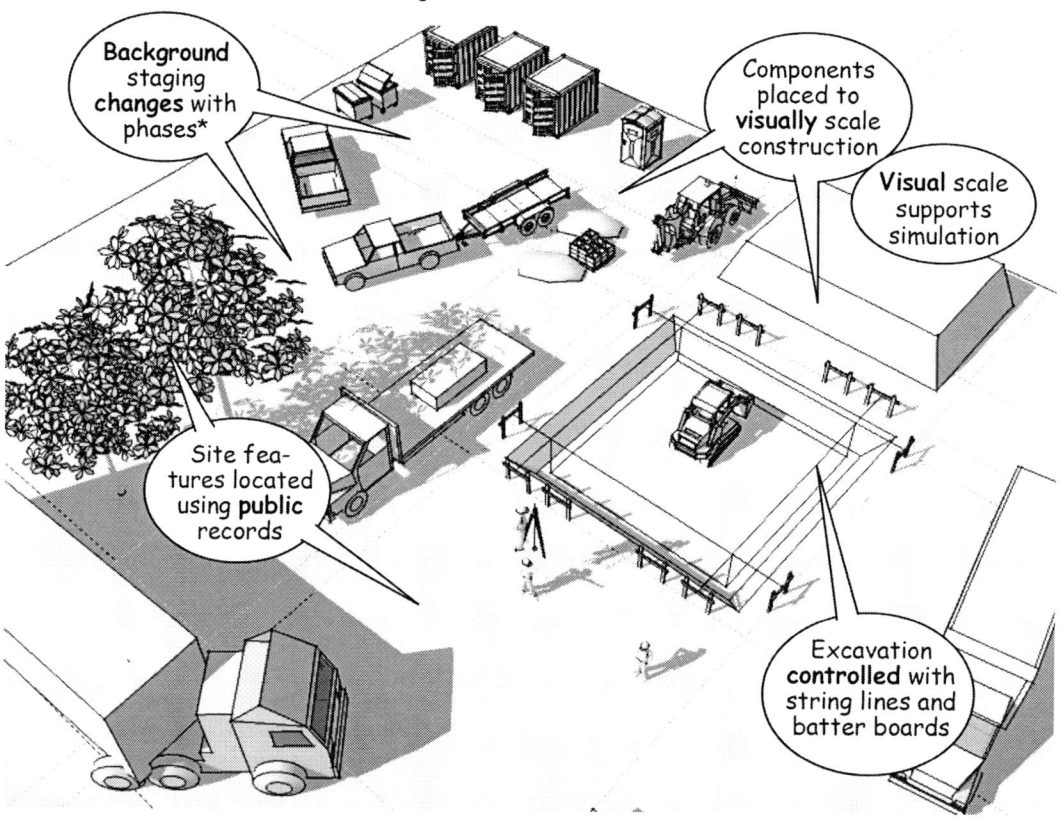

- **Background** staging **changes** with **phases***
- Components placed to **visually** scale construction
- **Visual** scale supports simulation
- Site features located using **public** records
- Excavation **controlled** with string lines and batter boards

• • • • • • • • • • • • • • • • • • • • • • • • • • • • • • • • • • • • • • • • • • • • • • • • • • • • • • • • • • •

## REVIEW SHORTCUT KEYS**

| | | | | | | | |
|---|---|---|---|---|---|---|---|
| **Space** > Select | c > Circle | **Shift z** > Zoom Previous |
| b > Move | v > Offset | **Ctrl-Shift s** > Pan |
| f > Tape | a > Arc | **Ctrl-Shift q** > Orbit |
| s > Scale | h > Hide | **Ctrl-Shift e** > Zoom Extents |
| t > Push/Pull | Alt h > Unhide | **Ctrl-Shift z** > Zoom |
| w > Line | Alt r > Rotate | **Ctrl-Shift w** > Zoom Window |
| r > Rectangle | Alt c > Hide Rest | |
| g > Group | Alt e > Erase Guides | |

*Scaled components set up screen captures and help visualize, plan, and stage each phase of the construction

**Shortcuts were imported into Preferences from the CD file, see the Shortcuts index at the back of the book

## CHECK THE WORKPOINT

Before starting construction verify the workpoint and setbacks are in the correct position.

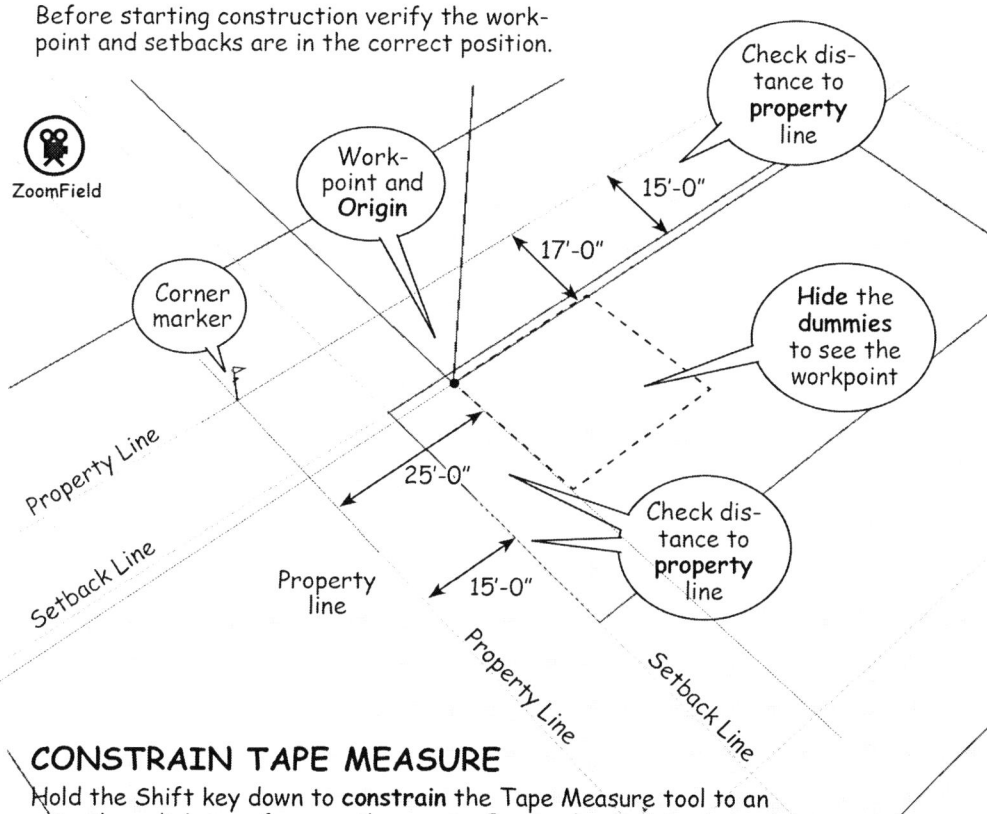

## CONSTRAIN TAPE MEASURE

Hold the Shift key down to **constrain** the Tape Measure tool to an axis, then click to reference the corner flag to check distance.

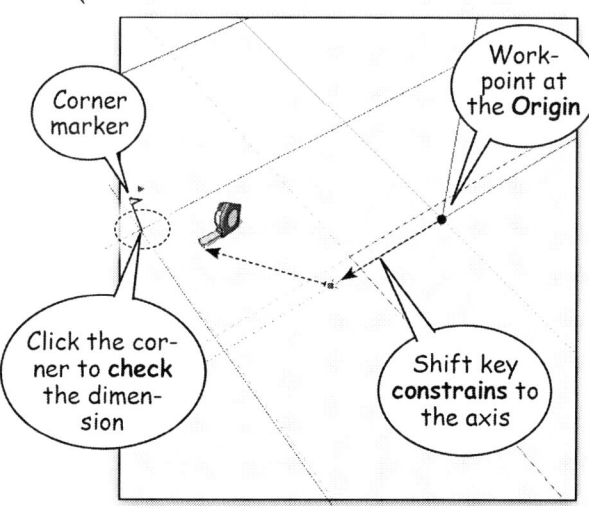

### WORKPOINT

The workpoint is located at the **Origin**. This sets the foundation corner reference at 0,0 and 0 elevation.

Just like the real-world the dimensions and elevations of the **excavation** and **foundation** are based on the location of the workpoint.

Prepare the area for excavation

PlaceBatterBoards

## LAY OUT THE BATTER BOARDS
Lay out the footprint of the excavation and **insert** and **place** batter board components.

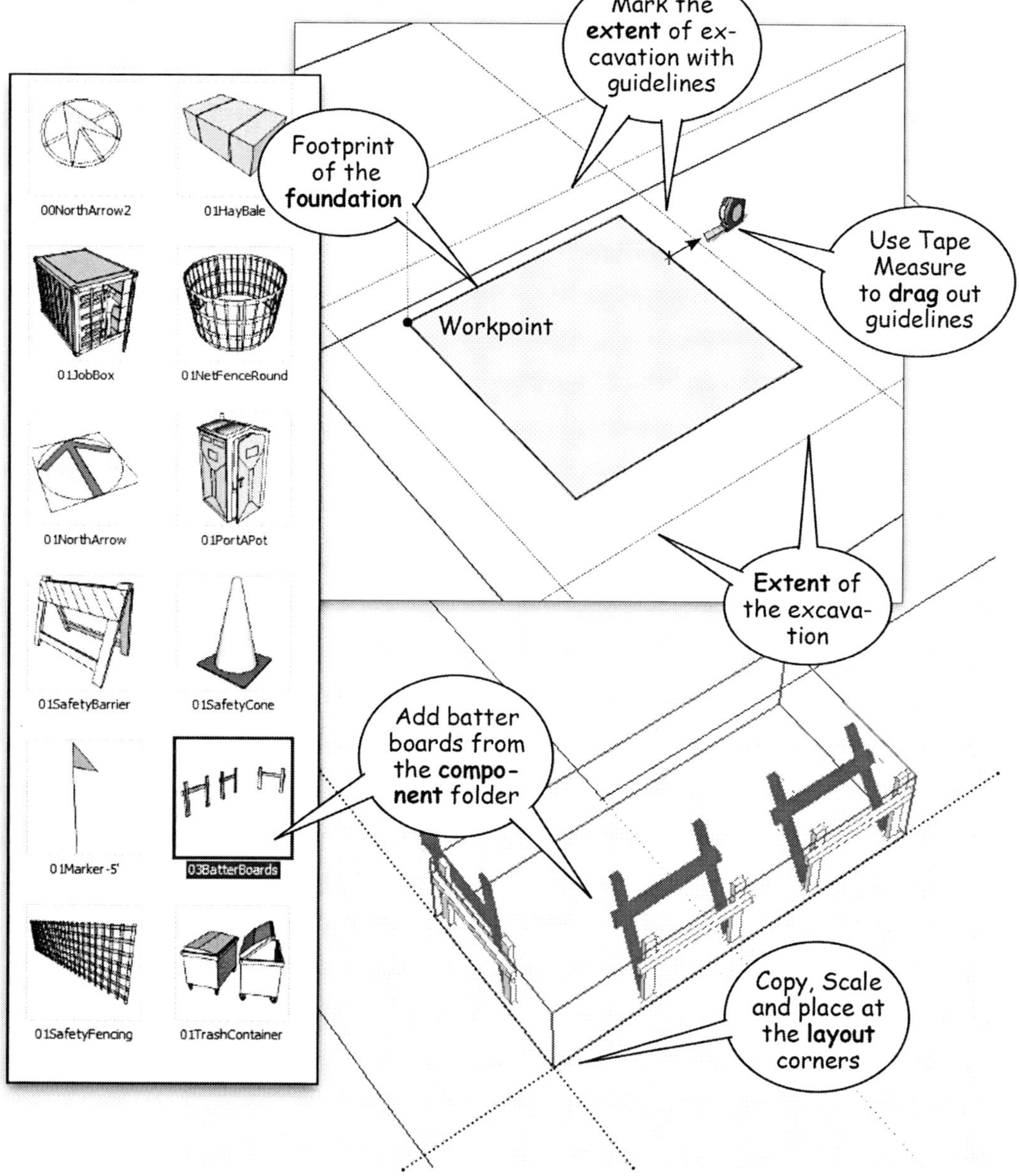

Mark the **extent** of excavation with guidelines

Footprint of the **foundation**

Use Tape Measure to **drag** out guidelines

Workpoint

**Extent** of the excavation

Add batter boards from the **component** folder

Copy, Scale and place at the **layout** corners

A batter board is a **horizontal** board securely fastened to vertical posts. They support the string lines used to **check** the excavation and foundation **layout**.

# Move, Copy, and Scale batter boards

## MOVE-COPY BATTER BOARDS

Use the Scale tool to copy and mirror-flip the batter board components.*

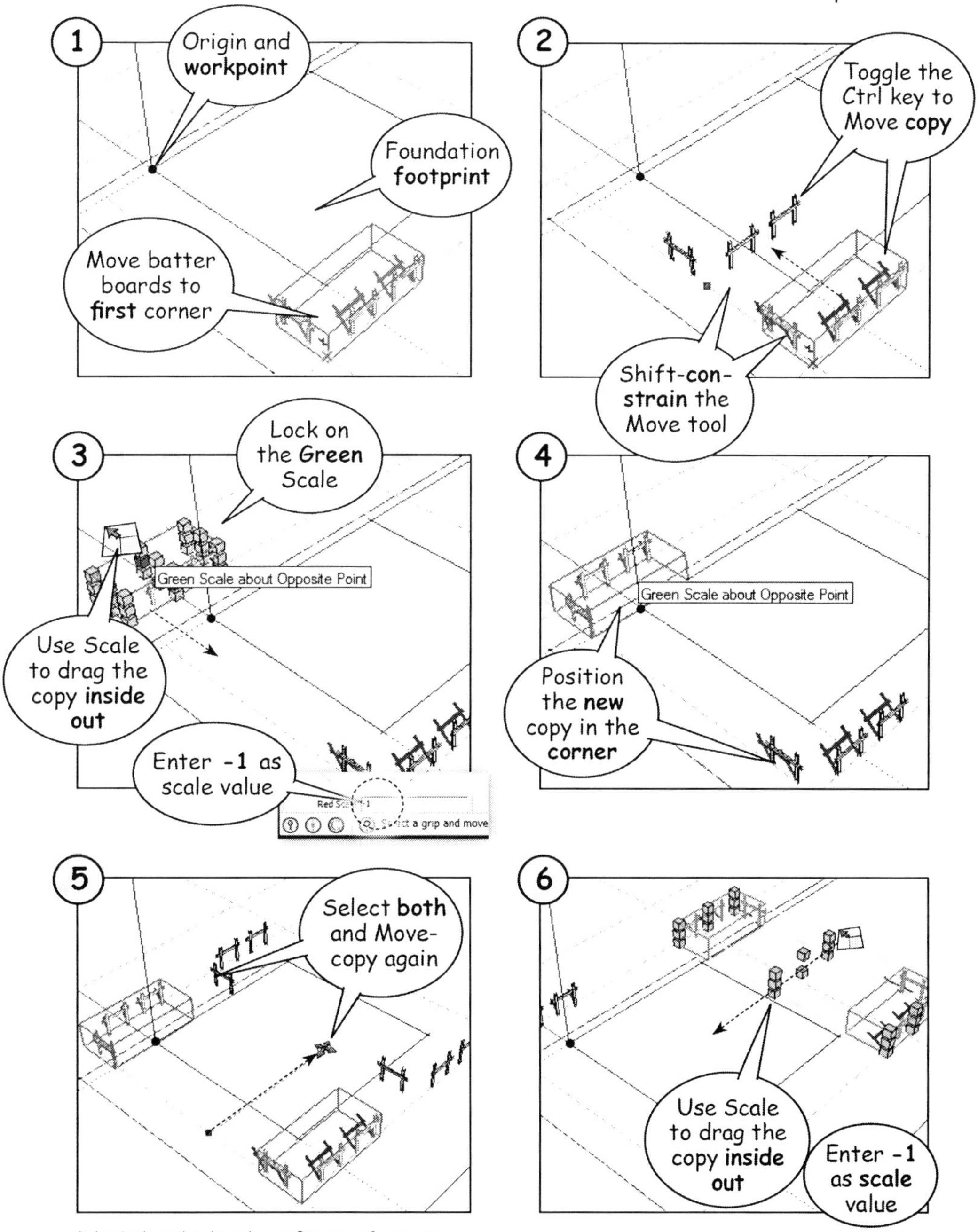

1. Origin and **workpoint**. Foundation **footprint**. Move batter boards to **first** corner.

2. Toggle the Ctrl key to Move **copy**. Shift-**constrain** the Move tool.

3. Lock on the **Green** Scale. Use Scale to drag the copy **inside out**. Enter -1 as scale value.

4. Position the **new** copy in the **corner**.

5. Select **both** and Move-copy again.

6. Use Scale to drag the copy **inside out**. Enter -1 as **scale** value.

*The Scale tool and inside-out flips are a fast way to copy and mirror groups of pieces and assemblies

Organize the jobsite for the excavation

## SET UP THE STRING LINES

To start the construction, Group the batter boards and **nest** them in the **foundation** component along with a new dummy group.

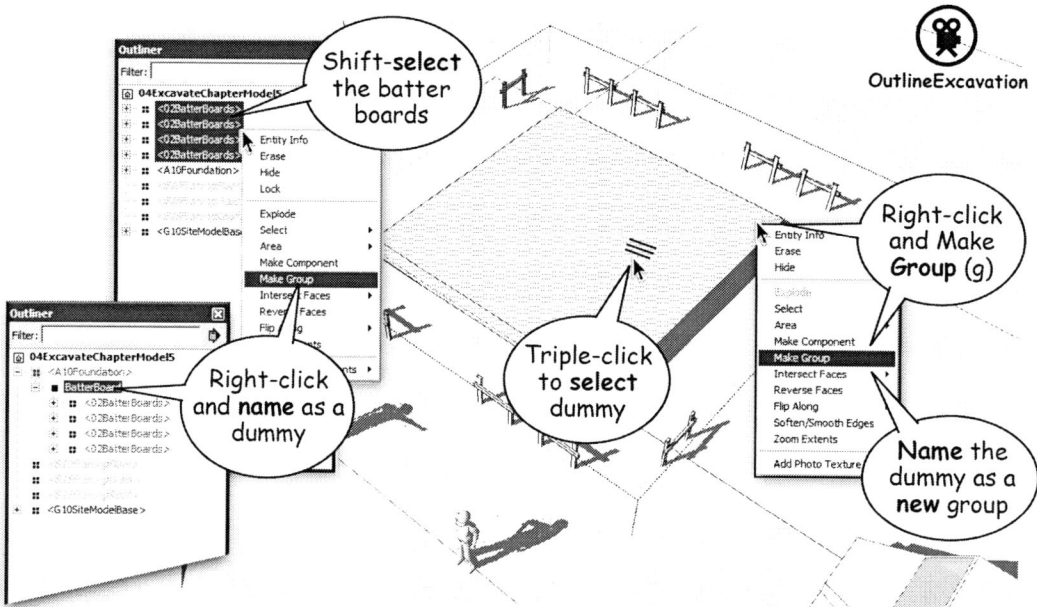

Use the workpoint to **lay out** the footprint and locate work areas, stockpiles, utility connections, and trenches to be **excavated** at the same time as the foundation.

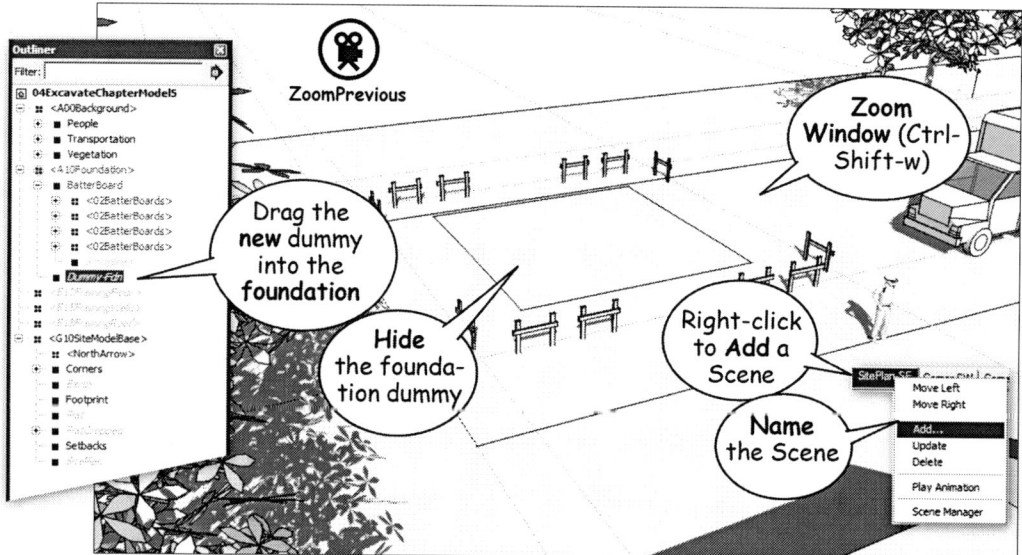

# String lines stretched across batter boards

String lines are stretched over the layout to locate corners. The strings are **removed** and **replaced** during construction for equipment and worker **access**.

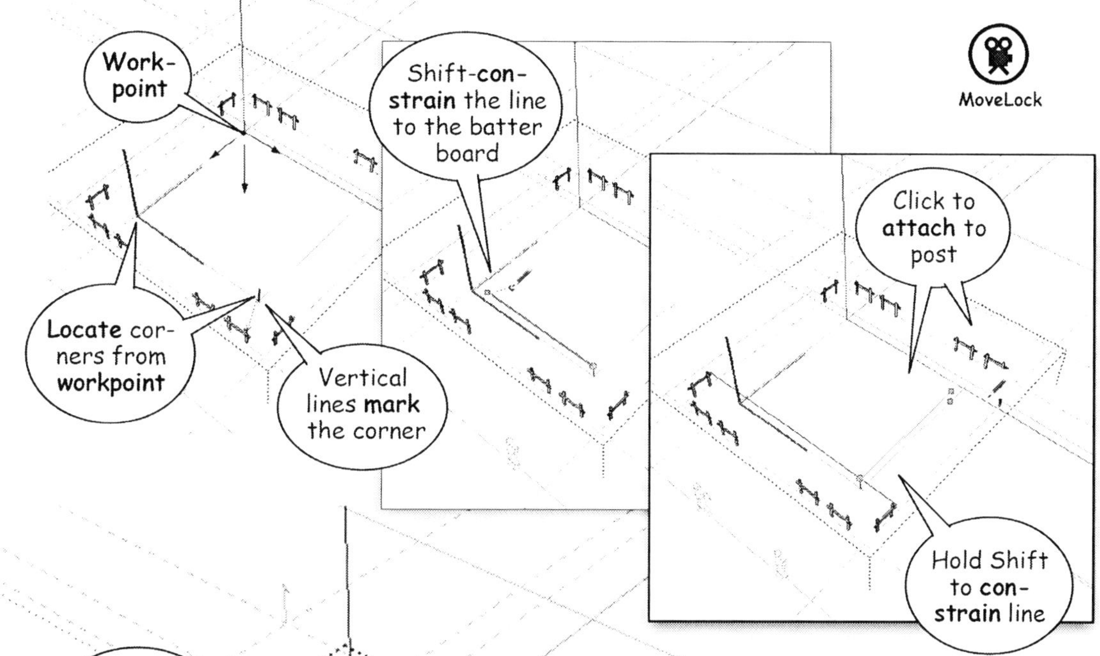

- Work-point
- Shift-**con-strain** the line to the batter board
- MoveLock 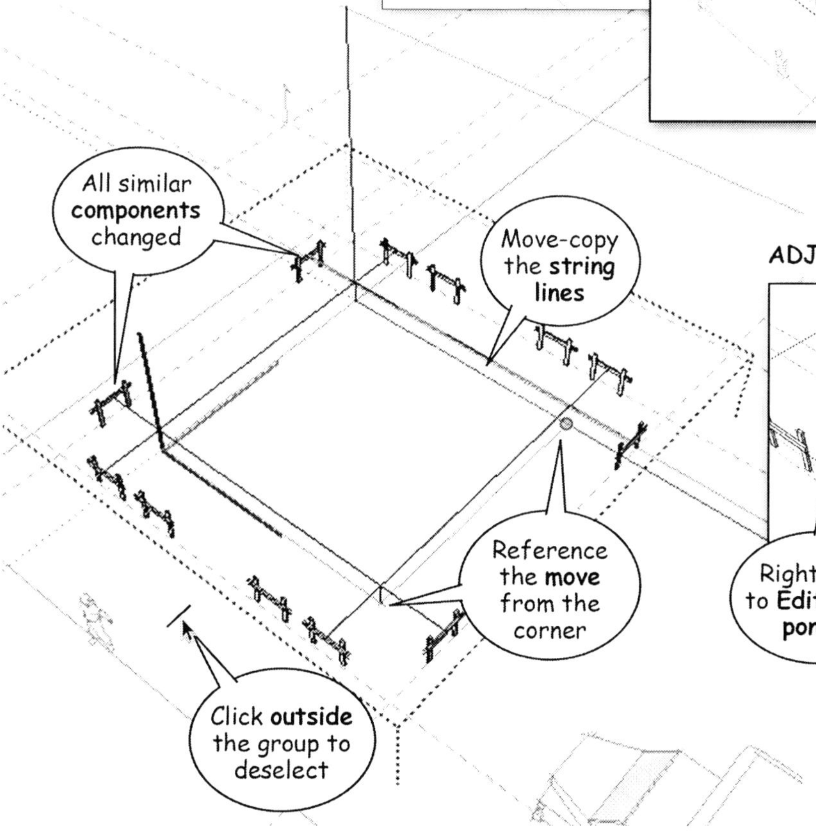
- Click to **attach** to post
- **Locate** corners from **workpoint**
- Vertical lines **mark** the corner
- Hold Shift to **con-strain** line
- All similar **components** changed
- Move-copy the **string lines**
- ADJUST BATTER BOARDS
- Move batter boards to **align**
- Reference the **move** from the corner
- Right-click to **Edit Component**
- Right-click to **Edit Group***
- Click **outside** the group to deselect

*Right or Double-click to edit group, Double-click to select a surface, Triple-click to select edges and surfaces

Excavate the model base for the foundation

## CUT INTO THE MODEL BASE
The Rectangle tool **cuts** the **surface** of the model base. The surface is then **pushed** down to the depth of the foundation and the top **edges** are **scaled** to shape the angle of repose.

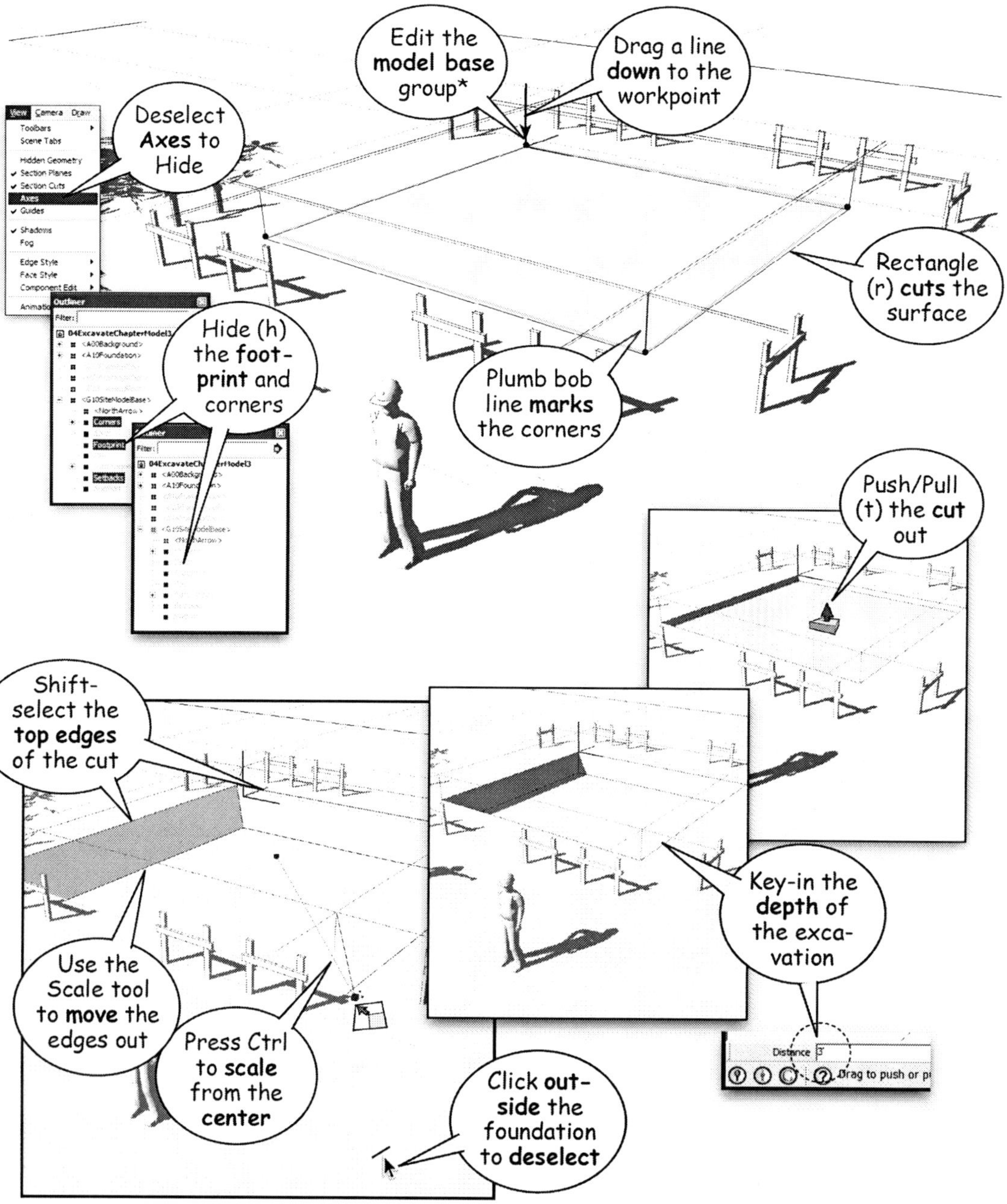

- Deselect **Axes** to Hide
- Edit the **model base group***
- Drag a line **down** to the workpoint
- Rectangle (r) **cuts** the surface
- Hide (h) the **footprint** and **corners**
- Plumb bob line **marks** the corners
- Push/Pull (t) the **cut** out
- Shift-select the **top edges** of the cut
- Key-in the **depth** of the excavation
- Use the Scale tool to **move** the edges out
- Press Ctrl to **scale** from the **center**
- Click **outside** the foundation to **deselect**

*To enter and Edit a group, double-click the group in the model or the name of the group in the Outliner

**64**

## Shape a massing model for the backfill

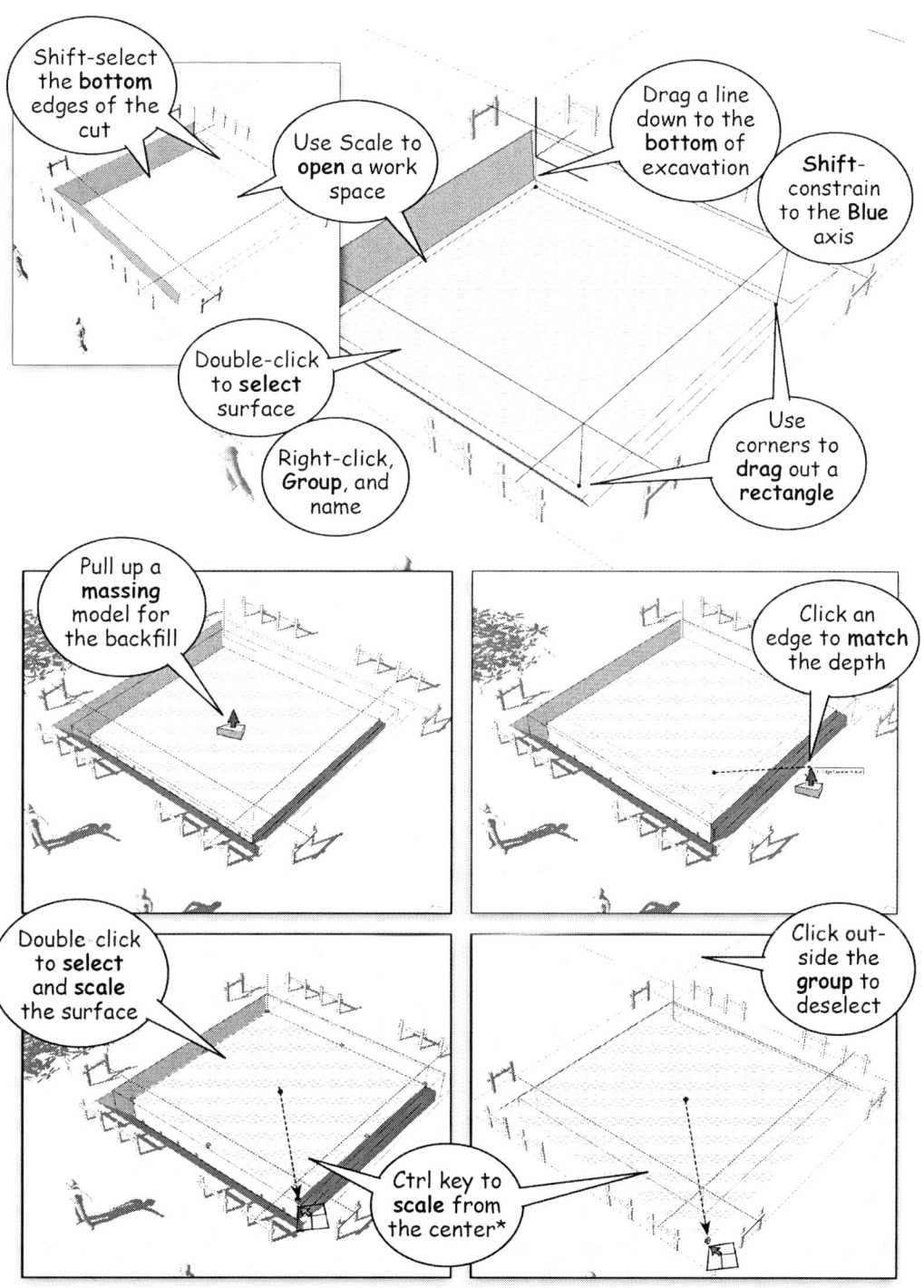

*Remember the Ctrl key modifies the action of the Scale tool by resizing the selection from the center

### Set up the jobsite for foundation

## STOCKPILE AND STAGE

Equipment is added for **visual** scale. This includes showing scaled stockpiles, storage, work areas, scrap bins, and the **general** organization of the jobsite.

Equipment Operation

- Shift-lock **Rotate** on the Red axis*
- Select the **backfill** and rotate
- Click Rotate (Alt-r) to **set axis**
- Click **again** to set the rotation **arm**
- Use Move (b) to **position** the backfill
- Reshape the **backfill** with the **Scale** tool
- Unhide and **populate** the background
- Use Scenes with **different** layers to illustrate and **animate** the excavation

LayerControls

*The Shift key locks the Circle, Protractor, and Rotate tools to match the slope of any axis or other surface

# Tips and tricks for construction modeling

## TIPS AND TRICKS

Position the viewpoint and set up the model for **different** Scenes.
You can then **Export** the Scene as a 2D image or as an **animation**
to illustrate movement or **steps** in the construction process.

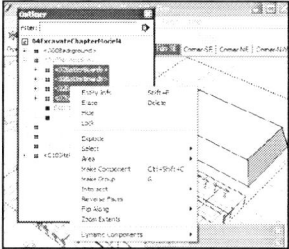

**01OutlineExcavation:**
take a look at the Outliner and organization of the excavation

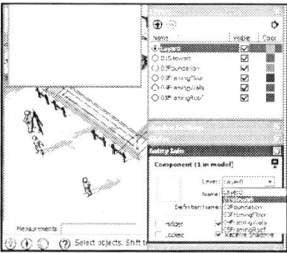

**02LayerControls:**
use Layer visibility controls to hide everything on that layer

**03ZoomField:**
hold the Shift key down to change the Zoom tool's field of view

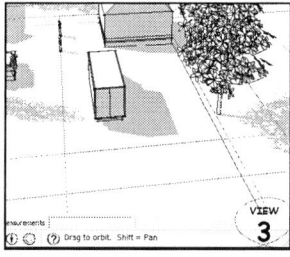

**04ZoomPrevious:**
Zoom Previous goes back to any of the last five points of view

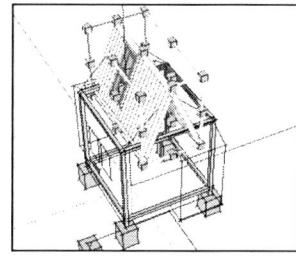

**05InsideOutFlip:**
reverse scale an object or entire assembly to flip a mirror copy

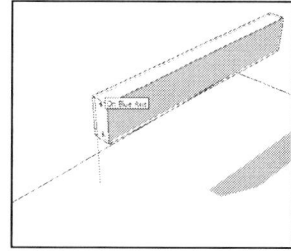

**06MoveLock:**
use the left, right, and up arrow keys to constrain moves and lines to any axis

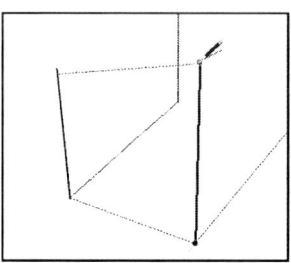

**07TypicalInferences:**
SketchUp's built-in Inferences speed fabrication and assembly

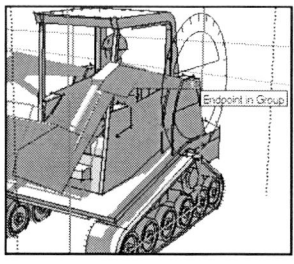

**08EquipmentOperation:**
use handles at pivot joints to operate equipment for staging

Keep in mind that a construction **model** is not static.

Construction models are organized to animate a **process** or illustrate a **sequence** of events.

# CHAPTER 4 CHECKLISTS - EXCAVATION

 ChecklistExcavation

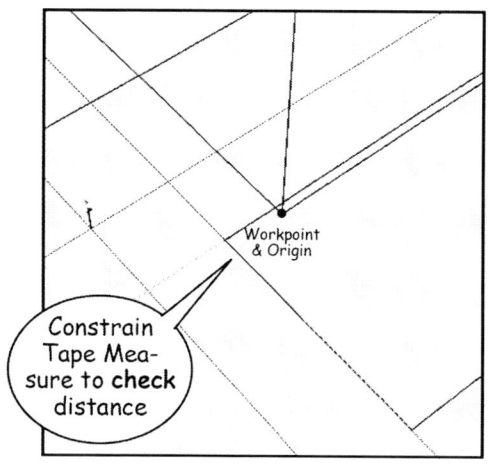

Constrain Tape Measure to **check** distance

## A. CHECK WORKPOINT
Like the real world, work on the jobsite starts with checking the location of the workpoint and setbacks.

- [ ] Tape Measure tool
- [ ] Verify the workpoint
- [ ] Drag along any axis
- [ ] Hold Shift key to constrain
- [ ] Constrained axis line darkens
- [ ] Click to reference corner
- [ ] Repeat to check layout lines

Workers add **visual** scale

## B. BATTER BOARDS
Batter boards are placed just outside the work area and used to guide the location and depth of the excavation.

- [ ] Workpoint locates the foundation
- [ ] Tape Measure tool for guidelines
- [ ] Drag a guideline to mark extent
- [ ] Offset depends on angle of repose
- [ ] Add batter board components
- [ ] Copy and scale using -1 flip
- [ ] Position batter boards in 4 corners

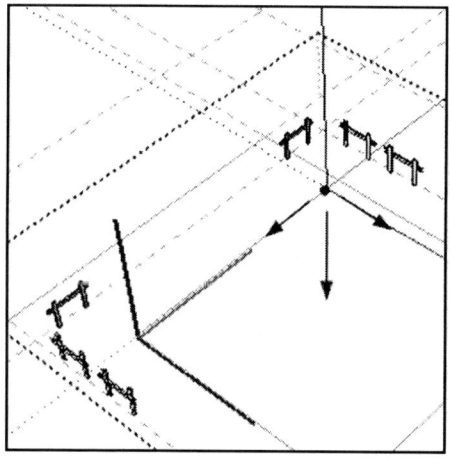

## C. STRING LINES
Stretch string lines across the work area using footprint corners to locate key points for the foundation.

- [ ] Organize assembly with Outliner
- [ ] Drag a line up from each corner
- [ ] Constrain and click to infer height
- [ ] Drag a string line from corners
- [ ] Stretch string line to boards
- [ ] Constrain and copy for layout
- [ ] Adjust batter boards to match

### D. CUT THE EXCAVATION
String lines are removed and replaced during excavation to check the progress of the work for the foundation.

- [ ] Drag a line down from corners
- [ ] Constrain to face of model base
- [ ] Edit the model base group
- [ ] Drag a rectangle from corners
- [ ] Push the surface down to cut
- [ ] Key-in the excavation depth
- [ ] Select & scale the top of cut
- [ ] Use Ctrl to scale from center

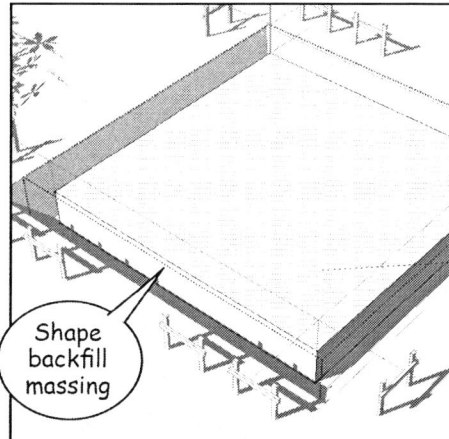

Shape backfill massing

### E. MASSING THE BACKFILL
Use the excavation in the model base to mold a massing model to represent the volume of backfill.

- [ ] Center-scale the bottom of the cut
- [ ] Exit the model base group
- [ ] Drag a rectangle from corners
- [ ] Group and name the rectangle
- [ ] Right-click to edit 2D rectangle
- [ ] Pull up to the top of the excavation
- [ ] Center-scale the top to match

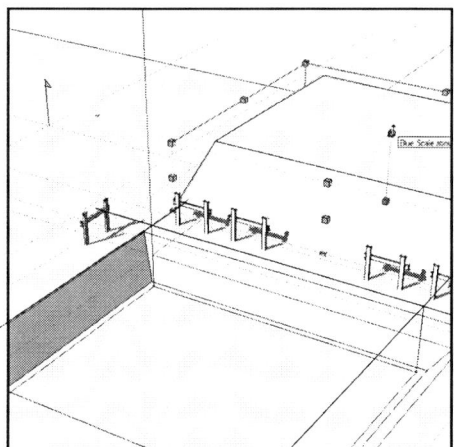

### F. STOCKPILE AND SET UP
Rotate the backfill and position it in the stockpile area. Unhide background features and populate the model.

- [ ] Shift-lock the Rotate tool
- [ ] Click to set rotation arm and axis
- [ ] Rotate 180 degrees and reshape
- [ ] Position the stockpile
- [ ] Unhide background components
- [ ] Populate the model for visual scale

# CHAPTER 5. FOUNDATION

## FABRICATING COMPONENTS

The key to building a construction model quickly is a well maintained **component library**. Every project is an opportunity to expand a **proprietary** collection of components because anything built for one job is more than likely going to be needed again.

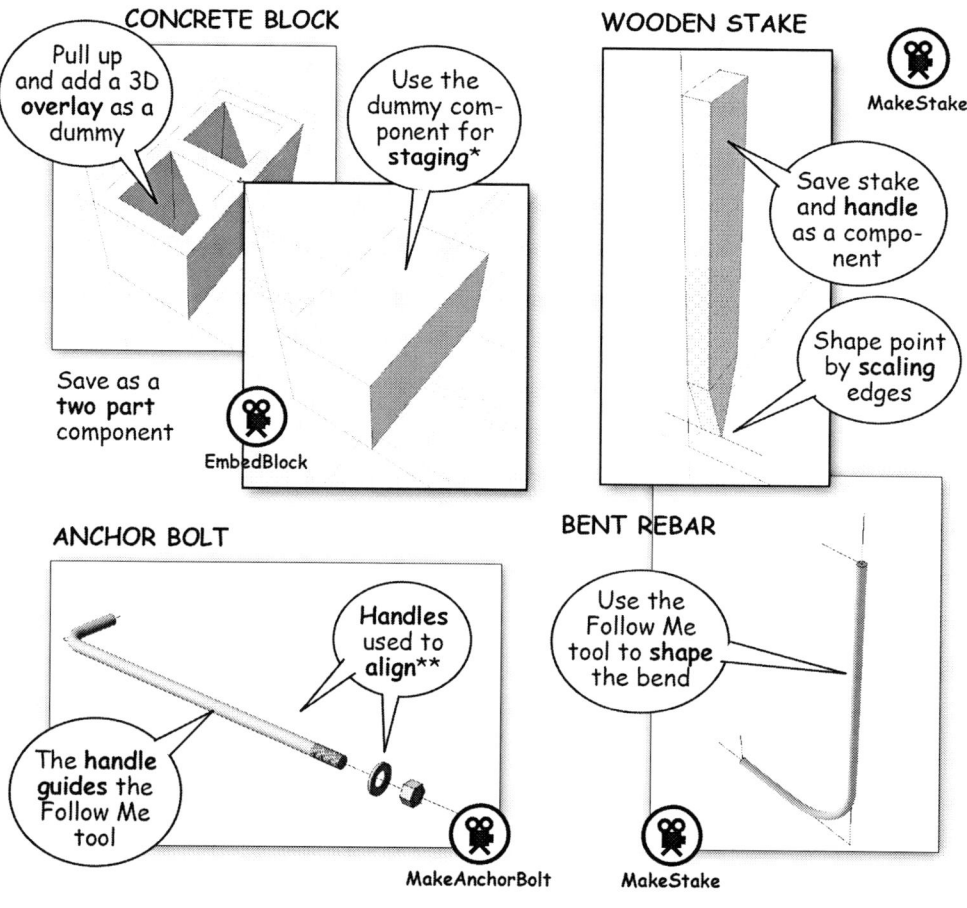

Remember to leave colors, textures, and excess details to design models. As the size of the **model file** increases, performance will slow.

1. Keep things **simple**, with **basic** shapes and forms.

2. Keep the focus on the construction process.

3. Use the phase dummies to simplify the display and model file.

*The dummy is a low poly, low resolution substitute to limit the level of detail and make the model faster

**Handles are guidelines that act as a wireframe for groups and components making them easier to assemble

## TIPS AND TRICKS

For speed, use the three-step modeling method to **fabricate** basic components and the Scale tool to **resize** the components to fit. Scaling avoids editing and trimming every piece as a unique component or **separate** group.

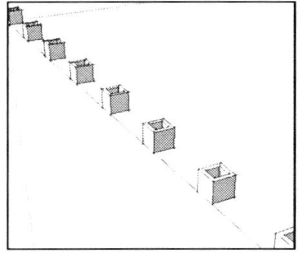

**01CopyArrays:**
make quickly spaced array-copies using a multiplier or a divider

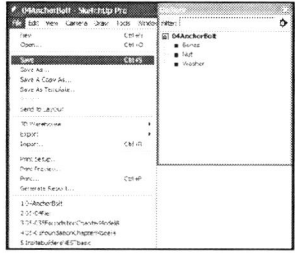

**02MaintainComponents:**
regularly save and update component changes to your own library

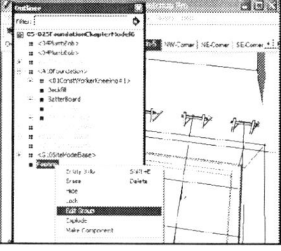

**03FoundationOrganized:**
the pieces of the Foundation are organized in the Outliner

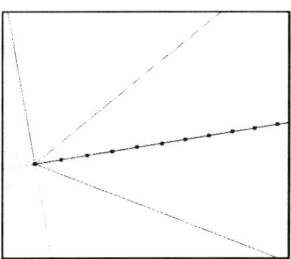

**04DividedAssemblies:**
Right-click to divide lines into equally spaced assembly points

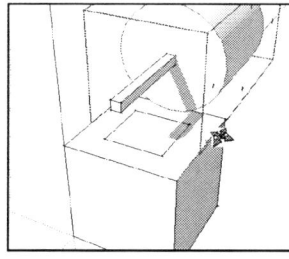

**05OffsetMove:**
select and move an object using a remote edge or inference axis

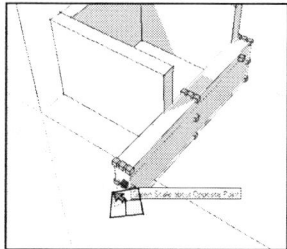

**06Scale2Fit:**
use the Scale tool to quickly reshape components to fit

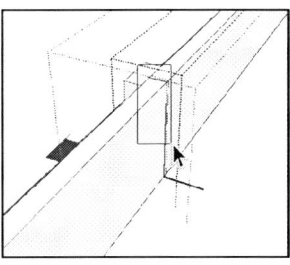

**07HideSplice:**
hide the common edges of a splice to make a seamless joint

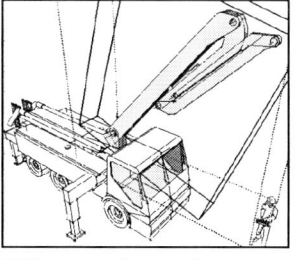

**08PumperOperation:**
use handles to position equipment and visually stage the jobsite

Remember, these pages are an **illustrated** index of the video **explanations** linked from the book's CD

71

Organize the jobsite for screenshots

## SET UP THE WORK AREAS
Thinking through lay down, staging, and work areas means **thinking** through **scope** and sequence.

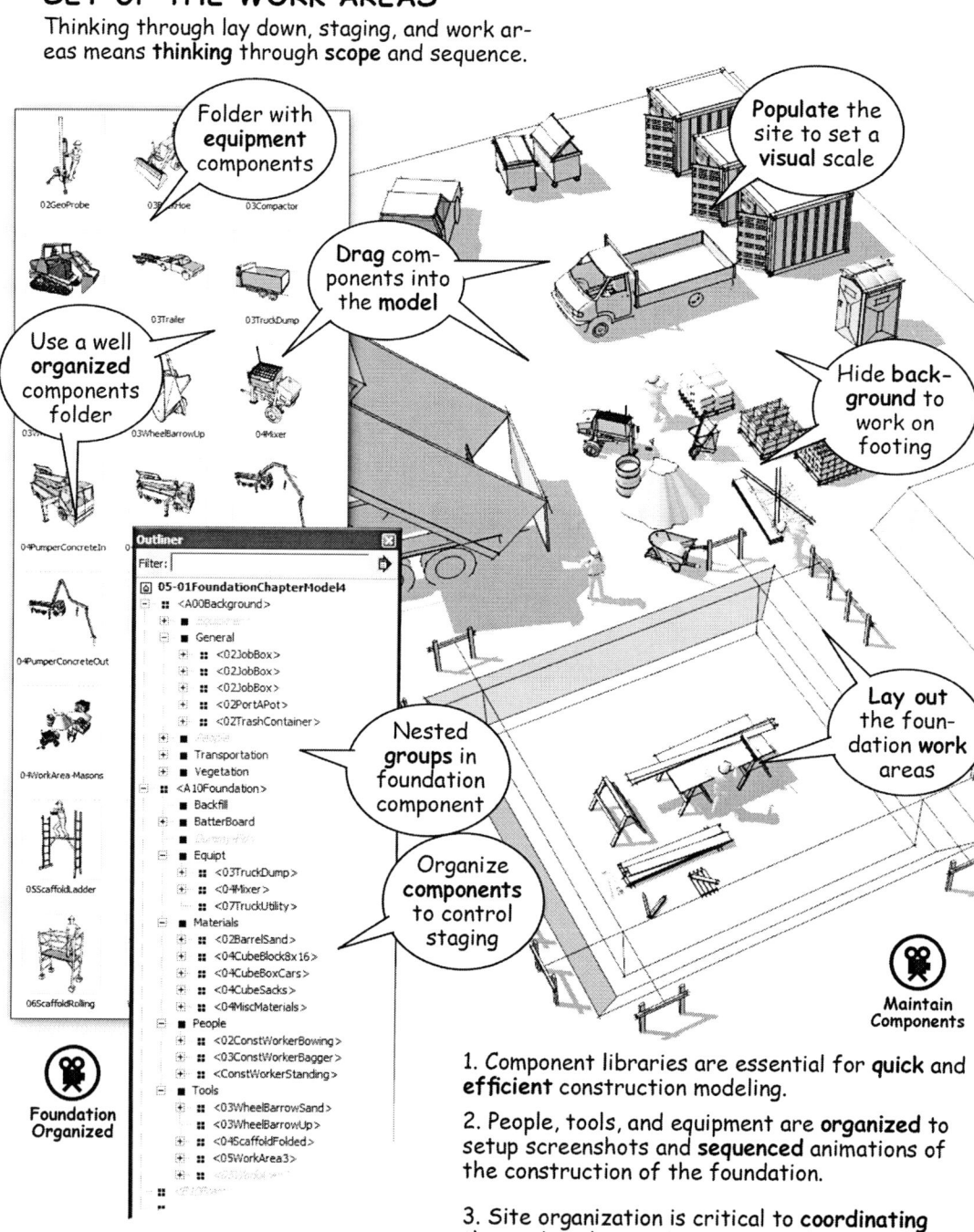

1. Component libraries are essential for **quick** and **efficient** construction modeling.

2. People, tools, and equipment are **organized** to setup screenshots and **sequenced** animations of the construction of the foundation.

3. Site organization is critical to **coordinating** the work and **managing** motion and sequence.

SetupScenes

Scenes speed movement around the model

## SET UP SCENES FOR THE WORK

Once **visual** scale and work areas are **staged**, update **Scenes** as new view points for the work.*

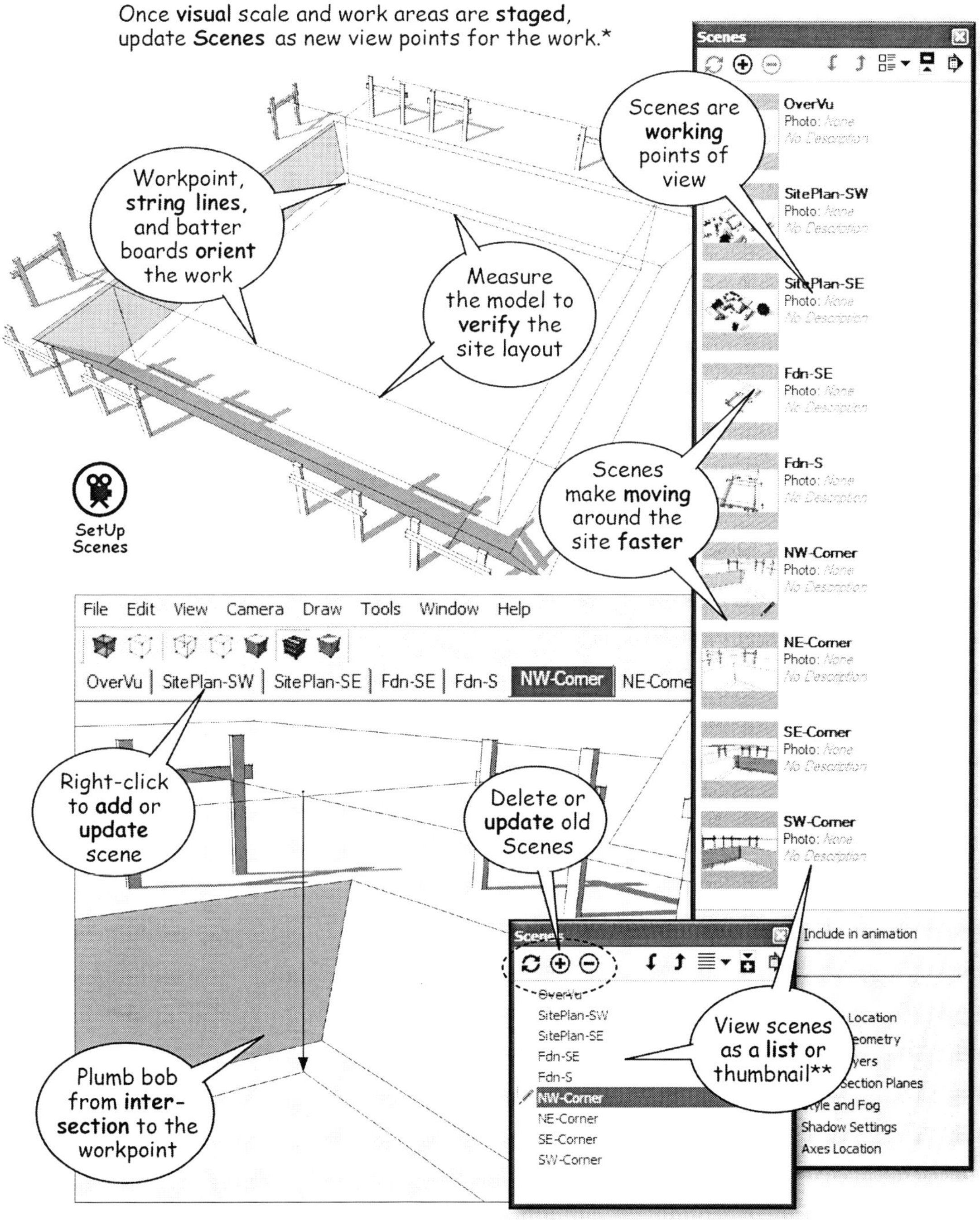

- Workpoint, **string lines**, and batter boards **orient** the work
- Scenes are **working** points of view
- Measure the model to **verify** the site layout
- Scenes make **moving** around the site **faster**
- SetUp Scenes
- Right-click to **add** or **update** scene
- Delete or **update** old Scenes
- Plumb bob from **inter-section** to the workpoint
- View scenes as a **list** or **thumbnail**\*\*

*Tool actions begun in any one Scene can continue in any other Scene as long as the tool remains active

**The list view is faster than thumbnails as a construction model changes and becomes more complex

Use string lines to lay out the formwork

PlaceFormwork

## SIMULATE FOOTING FORMWORK

A plumb bob **locates** the formwork from the same **intersecting** string lines used for the excavation.

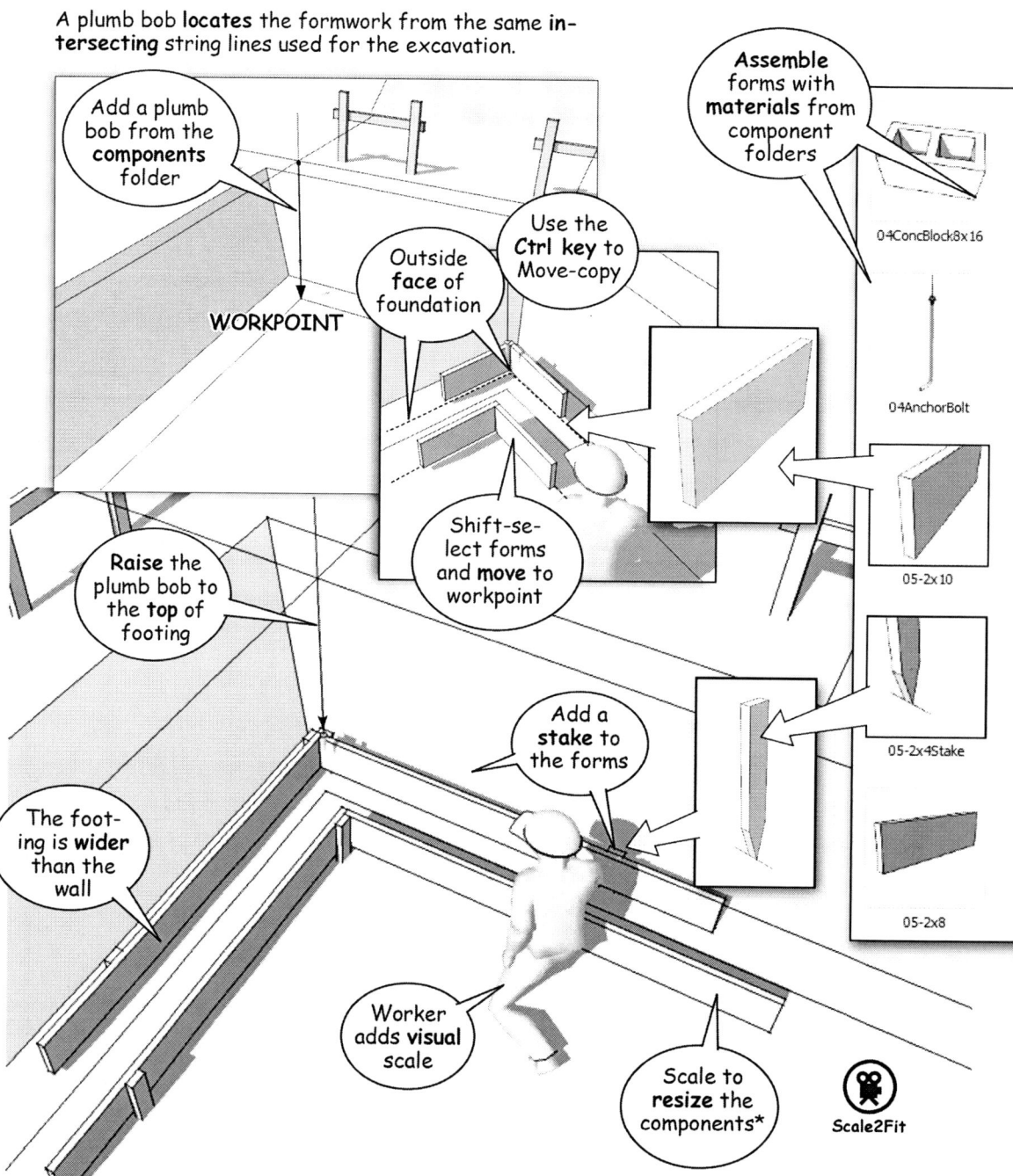

* Similar components do not change when resized with the Scale tool, but editing changes all similar components

# Placing rebar in the formwork

Move and place the rebar in the forms using **guidelines** drawn from **parallel** edges with the Tape Measure tool. The formwork and rebar are part of a construction **process** and used to **stage** illustrations or screenshots of the work sequence.

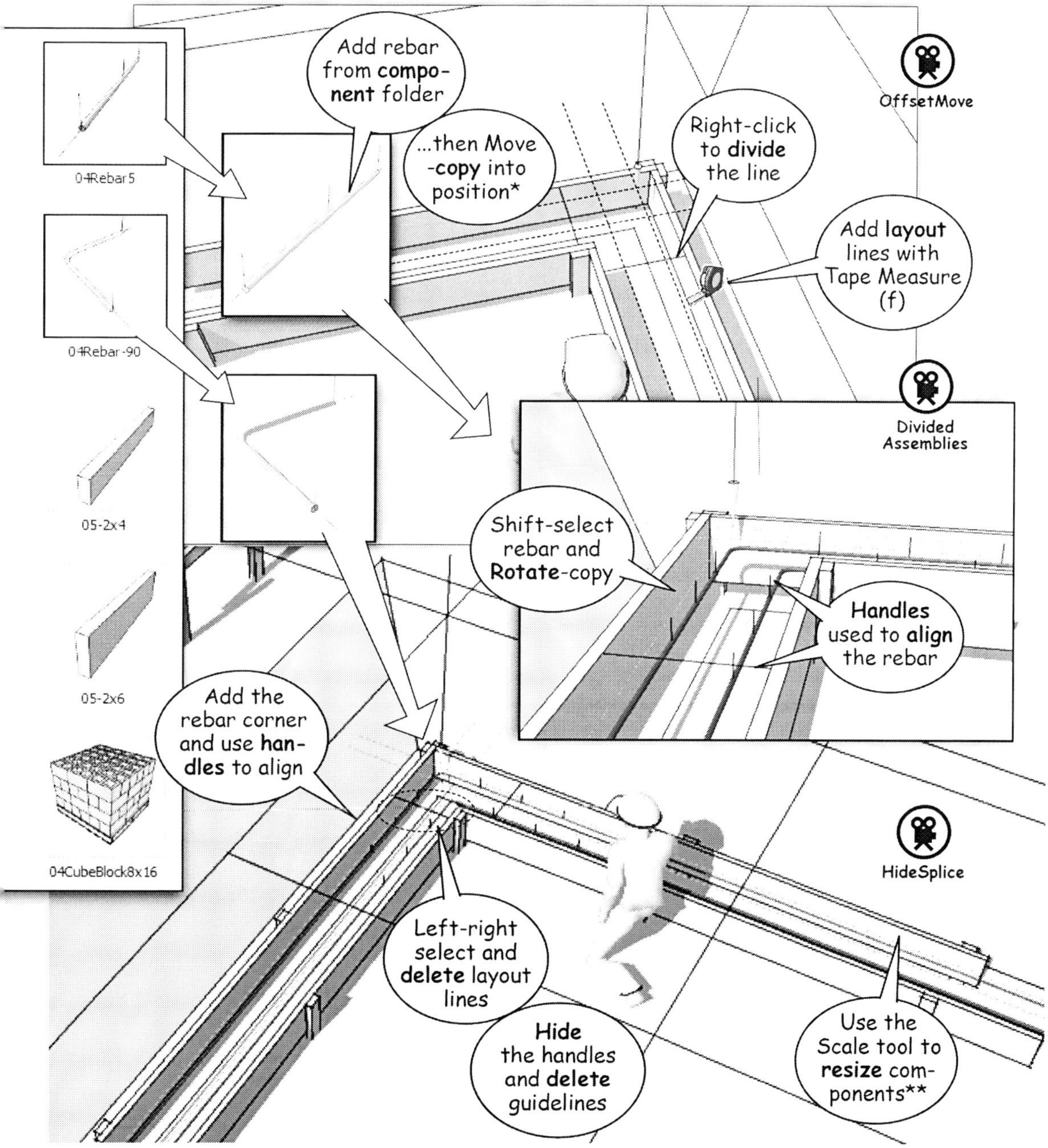

- Add rebar from **component** folder
- ...then Move-**copy** into position*
- Right-click to **divide** the line
- Add **layout** lines with Tape Measure (f)
- Shift-select rebar and **Rotate**-copy
- **Handles** used to **align** the rebar
- Add the rebar corner and use **handles** to align
- Left-right select and **delete** layout lines
- **Hide** the handles and **delete** guidelines
- Use the Scale tool to **resize** components**

PlaceRebar
OffsetMove
Divided Assemblies
HideSplice

04Rebar5
04Rebar-90
05-2x4
05-2x6
04CubeBlock8x16

*Use the Shift key to constrain moves and rotations and the Ctrl key to leave a copy in the same place

**The Scale tool stretches and reshapes one component without changing all similar components in the model

Footing reinforcing tied to J-bar

## ADDING J-BARS FOR THE WALL

Vertical rebar are **quickly** array-copied along the length of the forms to visually tie the **footing** to the foundation wall.

AddJbar

Divided Assembly

- Add J-bar from **component** folder
- Shift-select and move **into** concrete
- Draw a line to **divide** the width
- Move **copy** the rebar
- Constrain **drag** construction line to midpoint
- **Key-in** dimension
- ...or Key-in **dimension** to center*
- Drag into **Footing** group
- Select **formwork** and reinforcing
- ...then Rotate-copy around cen-ter 3 times
- Key-in **angle**
- Key-in **number** of copies

Angle 90

Angle 3x

CopyArrays

The J-bars are **separated** in the Outliner as a distinct group because the **upper** portion of the bar remains **visible** after the footing concrete is placed.

*Accurate placement can be shown in a detailed and dimensioned image at a typical location

PlaceConcrete

Placing the concrete in the forms

## CONCRETE FOOTING
Hide the footing formwork and rebar once the concrete is in place.*

- Plumb-bobs **mark** corners of the **foundation** wall
- Start a rectangle in **one** Scene
- Go to **another** Scene
- Click to **finish** in another Scene**
- Nest **groups** in foundation component
- Right-click to **Rename**
- **Hidden** pieces
- Key-in **height** of footing
- Delete the **inside** surface
- Right-click and **select** All Connected
- Group and **name**
- Set up **concrete** and J-bars for foundation wall

*Zoom in to the footing and hide layers to expose the rebar and formwork for a particular construction detail

**When you switch Scenes with a tool still active the tool remains active after the change of viewpoint

77

Placing concrete for the foundation wall

# FOUNDATION WALL: CONCRETE

Extrude the wall from a 2D **outline** on the footing. The concrete could also be **shown** in layers or sections to **simulate** special conditions.

Build
ConcreteWall

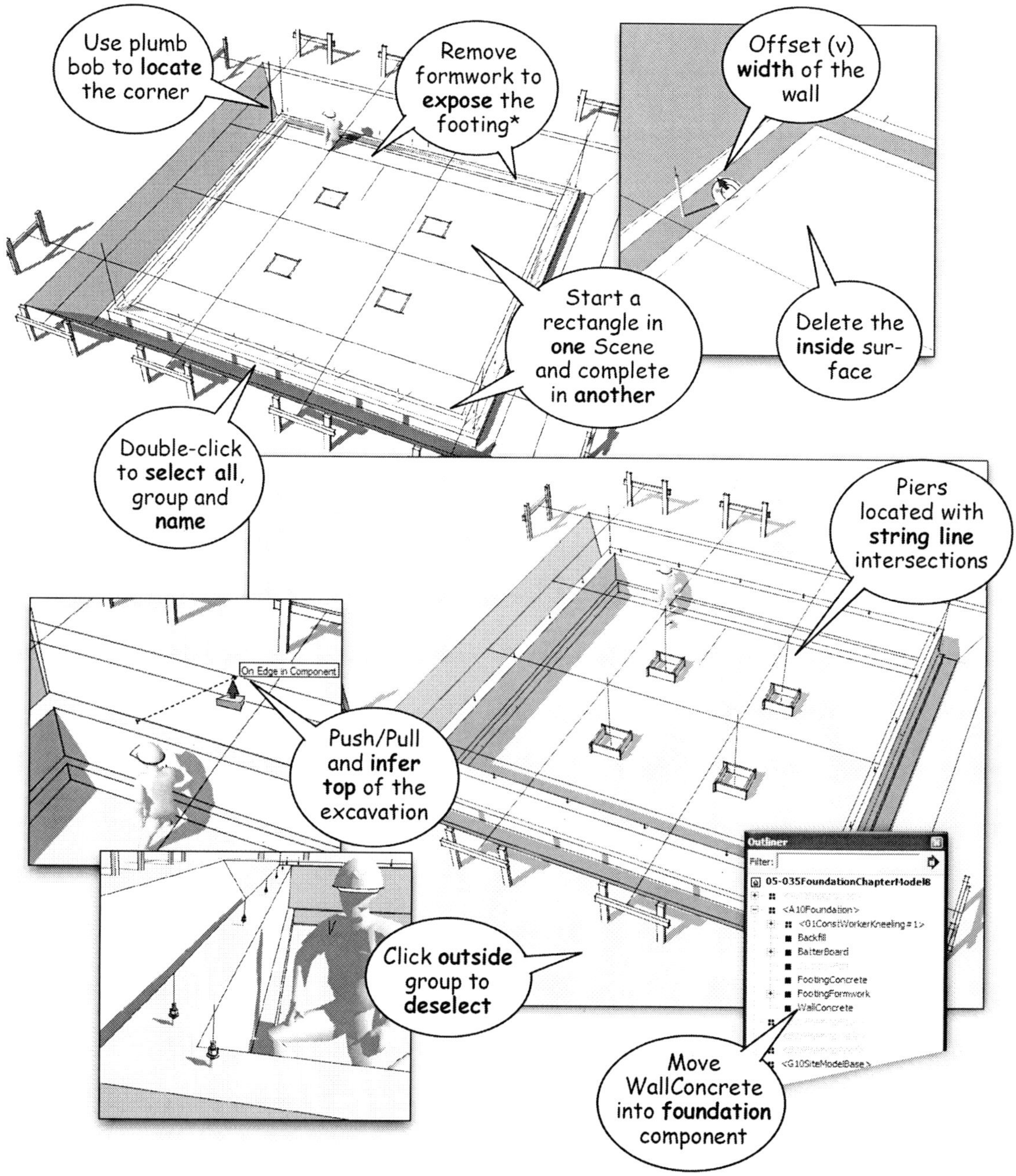

- Use plumb bob to **locate** the corner
- Remove formwork to **expose** the footing*
- Offset (v) **width** of the wall
- Start a rectangle in **one** Scene and complete in **another**
- Delete the **inside** surface
- Double-click to **select all**, group and **name**
- Piers located with **string line** intersections
- Push/Pull and **infer top** of the excavation
- Click **outside** group to **deselect**
- Move WallConcrete into **foundation** component

*Formwork and reinforcing could remain visible in a detail to illustrate a detail or sequence of tasks

Build MasonryWall

# Lay block for the masonry foundation wall

## FOUNDATION WALL: MASONRY

Lay the concrete block to **simulate** the assembly process. Group the block to illustrate **specific** sequences that might be necessary to add **detail** to the construction.

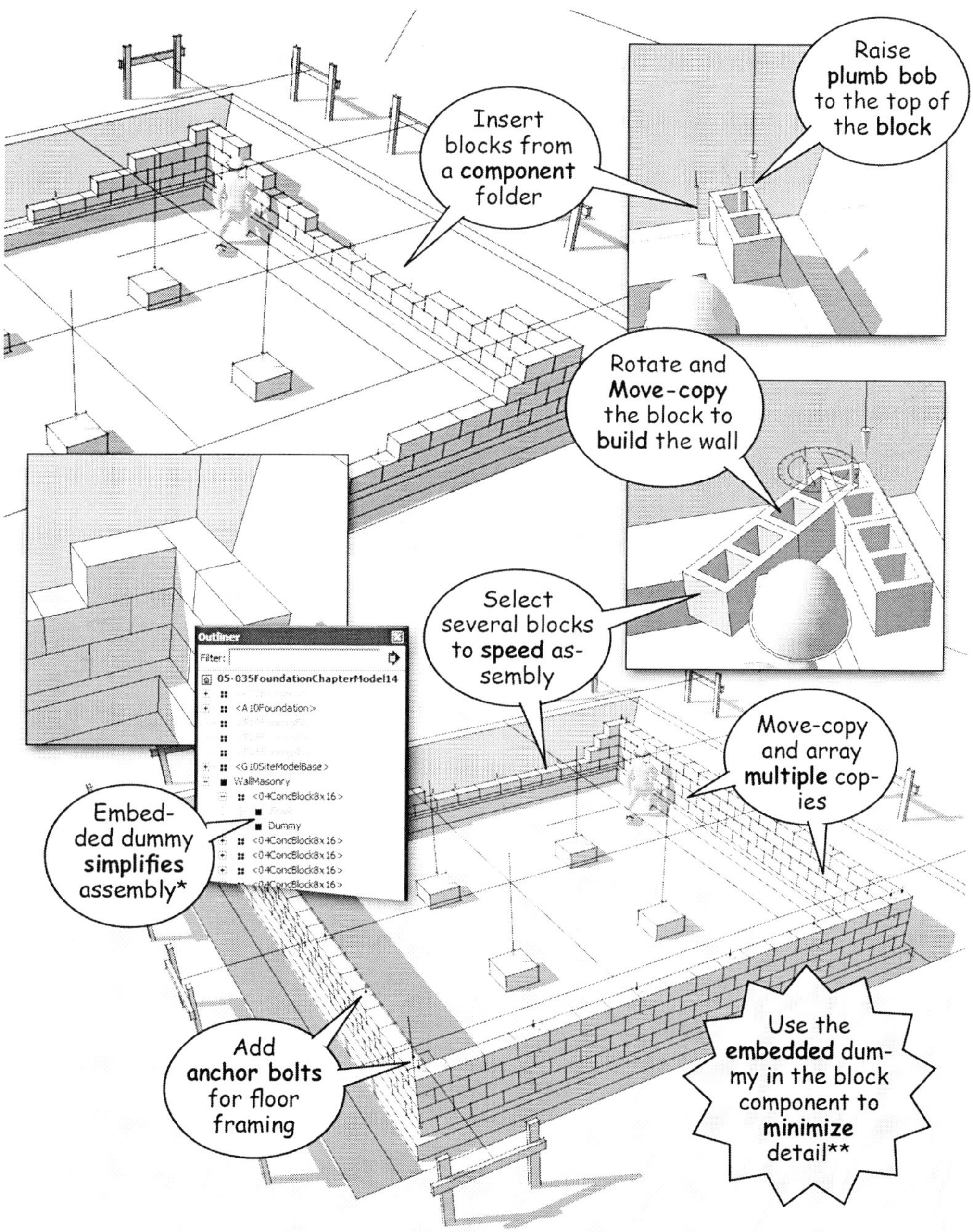

- Insert blocks from a **component** folder
- Raise **plumb bob** to the top of the **block**
- Rotate and **Move-copy** the block to **build** the wall
- Select several blocks to **speed** assembly
- Move-copy and array **multiple** copies
- Embedded dummy **simplifies** assembly*
- Add **anchor bolts** for floor framing
- Use the **embedded** dummy in the block component to **minimize** detail**

*See page 84 for more information on the embedded dummy and unhiding the details of the concrete block

**If there is too much detail, the model will slow down as the number of blocks and components increase

Insert anchor bolts for the sill plates

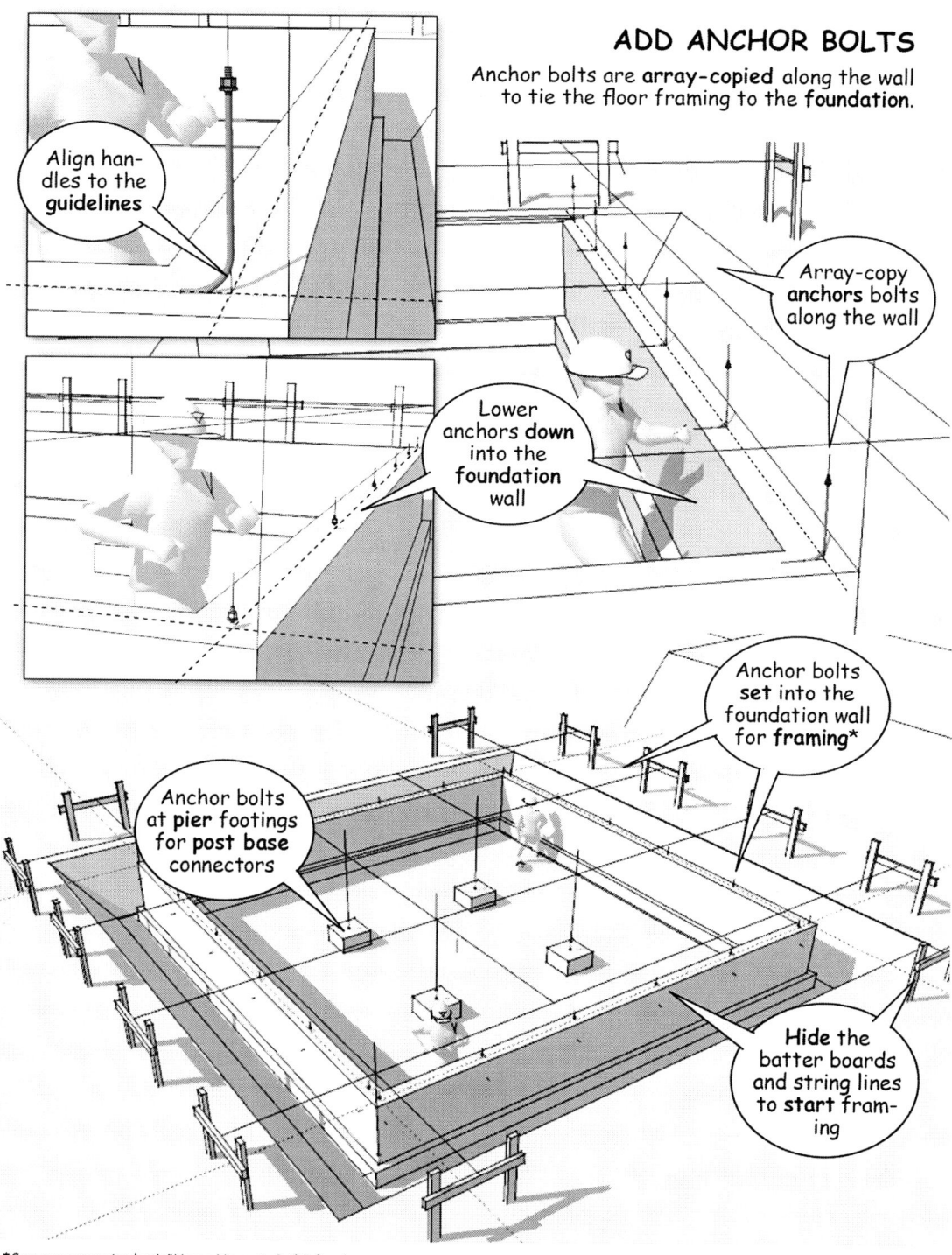

## ADD ANCHOR BOLTS
Anchor bolts are **array-copied** along the wall to tie the floor framing to the **foundation**.

Align handles to the **guidelines**

Array-copy **anchors** bolts along the wall

Lower anchors **down** into the **foundation** wall

Anchor bolts **set** into the foundation wall for **framing**\*

Anchor bolts at **pier** footings for **post base** connectors

**Hide** the batter boards and string lines to **start** framing

\*See our companion book "How a House is Built" for detailed illustrations and videos of foundation and framing

PumperOperation

Use annotated images to illustrate process

## SCREENSHOTS TELL THE STORY

Stage details and processes **embedded** in the construction model by changing the camera **viewpoint**, layer **visibility**, and hiding pieces of the assembly.

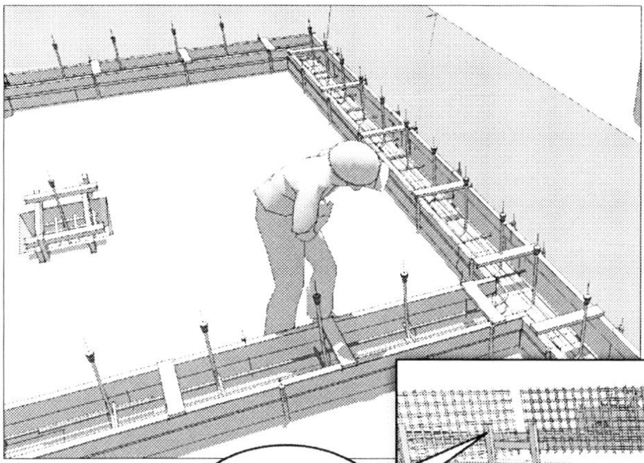

Use real-world details to add **credibility** to the image and the message.

Add objects to layers or in **groups** that can be **hidden** to display process.

Turn workers to **point** or **face** the area of focus for the screenshot.

Background components add **depth** and **scale** to the image

Use **bubbles** over the image to **separate** the message

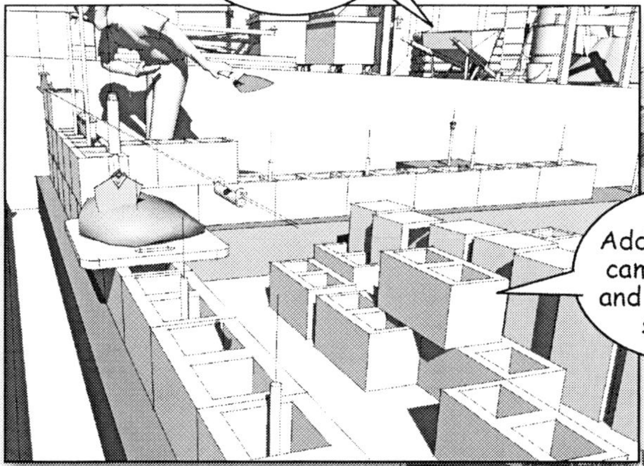

Add **time** with camera views and **shade** and shadow

You can **quickly** set the stage with materials and tools from **your** component library.

**Save** each setting as a Scene for **export** as a bitmap or animation.*

*Export PNG files for the web, JPEGs and TIFFs for illustrations, and bitmaps for text-based programs

# CHAPTER 5 CHECKLISTS - FOUNDATION

Foundation CheckList

Save components to a **component** library

## A. MAKING COMPONENTS
Construction models require simple components to minimize file size and maximize visual flexibility.

- [ ] Build simple components
- [ ] No color or texture
- [ ] Extrude 3D from 2D
- [ ] Embed stand-in dummies
- [ ] Use handles for alignment
- [ ] Save to a components folder
- [ ] Regularly update your collection

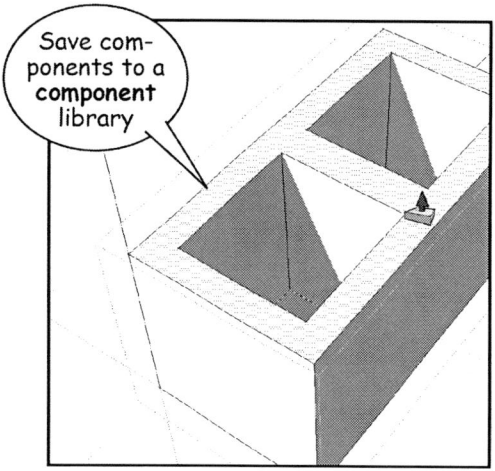

## B. WORK AREAS & SCENES
Set up work areas and scenes to both visually scale the model and simulate movement as you stage the process.

- [ ] Stage the jobsite in phases
- [ ] Use scaled equipment and tools
- [ ] Insert components from a library
- [ ] Outliner organizes the assembly
- [ ] Hide and unhide for staging
- [ ] Set Scenes for the work
- [ ] Use Scenes to move around

String lines **guide** the assembly

## C. FOOTING FORMWORK
Use string lines to align components and assemble the formwork and reinforcing for the footing.

- [ ] Plumb bob from the string lines
- [ ] Locate the workpoint
- [ ] Add components for formwork
- [ ] Copy and rotate into position
- [ ] Use segmented lines and guides
- [ ] Add reinforcing, copy and rotate
- [ ] Delete guides and layout lines

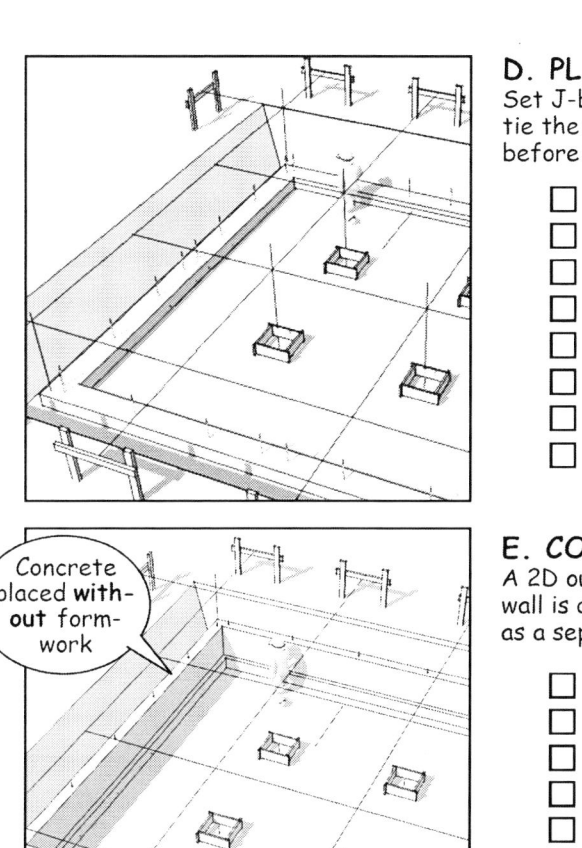

## D. PLACING CONCRETE
Set J-bars in the formwork to visually tie the footing to the foundation wall before placing the footing concrete.

- [ ] Add J-bar components
- [ ] Rotate and copy the J-bar
- [ ] Position with lines and guidelines
- [ ] Hide the formwork
- [ ] Drag out a rectangle
- [ ] Use Offset to outline the footing
- [ ] Push/Pull the 2D shape into 3D
- [ ] Group and name the footing

Concrete placed **without** formwork

## E. CONCRETE WALL
A 2D outline of the concrete foundation wall is drawn on the footing and extruded as a separate group with Push/Pull.

- [ ] Locate the corners of the wall
- [ ] Drag a rectangle out on the footing
- [ ] Use Offset tool to shape the wall
- [ ] Group and name the 2D wall profile
- [ ] Edit Group and Push/Pull to 3D
- [ ] Infer the top of the excavation
- [ ] Add and array anchor bolts

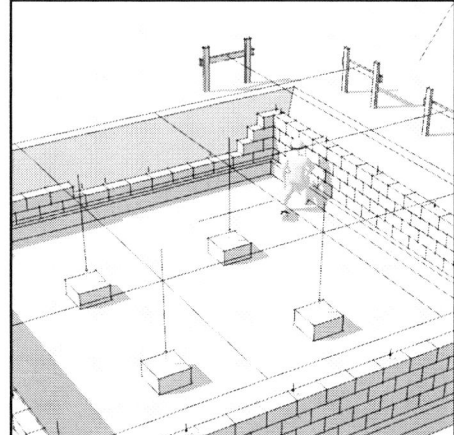

## F. MASONRY WALL
Build the wall from the corners using string lines and batter boards to simulate the assembly process.

- [ ] Plumb bob locates the corners
- [ ] Add a concrete block component
- [ ] Rotate and copy into position
- [ ] Unhide the embedded dummy
- [ ] Select multiple blocks for copy
- [ ] Add anchor bolts for framing
- [ ] Illustrate process with staging

# CHAPTER 6. FLOOR FRAMING

Foundation Dummy

## SET UP A FOUNDATION DUMMY

Embed dummies in components as **massing** models to reduce details in subassemblies and displays. The embedded dummy simplifies assembly and speeds regeneration time by **minimizing** program calculations as you **move** around the model.

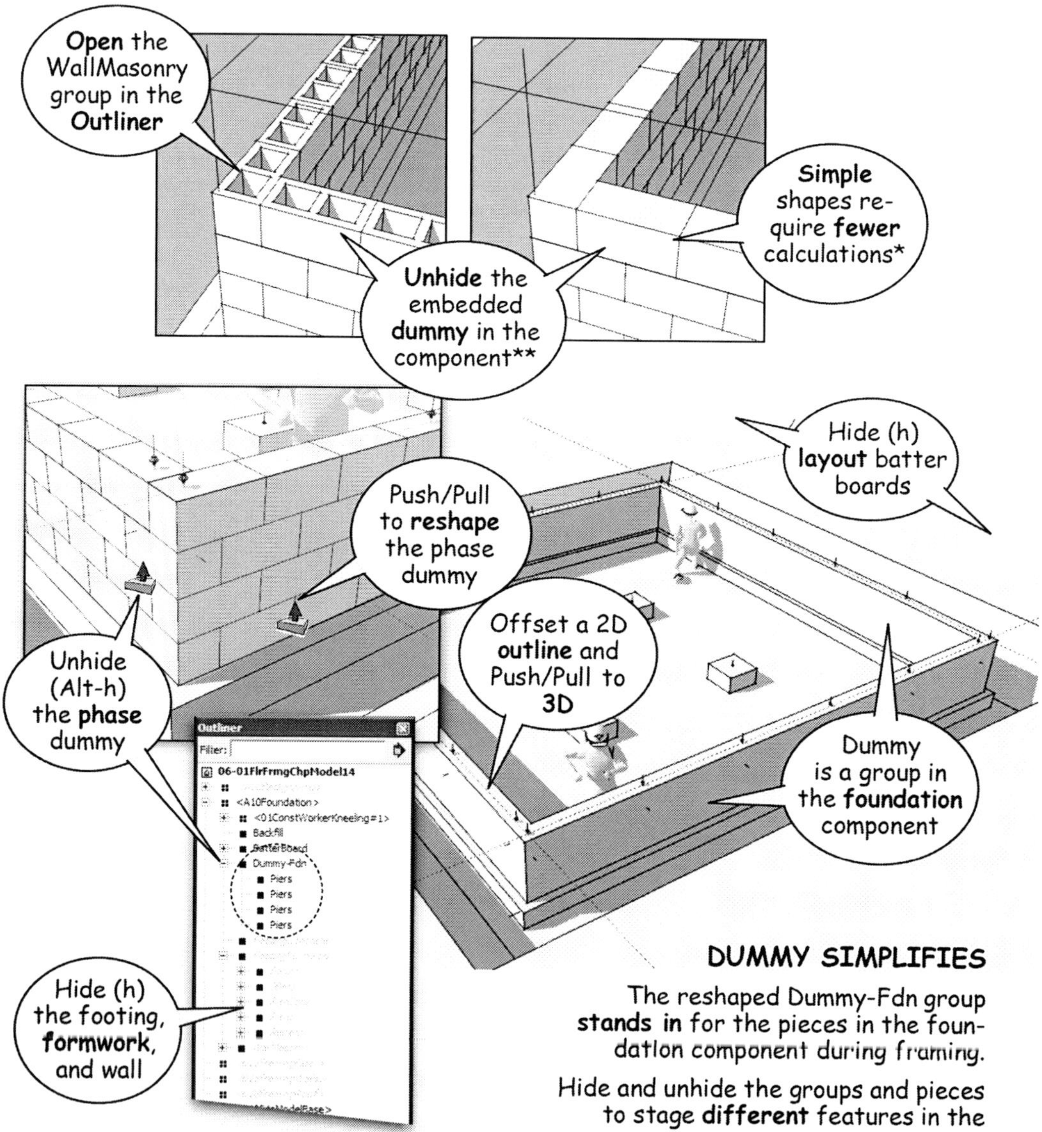

- Open the WallMasonry group in the **Outliner**
- Unhide the embedded **dummy** in the component**
- Simple shapes require **fewer** calculations*
- Push/Pull to **reshape** the phase dummy
- Hide (h) **layout** batter boards
- Unhide (Alt-h) the **phase** dummy
- Offset a 2D **outline** and Push/Pull to 3D
- Dummy is a group in the **foundation** component
- Hide (h) the footing, **formwork**, and wall

### DUMMY SIMPLIFIES

The reshaped Dummy-Fdn group **stands in** for the pieces in the foundation component during framing.

Hide and unhide the groups and pieces to stage **different** features in the construction model.

---

*Hide the Hollow block and unhide the Dummy block in any component and all similar components are changed

**The dummy acts as a low poly, lo resolution stand-in to make moving around the model faster and simpler

# Tips and tricks for faster modeling

## MORE TIPS AND TRICKS

Move a piece **out** of an assembly along any **axis** at a known **distance** to edit it. Then put the piece **back** into position by moving it along the **same** axis and same distance.

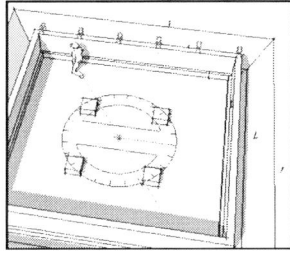

**01RotateCopies:** Rotate multiple copies around a common center similar to arrays

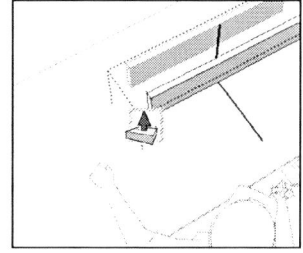

**02ReviewComponents:** add and scale components, any edit changes all copies

**COMPONENTS:** Components are valuable for fast construction modeling because they can be used as place markers.

Build them into a construction model as a **simple** massing element and edit them later to add details.

Any change to a component is reflected in **every** copy of that component in the model file.

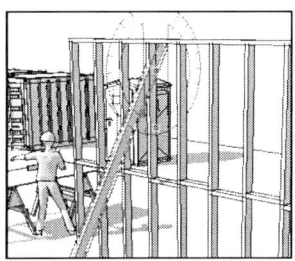

**03PasteInPlace:** cut to a new file for editing, then paste back to the original

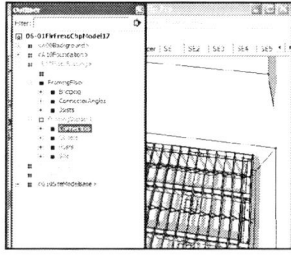

**04StayOrganized:** the Outliner keeps the pieces of the floor framing organized

## SKETCHUP HINTS

As you use SketchUp, watch the messages continually **posted** at the **bottom** of the interface for tips and options available for **different** tools and menu **selections**.

- Menu and tool hints
- Units for different measurements
- Modifier keys for the action
- Prompts for each step
- Options available for tools
- Icons link to other resources

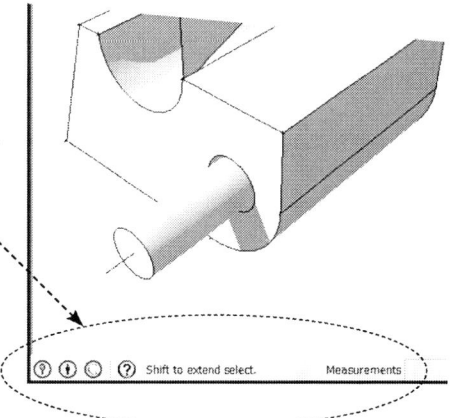

Scale the sill plates and bolt to the wall

# SILL PLATES AND ANCHOR BOLTS

Pressure treated sill plates are **installed** on the top of the foundation walls as bearing pads for the **floor** framing. The sills are components **scaled to fit** the standard lengths of the plates.

Sills&Anchors

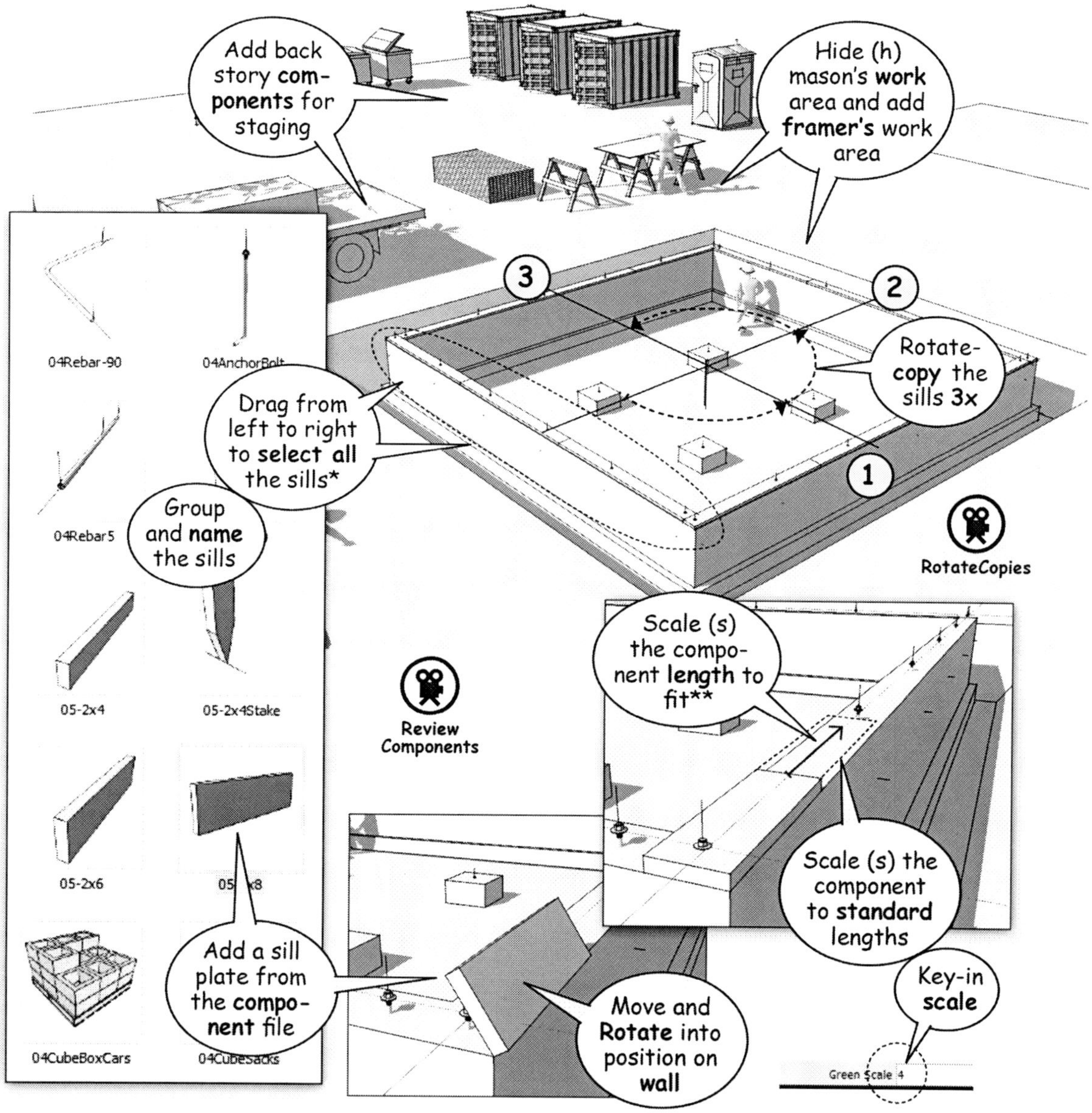

Add back story **components** for staging

Hide (h) mason's **work** area and add **framer's** work area

Rotate-copy the sills 3x

Drag from left to right to **select all** the sills*

Group and **name** the sills

04Rebar-90
04AnchorBolt
04Rebar5
05-2x4
05-2x4Stake
05-2x6
05-2x8
04CubeBoxCars
04CubeSacks

Review Components

Add a sill plate from the **component** file

Scale (s) the component **length** to fit**

Scale (s) the component to **standard** lengths

Move and **Rotate** into position on **wall**

Key-in **scale**

RotateCopies

*Use Shortcut keys, Scenes, and the Shift key to toggle Pan and Orbit and move around the model

**Unlike editing a component, scaling the component to fit does not affect other components in the model

SetGirders

Set the girders on the foundation

## SETTING THE GIRDERS

A composite girder is first **fabricated** and then **scaled** and **copied** to fit into post and hanger connectors.

- Draw a **line** up to the **bearing** height
- Draw a **guideline** at the girder centerline
- Add a post and **connectors** from the component folder
- Use the **handles** to align and position
- Add a **hanger** from components and **align** handles
- Rotate-**copy** the girder **and** connector
- Grouped **girder** fabricated with **scaled** components

PasteInPlace

- Scale the **girder** to fit into **connectors**
- Posts bear on **stand-off** base at anchor bolt
- Select and copy the pier **assembly** using an **offset** move
- Speed assembly with **multiple** selections and **offset** moves

Floor joists bear on the girder and sills

PlaceJoists

# PLACING THE FLOOR JOISTS

Rim joists are **tied** to the sill plates with standard framing **connectors**. Floor joists are then nailed or clipped to the rim joists and **bear** on the sills and girders.

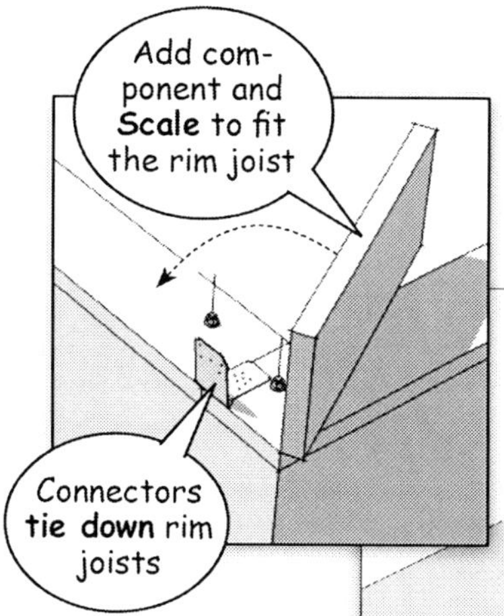

- Add component and **Scale** to fit the rim joist
- Connectors **tie down** rim joists
- Move-copy along the sill and **key-in** two copies
- Select the rim joist **and** tie downs
- Rotate and copy **around** the wall
- Copy and **array** connectors **along** the sill plate

StayOrganized

- Move-copy a rim joist and **array-copy** as floor joists*
- Key-in **multiple** copies
- Add components for **blocking**
- Use the framing **geometry** to position the pieces
- Use a guideline to position **bridging**\*\*

*Joist spacing and blocking and bridging locations vary with span, joist size, and anticipated loads.

\*\*Prefabricated bridging is spiked into the floor joists in a crossing pattern to stiffen the floor at mid-span

StaggerSubfloor

Subfloor works to stiffen the floor framing

### STAGGERED SUBFLOOR
A subfloor uses **interlocking** plywood or engineered sheet material laid out in a **staggered** pattern and glued and nailed to the joists with a specific nailing **spacing**.

- Add a **plywood** component
- Measure to **check** dimensions
- Key-in **scale** of component to **half** sheet
- Component **scaled** to a full sheet
- **Move** to corner
- Shift-**select** multiple pieces for **group** copy
- Key-in **multiple** copies
- Move (b) **scaled** pieces and fit to **corner**
- Solid blocking **under** bearing walls*
- **Shift-select** all to Group and name
- Drag subfloor group into **framing** component
- Backfill when **floor** framing is **finished**

*Additional blocking stiffens the floor framing and transfers wall and roof loads down to the foundation

## Connectors add detail to the frame

### FRAMING CONNECTORS
You can add a variety of framing connectors to a construction model from the **Insitebuilders** Component Library, but keep in mind that they are **memory** intensive when array-copied. Group and layer all components to **control** visibility.*

See Simpson **Strongtie** Framing Connectors at www.strongtie.com

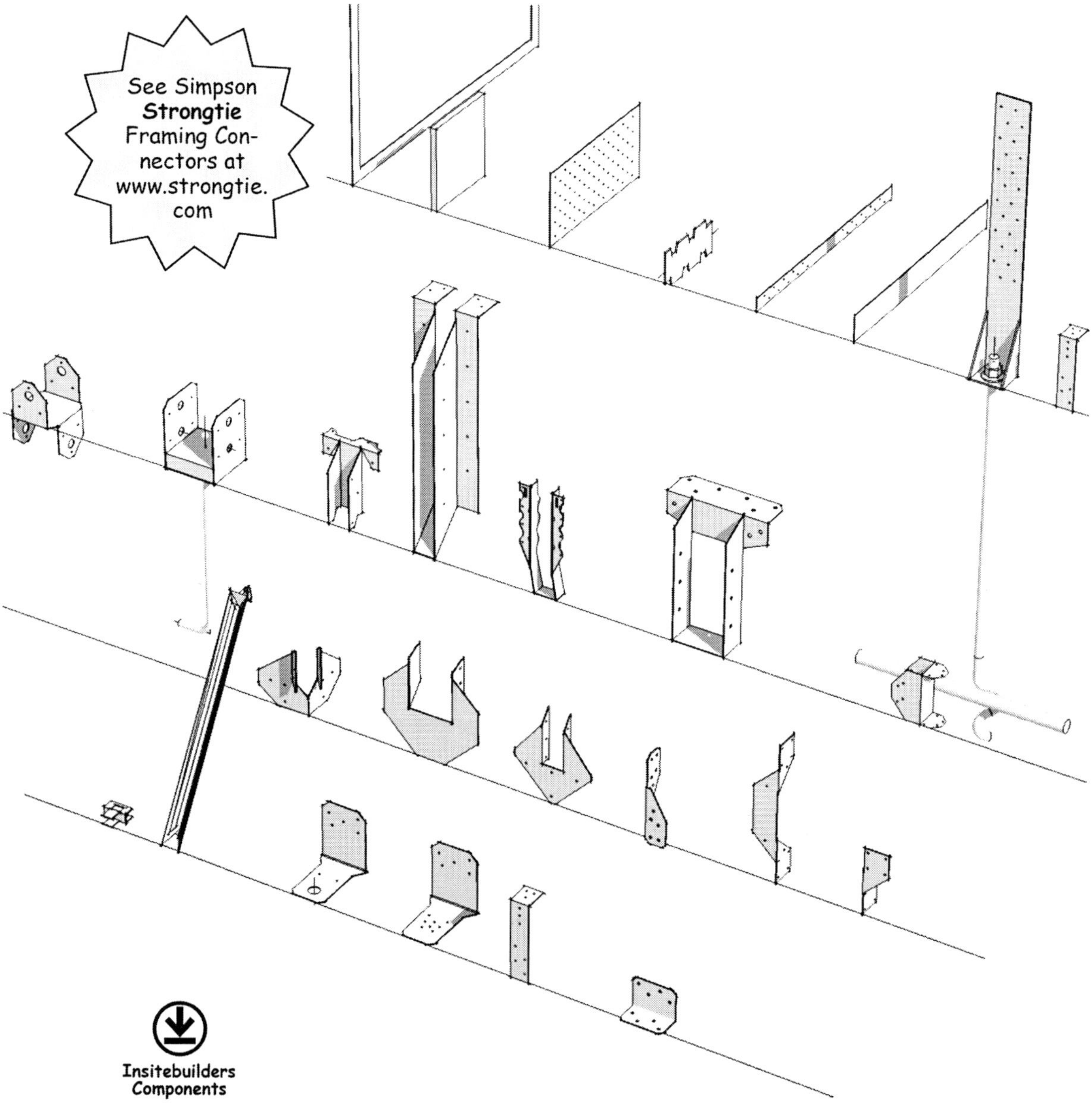

**Insitebuilders Components**

*The connectors in the Insitebuilders Component Library were fabricated from manufacturer's specifications

Staging pieces in the component

## MOISTURE PROTECTION

Add the waterproof membrane from the component folder and edit the pieces to **stage** the installation as a **detailed** screenshot.*

Moisture Protection

- Copy **dummies** and Paste-In-Place in a **new** file
- **Dimpled** membrane**
- Setup background **detail** for a screenshot
- Move to face of wall and **top** of footing
- Add the **membrane** component
- Use wall and footing **geometry** to align

## FOUNDATION DRAINS

Use component **handles** to align and sequence illustration of the construction **process**.

- Use **guidelines** to align the pieces
- Add **drain** pipe components
- Position pieces with **handles** to align
- **Scale** the straight pipe to **fit**

*Membranes and drains are installed as the floor framing is being completed just before foundation backfill

**For details and more information about the dimpled waterproof membrane in this mockup see www.superseal.ca

# CHAPTER 6 CHECKLISTS - FLOOR FRAMING

Floor Framing Checklist

Foundation pieces **shape** the dummy

## A. FOUNDATION DUMMY
Use the pieces of the foundation as a form to Push/Pull and reshape the foundation dummy.

- [ ] Open the masonry component
- [ ] Unhide the embedded block
- [ ] Hide the hollow block
- [ ] Unhide the phase dummy
- [ ] Reshape the phase dummy
- [ ] Outline the base of the wall
- [ ] Push/Pull to height of the wall

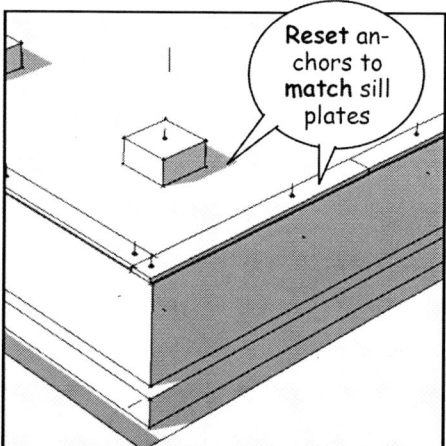
**Reset** anchors to **match** sill plates

## B. SILL PLATES AND ANCHORS
Set up the framing work area and add a sill to scale, move, rotate, and copy using the foundation anchor bolts.

- [ ] Unhide the framer's work area
- [ ] Add a lumber component as a sill
- [ ] Move and rotate into position
- [ ] Scale sills to stock lumber length
- [ ] Array-copy sills along one wall
- [ ] Select all and rotate 3 times
- [ ] Reset the bolts to top of the sill

Add posts to **support** girders

## C. SETTING THE GIRDER
Insert components to fabricate a composite girder and scale to bear on pier posts and framing connectors.

- [ ] Draw a centerline at the piers
- [ ] Add the post and connector
- [ ] Align handles with pier centerline
- [ ] Fabricate a composite beam
- [ ] Add a beam hanger for the girder
- [ ] Move and scale the girder to fit
- [ ] Group copy the girder to length
- [ ] Offset copy the girder and posts

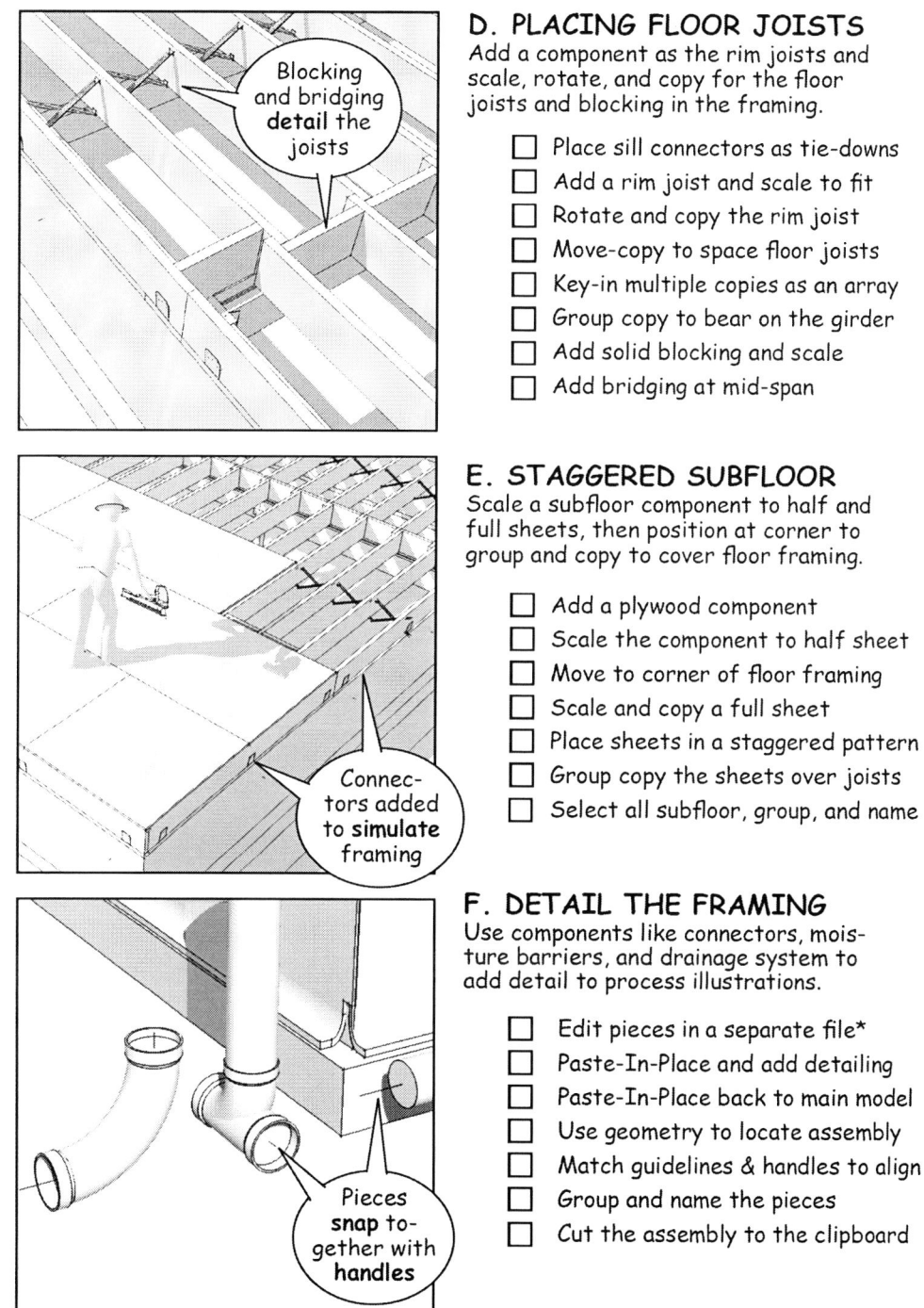

## D. PLACING FLOOR JOISTS
Add a component as the rim joists and scale, rotate, and copy for the floor joists and blocking in the framing.

- [ ] Place sill connectors as tie-downs
- [ ] Add a rim joist and scale to fit
- [ ] Rotate and copy the rim joist
- [ ] Move-copy to space floor joists
- [ ] Key-in multiple copies as an array
- [ ] Group copy to bear on the girder
- [ ] Add solid blocking and scale
- [ ] Add bridging at mid-span

## E. STAGGERED SUBFLOOR
Scale a subfloor component to half and full sheets, then position at corner to group and copy to cover floor framing.

- [ ] Add a plywood component
- [ ] Scale the component to half sheet
- [ ] Move to corner of floor framing
- [ ] Scale and copy a full sheet
- [ ] Place sheets in a staggered pattern
- [ ] Group copy the sheets over joists
- [ ] Select all subfloor, group, and name

## F. DETAIL THE FRAMING
Use components like connectors, moisture barriers, and drainage system to add detail to process illustrations.

- [ ] Edit pieces in a separate file*
- [ ] Paste-In-Place and add detailing
- [ ] Paste-In-Place back to main model
- [ ] Use geometry to locate assembly
- [ ] Match guidelines & handles to align
- [ ] Group and name the pieces
- [ ] Cut the assembly to the clipboard

*Open multiple copies of SketchUp to speed construction of subassemblies using dummies of the main model

# CHAPTER 7. WALL FRAMING

## FRAMING THE WALLS

Wall01 and Wall02 give an overview of the construction of a **simple** wall and a wall with a opening. Wall03 and Wall04 focus on the importance of **organizing** the pieces of the construction, while Wall05 and Wall06 **review** the assembly methods. The remaining walls demonstrate **short-cuts** and techniques to quickly copy and modify similar walls

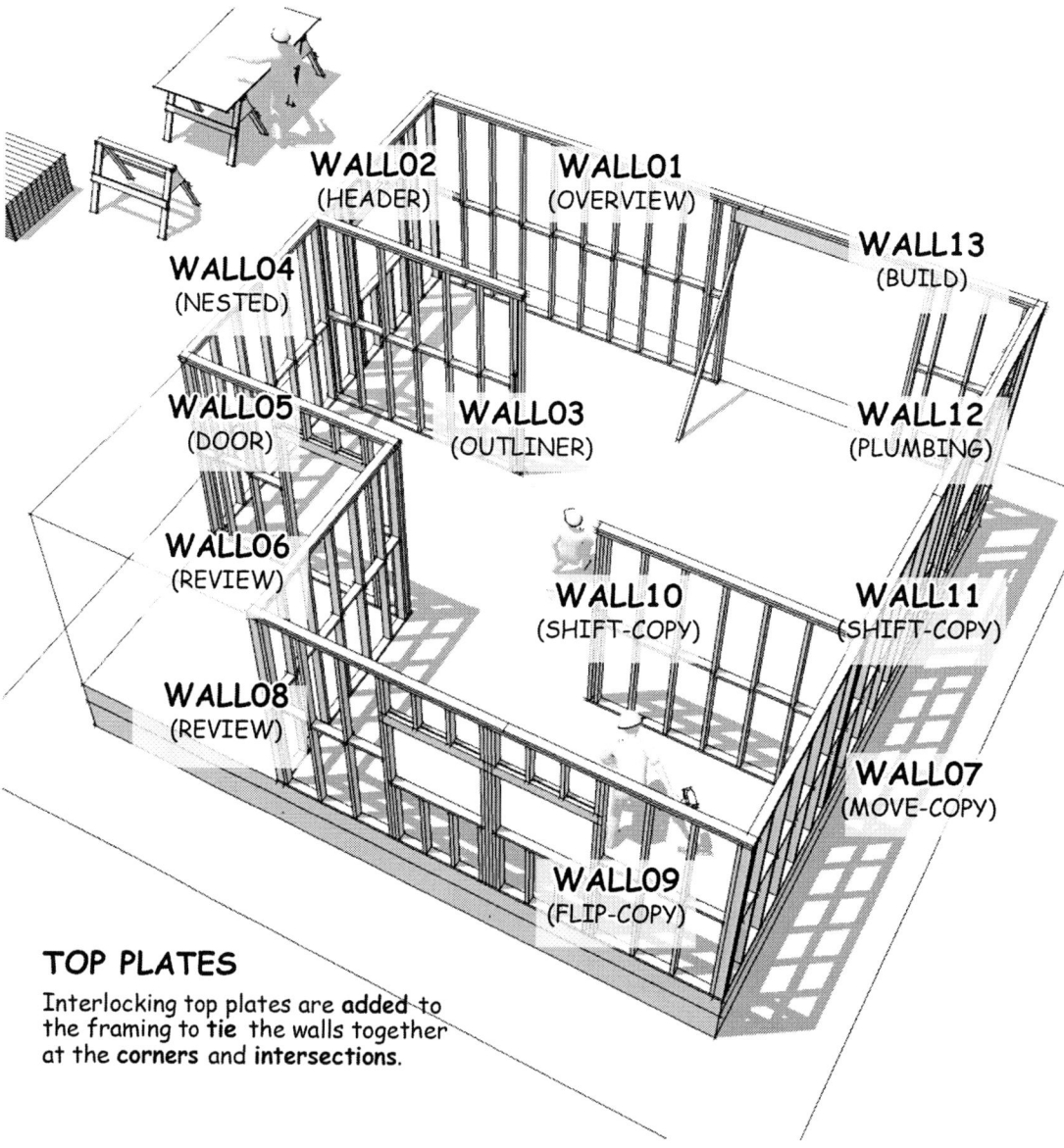

## TOP PLATES

Interlocking top plates are **added** to the framing to **tie** the walls together at the **corners** and **intersections**.

**FloorDummy** — Modify the floor framing phase dummy

## FLOOR FRAMING DUMMY
Use the floor framing dummy to **simplify** the floor framing assembly to **speed** the wall construction.

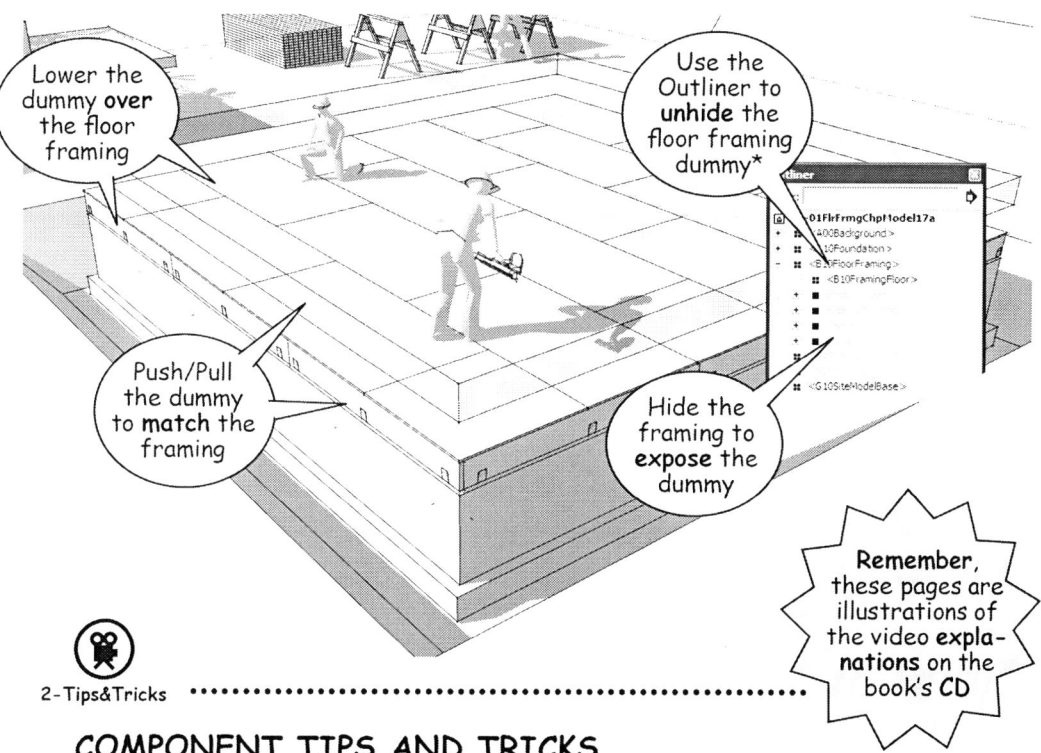

- Lower the dummy **over** the floor framing
- Use the Outliner to **unhide** the floor framing dummy*
- Push/Pull the dummy to **match** the framing
- Hide the framing to **expose** the dummy

*Remember, these pages are illustrations of the video explanations on the book's CD*

**2-Tips&Tricks**

## COMPONENT TIPS AND TRICKS
Use the Outliner to select pieces in the assembly, Double-click to edit the selection or Explode, Group and rename the assembly as a new object.

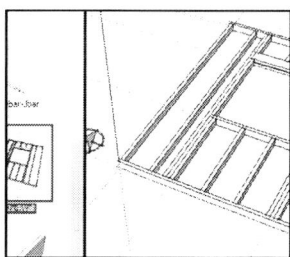

**01WallTypeComponents:** Add and modify walls from a library of typical wall types

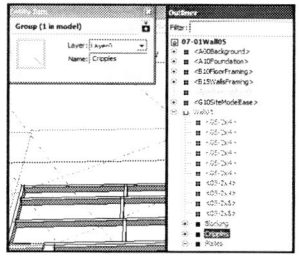

**02NestingGroups:** Group and drag nested objects from one group or component to another

*Paint the dummy with an edited transparent color to make it easier to reshape, return to white when done

# WALL01: Basics of the wall framing method

BasicWall01

## ASSEMBLE A WALL
A construction model is **built** to be technically **accurate**, with components inserted, placed, scaled, and copied to match **layout** lines.

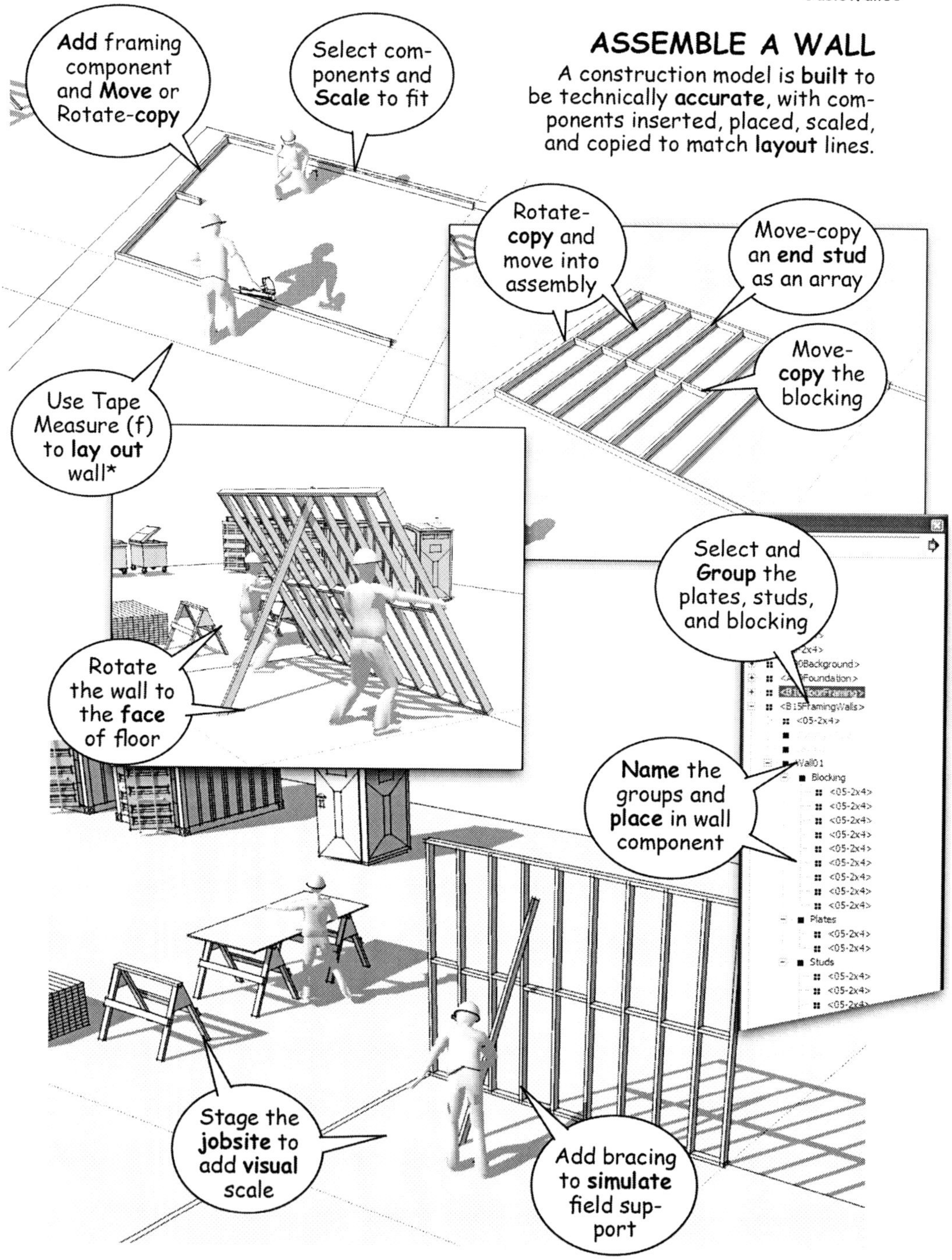

- **Add** framing component and **Move** or Rotate-**copy**
- **Select** components and **Scale** to fit
- **Rotate-copy** and move into assembly
- **Move-copy** an **end stud** as an array
- **Move-copy** the blocking
- Use Tape Measure (f) to **lay out** wall*
- **Rotate** the wall to the **face** of floor
- **Select** and **Group** the plates, studs, and blocking
- **Name** the groups and **place** in wall component
- **Stage** the **jobsite** to add **visual** scale
- Add bracing to **simulate** field support

*Remember left, right, and up arrow keys constrain cursor movement to the red, blue, and green axes

OpeningWall02

# WALL02: Framing a wall with an opening
## FRAMING AN OPENING

Lay out the overall dimension of the wall and the rough opening on the subfloor

- Lay out rough opening on the subfloor
- Move the plate to **height** of the top **plate**
- Move-copy **jambs** and end **studs**
- Drag in a header from the **component** folder
- Double the header and **scale** to fit layout lines
- Move-copy to **opposite** side and divide copy
- Rotate the wall to **align** with the foundation
- Shift-select to **group** and name the wall
- Drag the wall into the **framing component**
- Rough opening **matches** window frame
- Frame the corner or **add** panel clips*

*A detail showing drywall clips, nailers, or a typical 3 stud corner may only be necessary in one location

## WALL03: Outliner organizes the assembly

OutlinerWall03

### OUTLINER ORGANIZES
The Outliner is the key to **organizing** the pieces of an assembly for future display.

- Shift-select and **Scale** the plates
- Drag in a **stud** and Rotate-copy
- Move and array **multiple** copies
- Shift-select **studs** and Scale to **fit** plates
- Move-copy blocking in **staggered** pattern
- Lay out the wall with **guidelines**
- Select and Group in the **Outliner** or model
- Select **Wall03** in Outliner and **rotate**
- **Name** the groups then **group** the groups
- Name the group **Wall03** and drag into **framing** component
- Add reinforced end for **bearing**
- Delete the guidelines

# WALL04: Nesting groups in the Outliner

## NESTED GROUPS
Groups and components are **selected**, grouped, and **named** in nested assemblies

*Double-click the piece or group names in the Outliner to edit the objects in the construction model

# WALL05: Framing a door with a twist

TwistWall05

## LAY OUT AT AN ANGLE
Use the Protractor (p) to lay out **guidelines** for the **wall** and rough **opening** for the door.

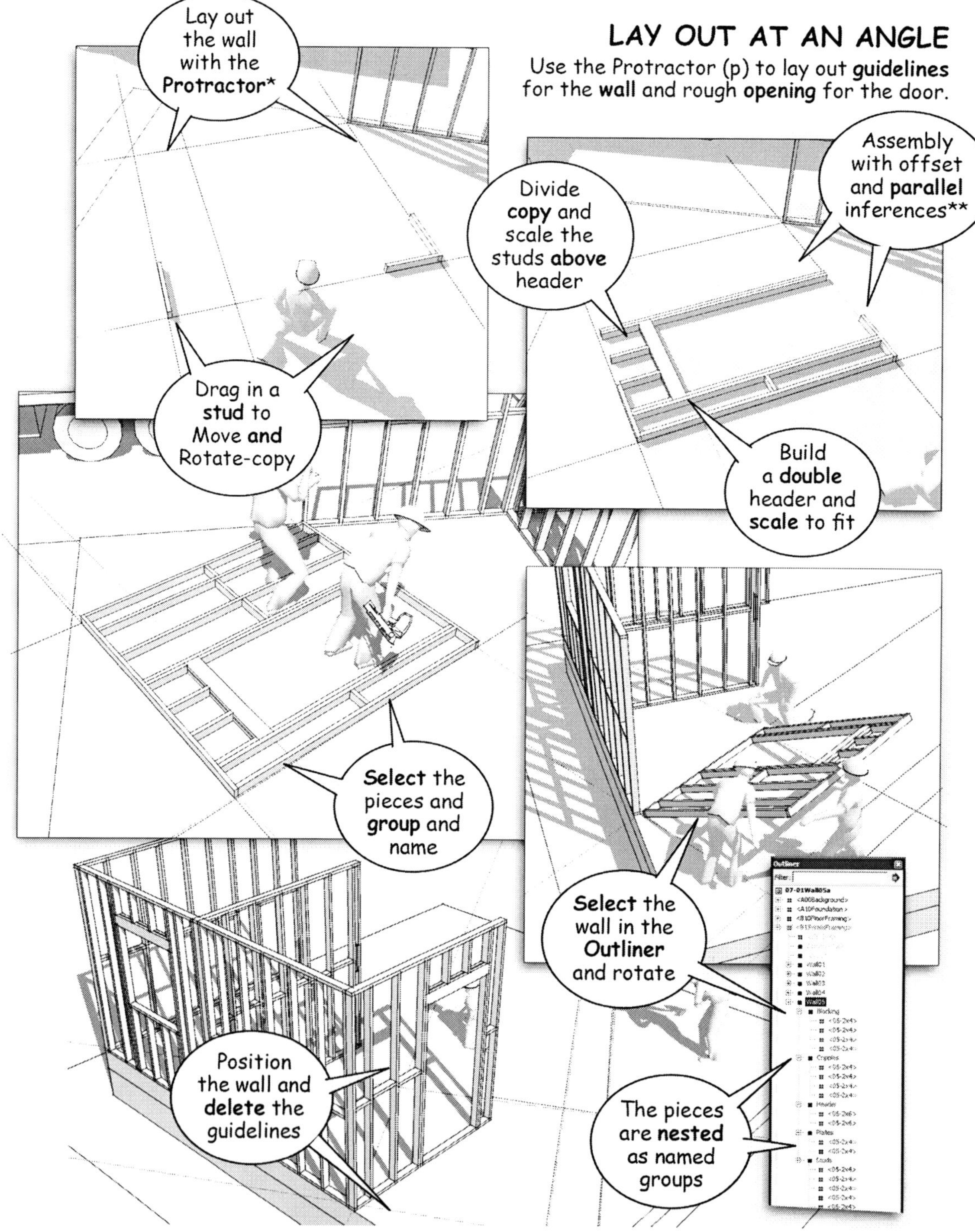

- Lay out the wall with the **Protractor***
- Divide **copy** and scale the studs **above** header
- Assembly with offset and **parallel** inferences**
- Drag in a **stud** to **Move** and **Rotate-copy**
- Build a **double** header and **scale** to fit
- **Select** the pieces and **group** and name
- **Select** the wall in the **Outliner** and rotate
- The pieces are **nested** as named groups
- Position the wall and **delete** the guidelines

*Key-in angles and dimensions as you rotate or drag out layout lines using units of measure or formulas

**Purple parallel inferences follow a referenced edge or guideline instead of one of the three SketchUp axes

WALL06: Review the framing sequence

## WALL06: REVIEW STEPS TO BUILD A WALL

Keep the walls and framing members well **organized** so that they can be modified, sequenced, and displayed in **future** illustrations and animations.

A. **Lay out** the wall on the subfloor
- ☐ Check the dimensions
- ☐ Use Tape Measure tool
- ☐ Drag out guidelines
- ☐ Guidelines are layout lines

B. **Add** framing components
- ☐ Match layout lines
- ☐ Move and Rotate-copy
- ☐ Scale components
- ☐ Fit to the assembly

C. **Organize** pieces as an assembly
- ☐ Group and name pieces
- ☐ Group the groups
- ☐ Name as a wall
- ☐ Drag into phase component

D. **Rotate** the wall into position
- ☐ Select the wall
- ☐ Rotate to vertical
- ☐ Move to layout lines
- ☐ Stage as a process

E. **Square** and plumb the wall
- ☐ Match layout guidelines
- ☐ Align with framing
- ☐ Check for fit
- ☐ Delete the guidelines

# WALL07: Move-copy a wall and rename

CopyWall07

## QUICK MOVE AND COPY
Use the Shift key to **constrain** and align the copy, then **rename** the wall assembly.

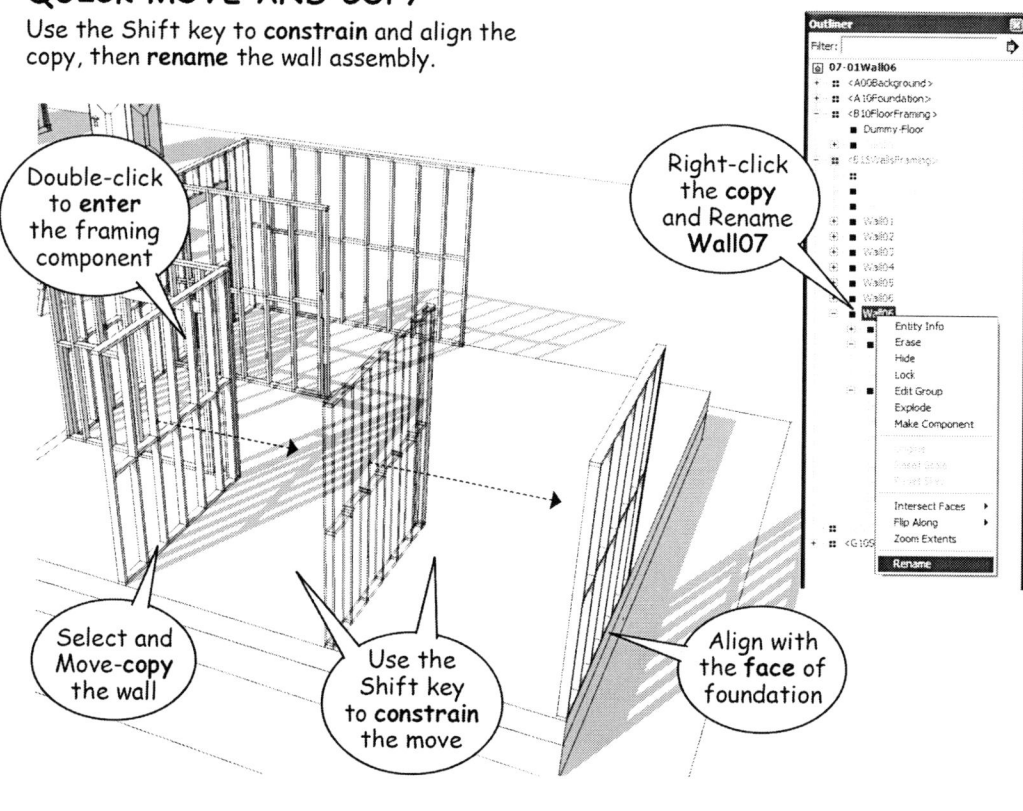

## SIMPLE THINGS TO KEEP IN MIND

- Use the Outliner to organize
- Group and name immediately

- Click once to select
- Double-click to select a surface
- Triple-click to select all connected

- Shift-select multiple objects
- Left-right select all inside box
- Right-left select all touched by box

- Toggle Ctrl key to leave a copy
- Toggle Shift key to Orbit and Pan

- Use a Component Library folder
- Save modified components to a library
- Scale simple components to fit
- Edit one component to edit all

- Arrow keys lock movement to an axis
- Key-in dimensions as you drag
- Add and update Scenes regularly

- Use offset moves in tight spots
- Even increments to move and rotate

- Right-click for context menus

# Insitebuilders Shortcut keys

## REVIEW SHORTCUT KEYS*

### TOOL COMMANDS

 Select (Space)   Orbit (Ctrl-Shift q)

 Line (w)   Pan (Ctrl-Shift s)

 Rectangle (r)   Zoom (Ctrl-Shift z)

 Offset (v)   Zoom Window (Ctrl-Shift w)

 Move (b)   Zoom Extents (Ctrl-Shift e)

 Rotate (Alt r)   Zoom Previous (Shift z)

 Scale (s)

Push/Pull (t)   Tape Measure (f)

 Protractor (p)

 Components (Ctrl-Shift c)

### MENU COMMANDS

Undo   Ctrl z
Redo   Ctrl y

Cut    Ctrl x
Copy   Ctrl c
Paste  Ctrl v
PasteInPlace  Ctrl-Shift v

Group  g

Hide        h
UnhideLast  Shift h
UnhideAll   Ctrl-Shift h

Explode     Alt x
EraseGuides Alt e

*See the Shortcuts Index at the back of the book for a complete list of the Insitebuilders Shortcuts

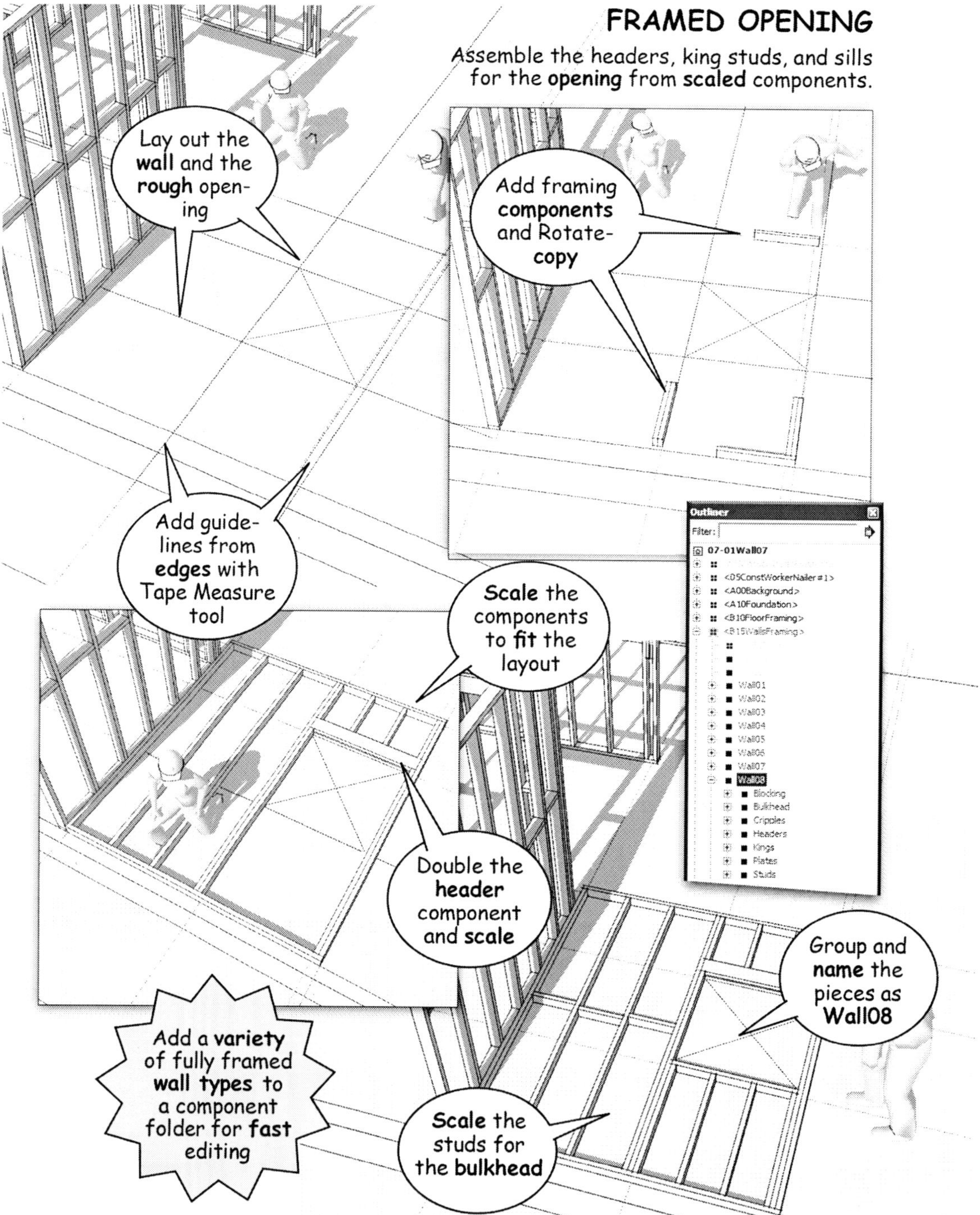

WALL09: Rotate and copy a wall

RotateWall09

## FAST FLIPS

After a few walls have been constructed, many of the **later** walls can be quickly **copied** and renamed.

Hold the **Ctrl key** to Move-copy or Rotate-copy.

Select **Wall08** and Rotate-copy

Right-click to **rename** the copy

Align the **bottom plates** of the **wall**

WallType Component

Check **corners** for alignment

**Tilt** the walls into **position**

Align with the **face** of the foundation

WallType Components

# Wall10 and Wall11: More quick copies

AlignWall10n11

## ROTATE AND MOVE-COPY
Quickly copy **similar** walls to speed assembly and construction.

- Double-click to **edit** the **wall** framing component
- Rotate-copy **Wall03** and rename **Wall10**
- Rename the wall in **Outliner** or **Entity** box
- Move-copy **Wall04** and rename **Wall11**
- Rename the wall in **Outliner** or **Entity** box
- Constrain the move with the **Shift** key

106

ModifyWall12

## Wall12: Modify a copy of an existing wall

### FAST FABRICATION
The pieces in an assembly are exploded, resized, and renamed to form a new entity.

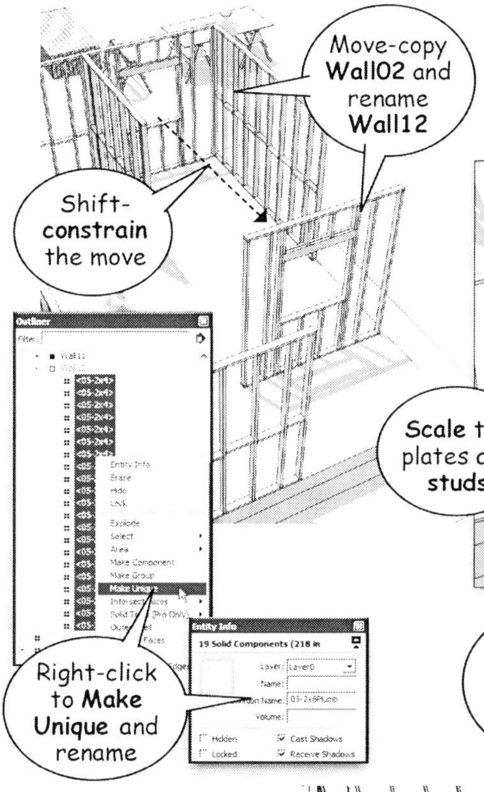

Move-copy **Wall02** and rename **Wall12**

Shift-**constrain** the move

Right-click to **Explode** the wall

Scale the plates and **studs**

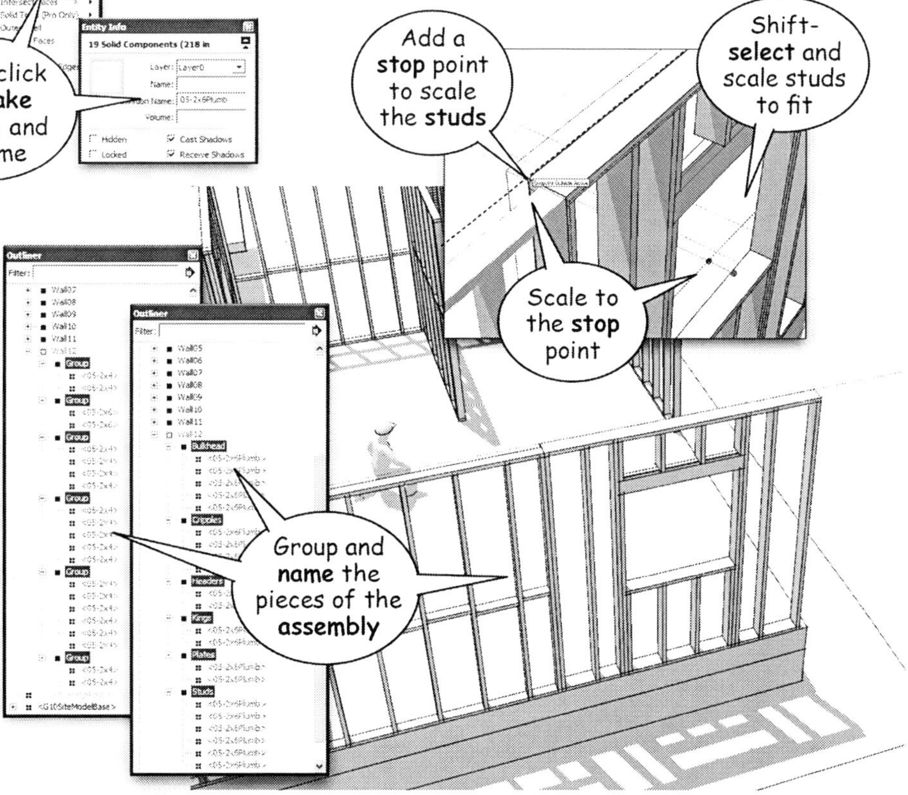

Right-click to **Make Unique** and rename

Add a **stop** point to scale the **studs**

Shift-**select** and scale studs to fit

Scale to the **stop** point

Group and **name** the pieces of the **assembly**

Wall13: Build the wall in place

BuildWall13

# BUILD TWO SIDES

Build a wall to inset into the **corner** then Rotate-**copy** the wall and modify the plates and studs to support the **other** side of the opening.

Lay out **guidelines** for the walls and **opening**

Add a line to **mark** the **corner** and start the layout

Rotate and Move-**copy** plates and **studs**

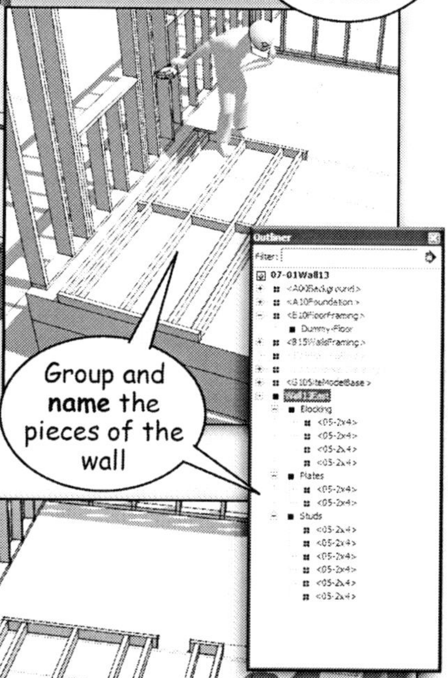

Group and **name** the pieces of the wall

Rotate-copy the **east** wall and rename as **west** wall

**Explode** the west wall and **modify**

**Delete** studs and **resize** the plates to fit

Rotate and **modify** the framing for the new wall as a series of **staged** assemblies to illustrate the construction **process**.

108

## Wall13: Size a header to the opening

### ADD THE HEADER
Rotate the walls then **add** and group components for a double header **scaled** to the size of the **rough** opening.

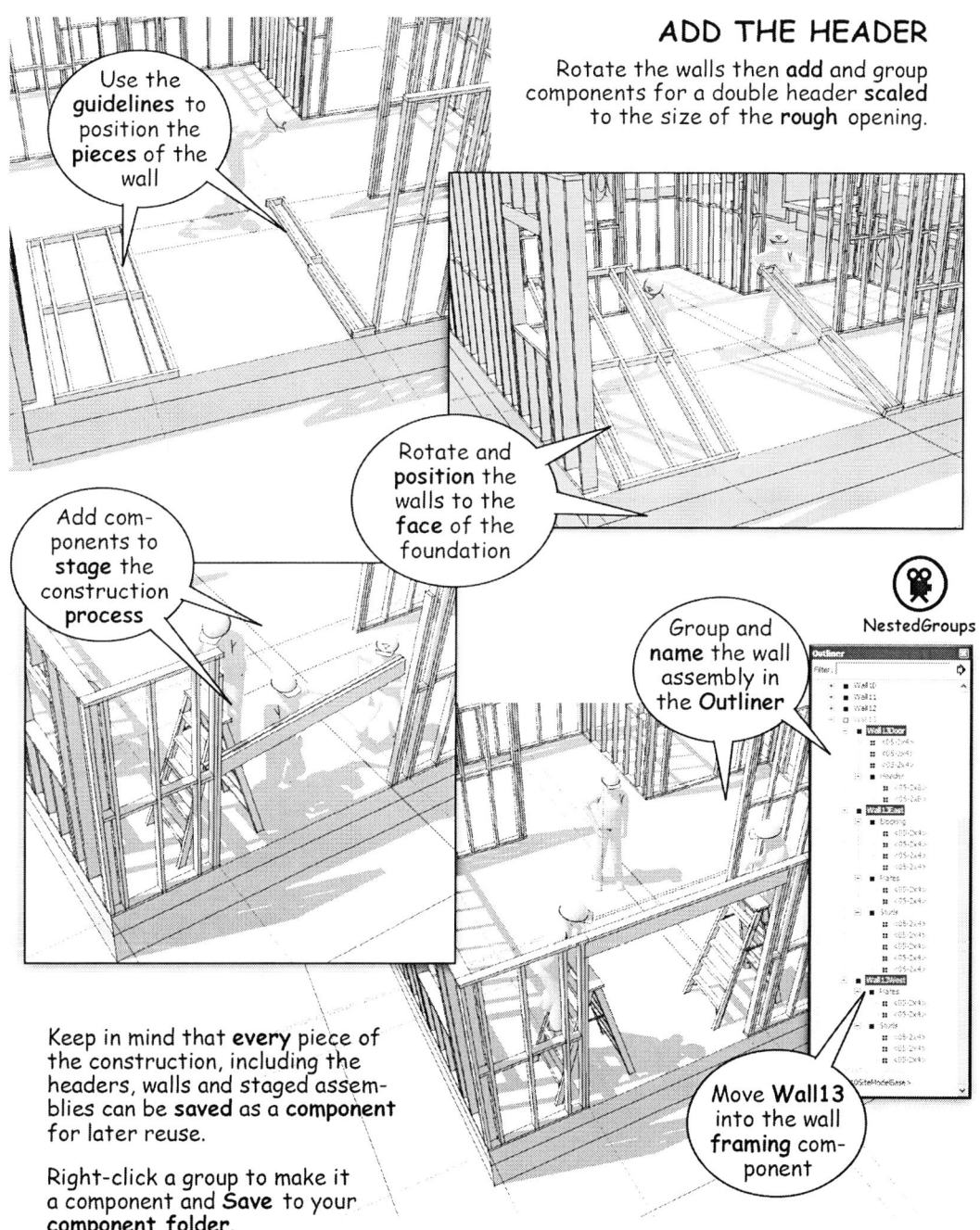

Use the **guidelines** to position the **pieces** of the wall

Rotate and **position** the walls to the **face** of the foundation

Add components to **stage** the construction **process**

Group and **name** the wall assembly in the **Outliner**

NestedGroups

Move **Wall13** into the wall **framing** component

Keep in mind that **every** piece of the construction, including the headers, walls and staged assemblies can be **saved** as a **component** for later reuse.

Right-click a group to make it a component and **Save** to your **component folder**.

109

### Add interlocking top plates

## SCALE TOP PLATES

Use Scenes, and Orbit and Pan with the **Shift key** to move around the model and **quickly** add and **resize** interlocking top plates.

WallTopPlates

*Add a component and **Scale** to a stock length*

*Add and **update** Scenes to jump **around** the model*

*Toggle Shift to **Pan** and Orbit*

*Rotate and **Move**-copy the plates to **interlock** corners*

*Scale to **resize** stock lengths and **match** the framing*

*Top plate **overlaps** the joint to tie to **outside** wall*

*Interlock top **plates** to **tie** the walls **together***

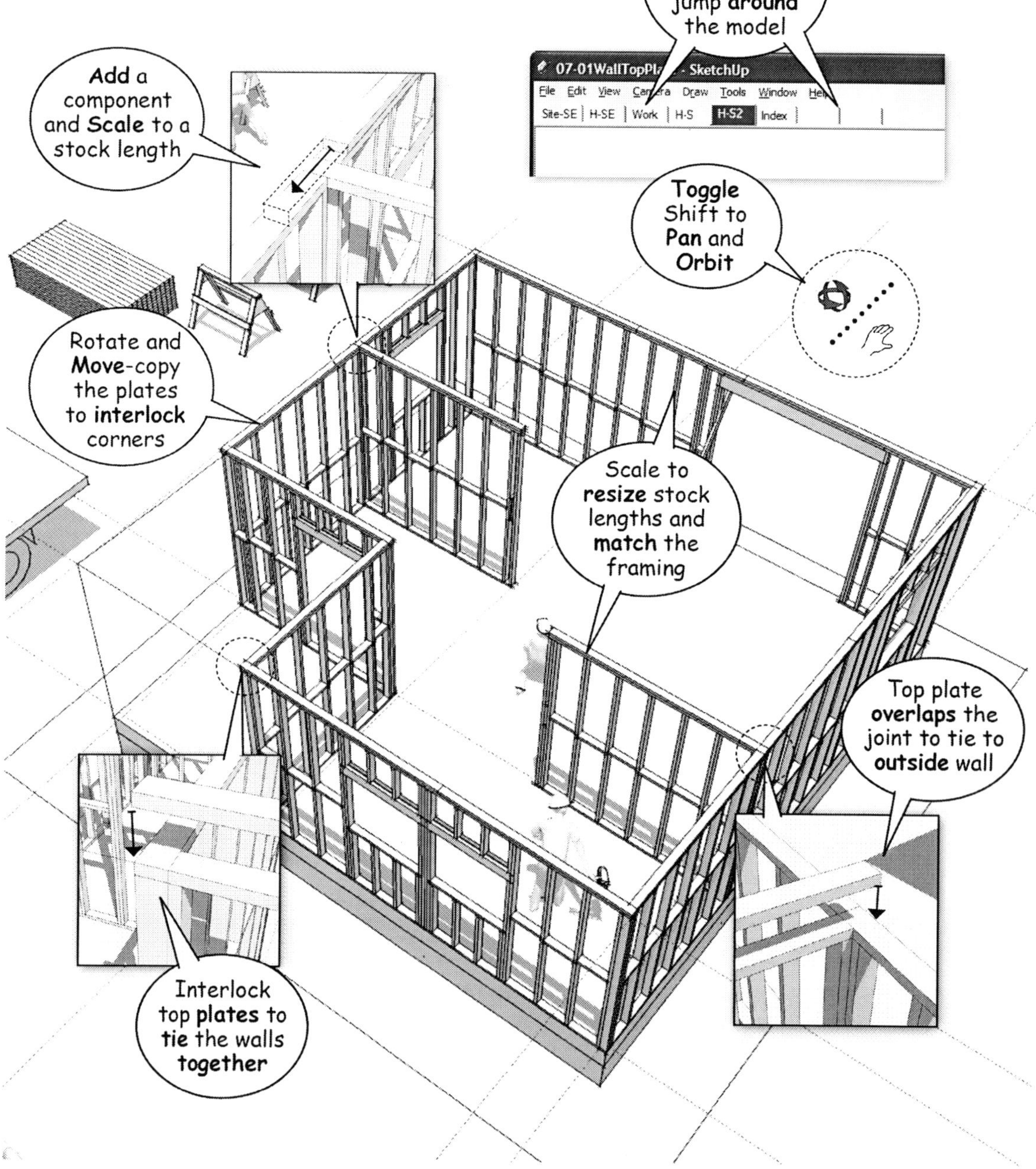

Typical wall framing details

## WALL FRAMING DETAILS

Construction models are **built** to be annotated and dimensioned. That means they must also **accurately** illustrate the **visual details** of the construction system.

- Framing connectors **tie** studs to the **plates**
- Wind loads **may** require connectors at **headers**
- Solid plywood **filler** between **double** headers
- Sheathing **ties** the wall to the **rim** joists
- Clips used at **reinforced** openings with **double** sill
- **Structural** connectors used to tie **walls** to the foundation
- **Square** structural **washers** at anchor bolts

# CHAPTER 7 CHECKLISTS - WALL FRAMING

WallFraming Checklist

*Color **trans-parent** and shape dummy to **match***

## A. FRAMING A WALL
Reshape the floor phase dummy with the Push/Pull tool, then hide the floor framing to start wall layouts.

- [ ] Lay out guidelines on subfloor
- [ ] Add framing component
- [ ] Rotate and Move-copy
- [ ] Scale the components to fit
- [ ] Organize in the Outliner
- [ ] Rotate the wall into position
- [ ] Square and plumb the wall

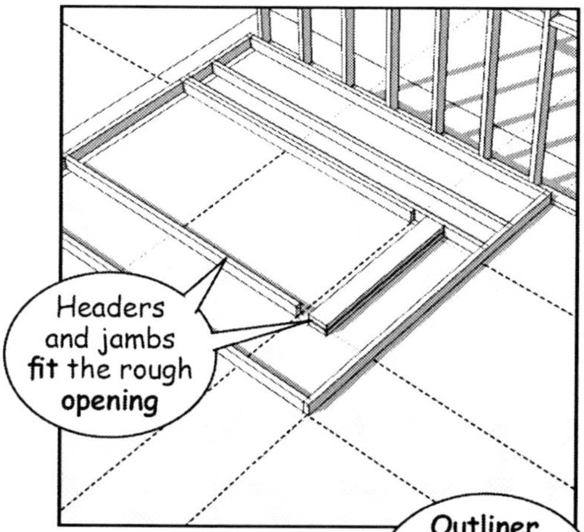

*Headers and jambs fit the rough opening*

## B. FRAMING AN OPENING
Use the Tape Measure tool again to drag out guidelines to lay out the wall and the rough opening.

- [ ] Lay out the wall and rough opening
- [ ] Add framing components
- [ ] Rotate and Move-copy
- [ ] Place king studs at opening
- [ ] Add a double header and scale
- [ ] Organize in the Outliner
- [ ] Rotate and square the wall

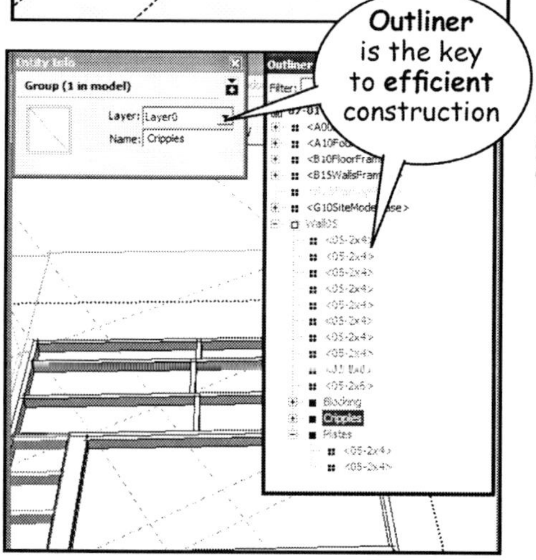

*Outliner is the key to efficient construction*

## C. ORGANIZE THE OUTLINER
Use the Outliner to quickly select, group, name, and organize the nested assemblies for each wall.

- [ ] Select studs, plates, and blocking
- [ ] Group and name the pieces
- [ ] Name according to type of pieces
- [ ] Select the different group types
- [ ] Group and name the wall assembly
- [ ] Select the wall to reorganize
- [ ] Move into the framing component
- [ ] Walls nested in phase component

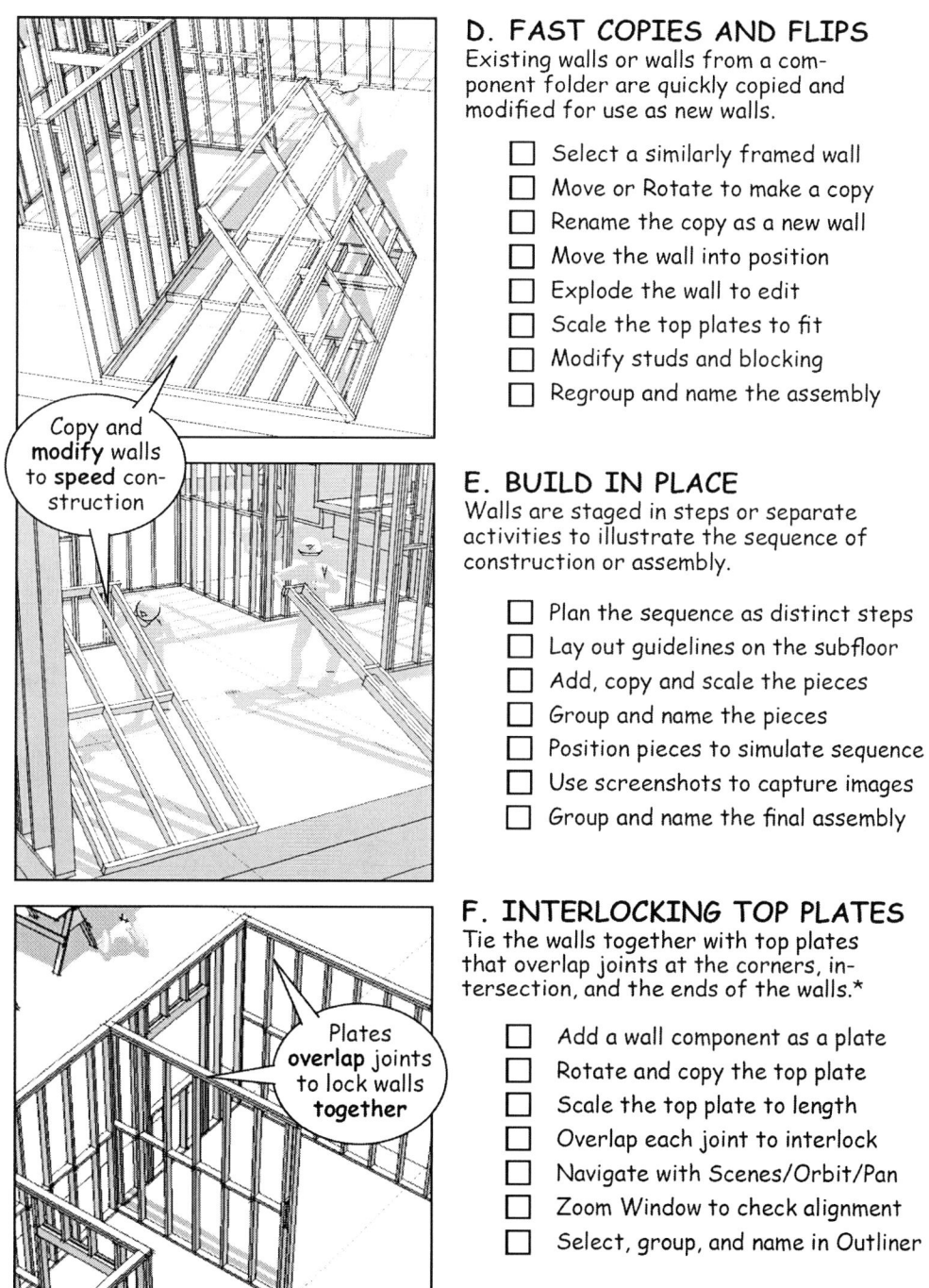

### D. FAST COPIES AND FLIPS
Existing walls or walls from a component folder are quickly copied and modified for use as new walls.

- ☐ Select a similarly framed wall
- ☐ Move or Rotate to make a copy
- ☐ Rename the copy as a new wall
- ☐ Move the wall into position
- ☐ Explode the wall to edit
- ☐ Scale the top plates to fit
- ☐ Modify studs and blocking
- ☐ Regroup and name the assembly

### E. BUILD IN PLACE
Walls are staged in steps or separate activities to illustrate the sequence of construction or assembly.

- ☐ Plan the sequence as distinct steps
- ☐ Lay out guidelines on the subfloor
- ☐ Add, copy and scale the pieces
- ☐ Group and name the pieces
- ☐ Position pieces to simulate sequence
- ☐ Use screenshots to capture images
- ☐ Group and name the final assembly

### F. INTERLOCKING TOP PLATES
Tie the walls together with top plates that overlap joints at the corners, intersection, and the ends of the walls.*

- ☐ Add a wall component as a plate
- ☐ Rotate and copy the top plate
- ☐ Scale the top plate to length
- ☐ Overlap each joint to interlock
- ☐ Navigate with Scenes/Orbit/Pan
- ☐ Zoom Window to check alignment
- ☐ Select, group, and name in Outliner

*To simulate placement and quantities, scale each plate to match the length of a standard lumber dimension

# CHAPTER 8. ROOF FRAMING

## FRAMING THE ROOF AND SUPPORTS

Roof framing **begins** with gable walls, clerestories, and the ridge beam. **Next**, rafters are installed along with the rakes, outlooks, blocking, and the fascia. Sheathing is then **placed** on the rafters in a **staggered** pattern to help resist lateral loads.

Traditional beam and rafter roof framing **increases** design and construction flexibility, **maximizing** the volume of the interior space, and making it possible to add clerestories and other architectural **features**.

Once in place, traditional framing is also **easier** to change and **expand** in the future.

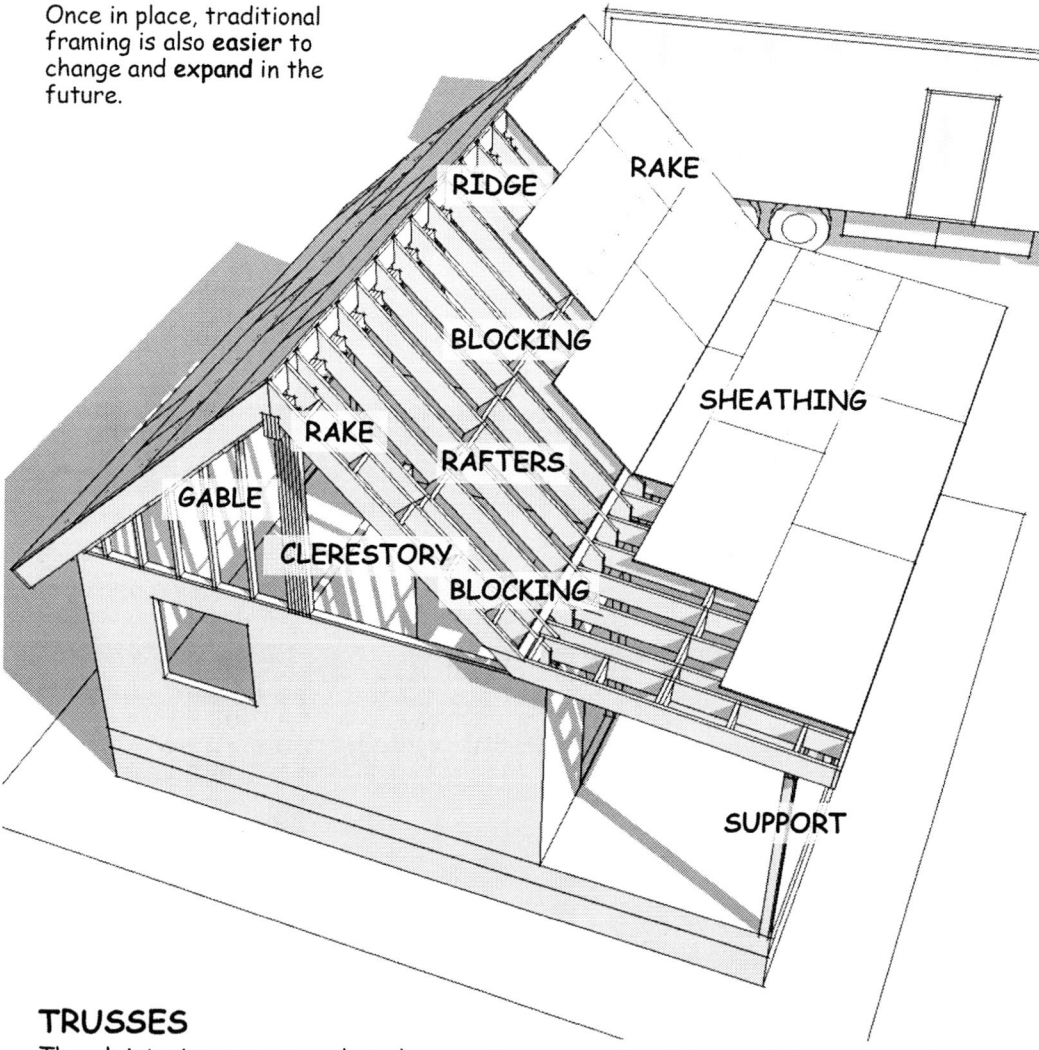

## TRUSSES

Though interior spaces are less dynamic, **trusses** reduce labor and the number of structural components while **increasing** efficiency and maximizing spans. They also make it **easier** to install mechanical systems because of the otherwise **unusable** attic.

WallDummy

Phase dummy for the walls

## WALL FRAMING DUMMY

Resize and shape the wall phase dummy to **simplify** the framing members while working on the roof. Remember, the dummy **reduces** the level of detail while modeling.

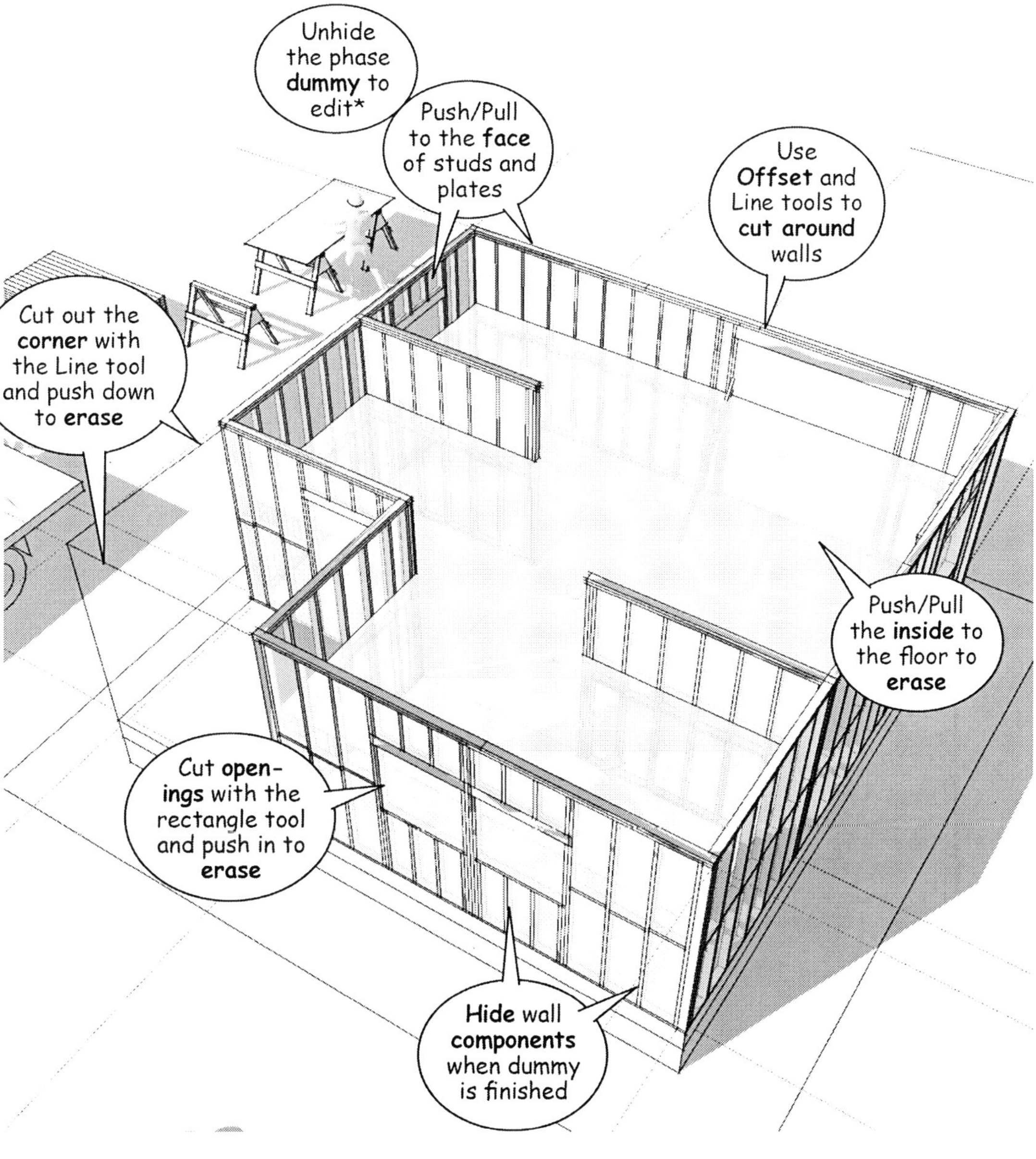

- Unhide the phase **dummy** to edit*
- Push/Pull to the **face** of studs and plates
- Use **Offset** and Line tools to **cut around** walls
- Cut out the **corner** with the Line tool and push down to **erase**
- Push/Pull the **inside** to the floor to **erase**
- Cut **openings** with the rectangle tool and push in to **erase**
- **Hide** wall **components** when dummy is finished

*Paint the dummy with an edited transparent-white to make it easier to reshape, return to white when done

A few more tips and tricks

7-Tips&Tricks

## SOME FINAL TIPS AND TRICKS

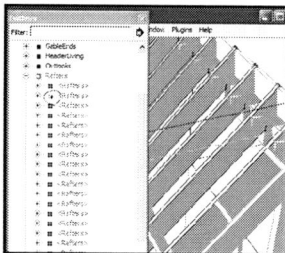

**01LockUnlock:**
Right-click to lock objects in three-dimensional space while editing

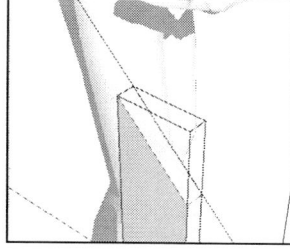

**02GuidelinesAsRails:**
Add a guideline and use it as an rail to guide movement in open space

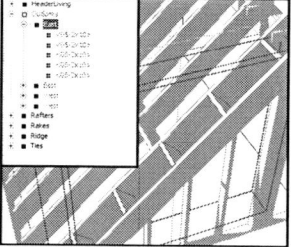

**03DoubleClickEdit:**
Double-click to edit assemblies and pieces in the Outliner

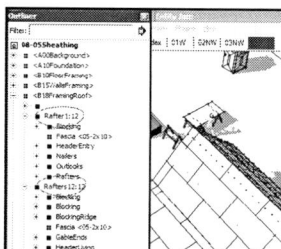

**04NestedOutliner:**
Review the organization of the roof framing in the Outliner

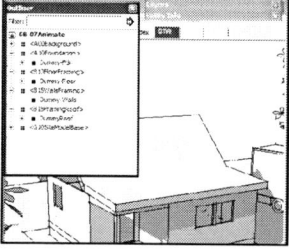

**05SetUpSequence:**
Set up a series of Scenes as a sequence animation of the construction

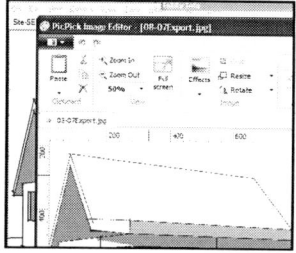

**06ExportIllustrations:**
Export illustrations and animation from the construction model

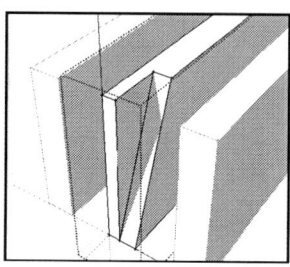

**07FastFabrication:**
Explode and regroup or Make Unique to modify a single component

### FAST FABRICATION

The fastest way to change a group or component is to **select** it, then **Explode** it, and while the pieces are still selected, immediately **Group** or Make **Component** of the pieces. **Rename** the new object in the Component or Entity Info box.

You can do this with **four quick steps**:
1. Select the piece or assembly
2. Explode (Alt x)
3. Group (g) or Make Component (Ctrl Alt c)
4. Rename the new assembly/object

**116**

**BuzzwordIndex**

## Review construction modeling buzzwords

## BUZZWORDS YOU NOW KNOW*

Use these words to **check** your understanding of the three step modeling **method**, sequencing an assembly **process**, and setting up the **organization** of a construction model.

**Array-copy**: line of multiple copies

**Axis**: red, green, blue directions in 3D space

**Camera**: view point of observer in 3D space

**Component**: a remotely saved SketchUp file

**Ctrl key**: generally used to leave a copy

**Ctrl-scale**: resize objects from the center

**Divide-copy**: line of divided copies

**Dummy**: acts as a low poly substitute for details

**Edges**: the lines that define an object

**Edit-group**: Right or Double-click to edit

**Embed**: dummy object or group within a group

**Entity**: an object as a piece of an assembly

**Explode**: breakdown a group or component

**Flip-copy**: flip a copy along an axis

**Group**: a named collection of pieces or assemblies

**Guidelines**: temporary construction chalk lines

**Handle**: the bones or wireframe of an entity

**Inferences**: built-in guides and snap points

**Inside-Out**: Scale tool used to mirror copy

**Key-in**: input values while a tool is active

**Layers**: distinct blocks or subassemblies

**Make unique**: a new copy of a component

**Modeling method**: 2D+3D+Group&Name

**Move-copy**: toggle the Ctrl key with Move tool

**Nested**: a piece or group in a group in the Outliner

**Object**: an entity or piece in 3D space

**Offset**: move or copy with an isolated cursor

**Origin**: the zero point for the 3 axes of 3D space

**Phase-dummy**: used to simplify level of detail

**Pieces**: entities or objects ready for assembly

**Plumb&Level**: parallel to an axis or flat on a plane

**Poly count**: number of edges and surfaces

**Reshape**: edit a component with Push/Pull tool

**Resize**: stretch component with Scale tool

**Rotate-copy**: toggle Ctrl key with Rotate tool

**Scale**: resize objects without editing

**Screenshot**: captured image for an illustration

**Shape**: edit a group or object to trim

**Shift key**: generally constrains or locks to an axis

**Shift-scale**: constrained resize with Scale tool

**Snaps**: object inference points for assembly

**Staging**: set up the model for a screenshot

**Surface**: the skin or plane between edges

**Visual scale**: components to simulate process

**Workpoint**: point of reference set to Origin

*See the Buzzword Index at the back of the book for a complete list of the construction modeling buzzwords

# Frame the clerestory opening

GableClerestory

## FRAMING THE CLERESTORY
Add and explode components to shape sills and jambs for the clerestory and lift into place.

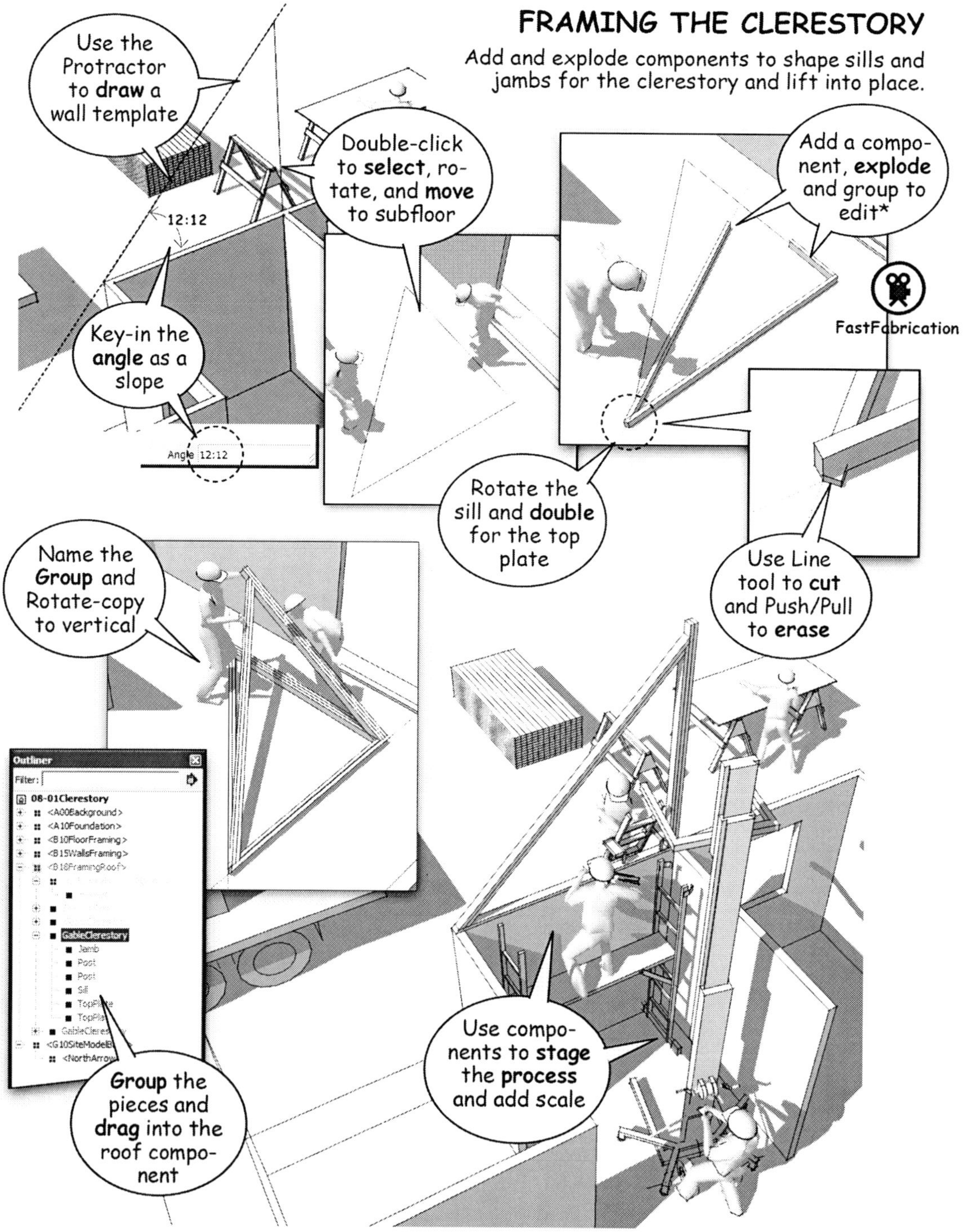

- Use the Protractor to **draw** a wall template
- Double-click to **select**, rotate, and **move** to subfloor
- Add a component, **explode** and group to edit*
- Key-in the **angle** as a slope
- Rotate the sill and **double** for the top plate
- Use Line tool to **cut** and Push/Pull to **erase**
- Name the **Group** and Rotate-copy to vertical
- **Group** the pieces and **drag** into the roof component
- Use components to **stage** the **process** and add scale

FastFabrication

*Explode returns a component to edges and surfaces, so it can be grouped and renamed as a new entity

GableWall

Add studs for the gable end

## FRAMING THE GABLE WALL

Use the copy of the clerestory frame on the **subfloor** to build the **gable** wall.

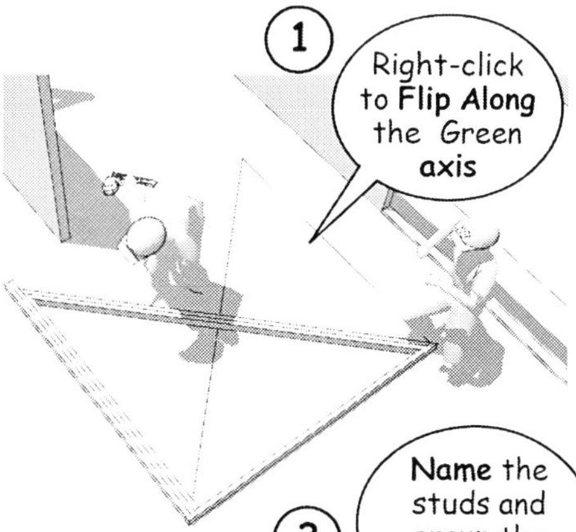

1. Right-click to **Flip Along** the Green axis

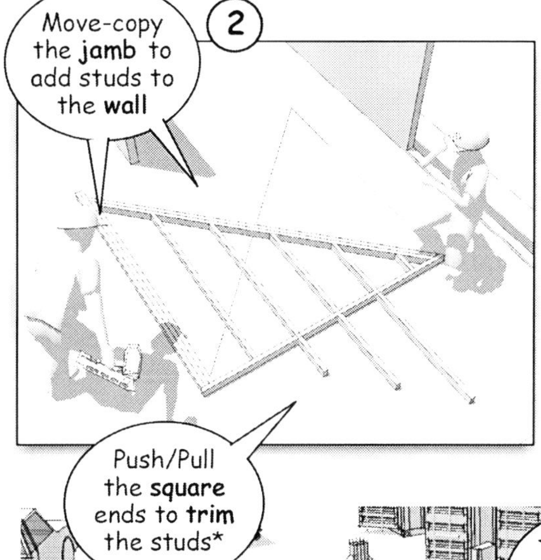

2. Move-copy the **jamb** to add studs to the **wall**

Push/Pull the **square** ends to **trim** the studs*

3. **Name** the studs and **group** the gable wall

Tilt up the **wall** and **lift** into position

Move-copy the clerestory and **gable** walls

Group the **pieces** and drag into the **roof** component

Move the **copies** into place over the **east** wall

*The studs were exploded, grouped, and renamed from a component file and can now be individually edited

# Add entry and interior support beams

HeaderSupports

## HEADER BEAMS FOR RAFTERS

Rafter supports are **fabricated** along the interior **bearing** points and the front entry.

- Add components for **headers** and studs
- Assemble the **components** as a double header
- Scale the **header** to fit the opening
- Place studs against **existing** wall framing for **bearing**
- Scale the studs to **fit** under header for **bearing**
- Move-copy the **header** and studs to the **entry**
- Add a **post** component and **scale** to fit the header
- Scale the header to fit the **post**
- Stud aligns with **existing** framing
- Move-copy the stud to the **post**

120

RidgeBeam

Set the ridge beam in beam pockets

# SETTING THE RIDGE BEAM

Use the gable layout and a wireframe to determine the position of the ridge beam.

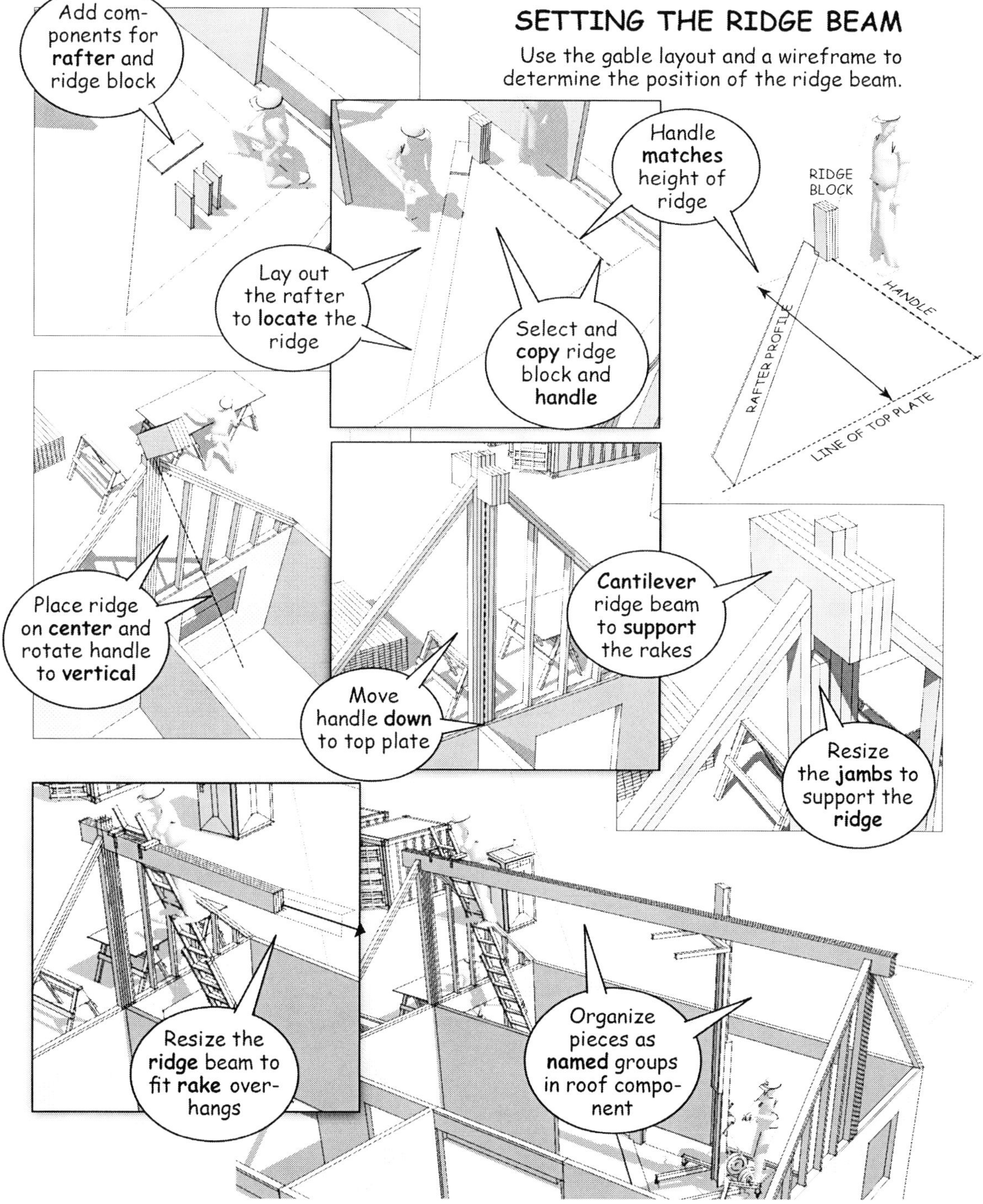

- Add components for **rafter** and ridge block
- Lay out the rafter to **locate** the ridge
- Select and **copy** ridge block and **handle**
- Handle **matches** height of ridge
- Place ridge on **center** and rotate handle to **vertical**
- Move handle **down** to top plate
- Cantilever ridge beam to **support** the rakes
- Resize the **jambs** to support the **ridge**
- Resize the **ridge** beam to fit **rake** overhangs
- Organize pieces as **named** groups in roof component

RIDGE BLOCK

RAFTER PROFILE

HANDLE

LINE OF TOP PLATE

Lay out rafters for the upper roof

## SET RAFTERS ON THE RIDGE BEAM

Use the gable wall **layout** to fit a rafter to the ridge beam and **trim** overhangs.
Flip-copy the **rafter** and array-copy both rafters along the **top** of the ridge beam.

ShapeRafters

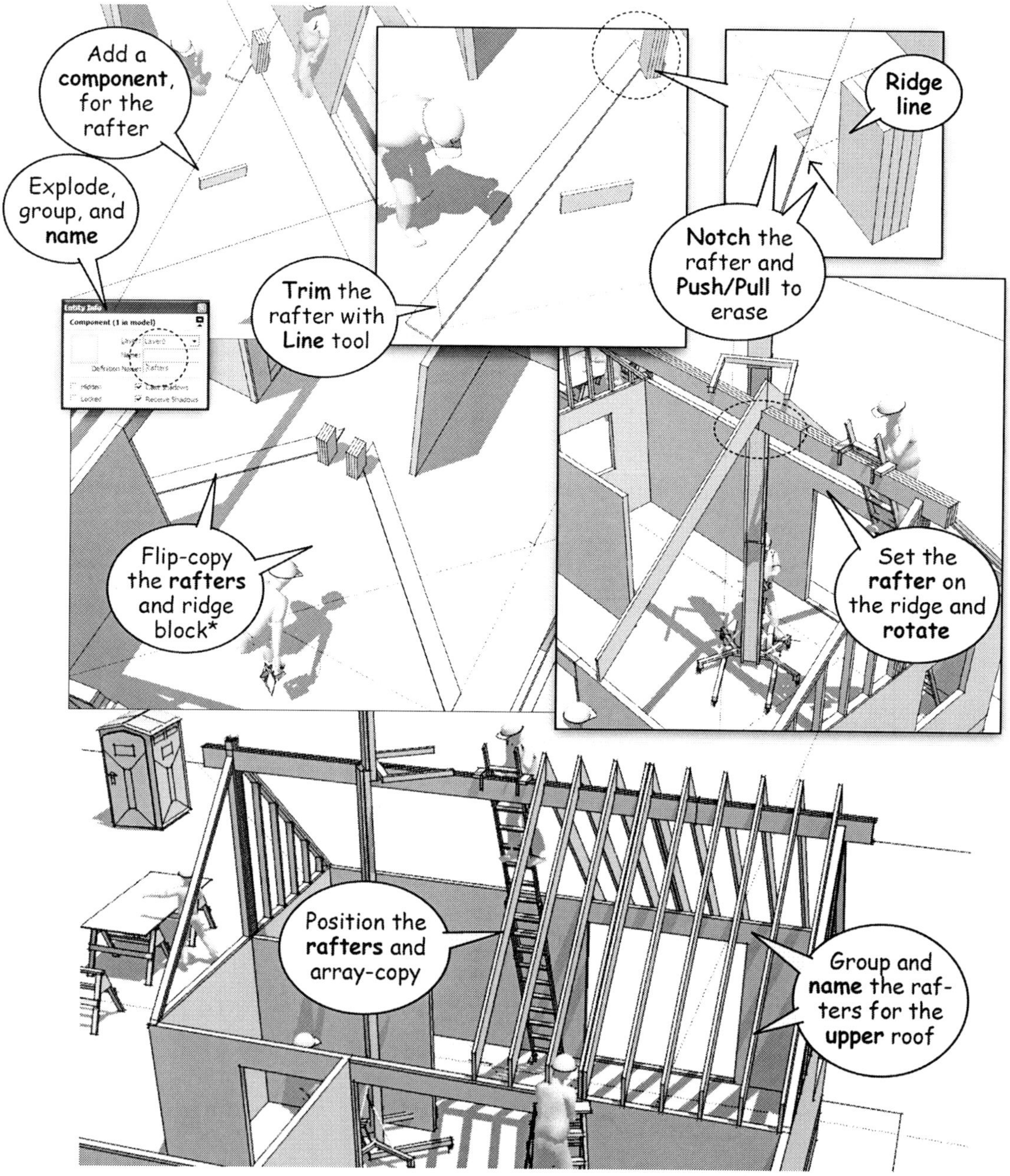

*The ridge blocks are common to both groups and help quickly align the rafters to the ridge (before deleting)

Array-copy the lower rafters

## RAFTERS FOR THE LOWER ROOF

Add a **component** and scale and **slope** it as a rafter to fit the **lower** roof. Explode and name the rafter as a new **component** and array-copy across the bearing walls.

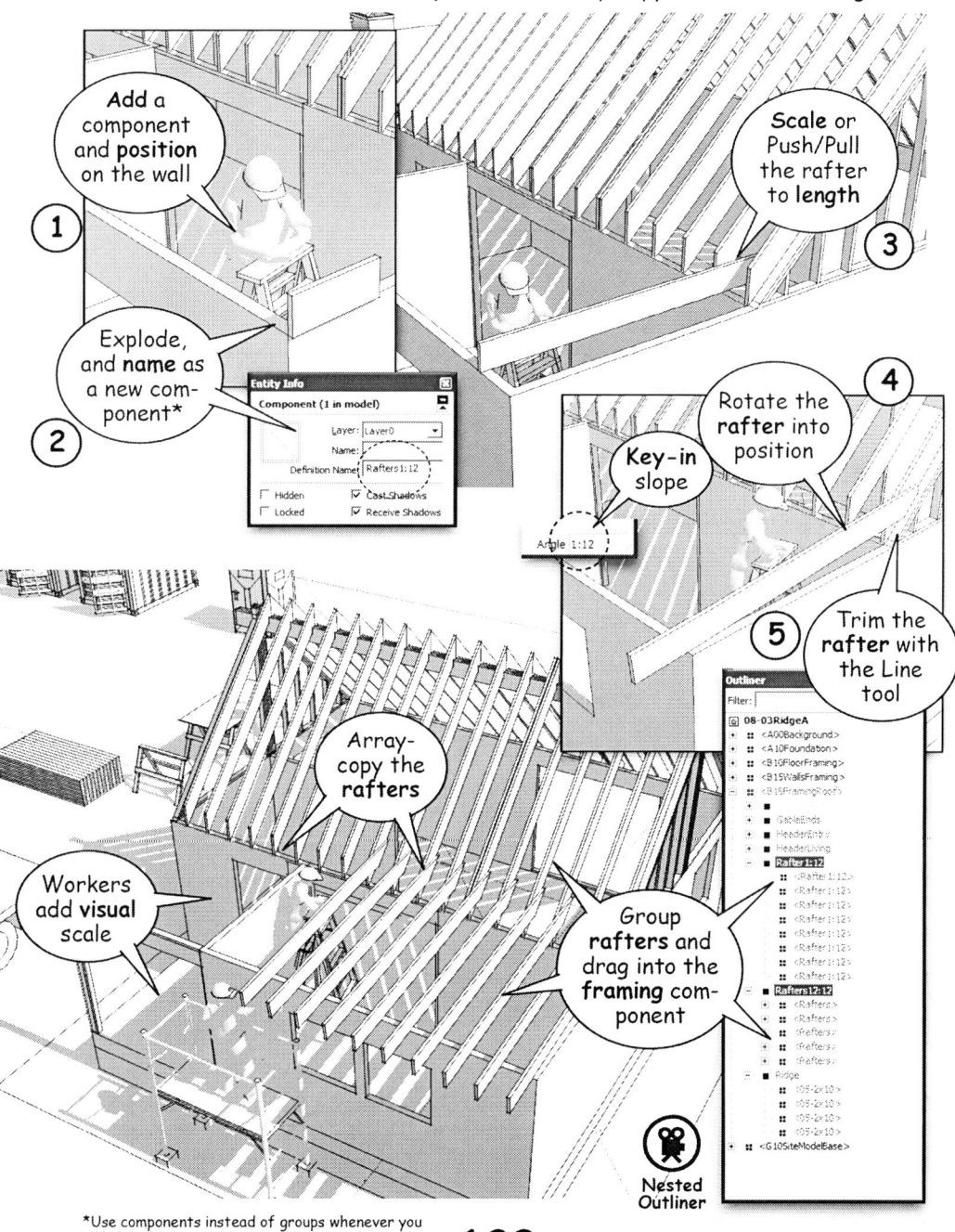

*Use components instead of groups whenever you anticipate changes that will effect multiple copies

## Rake overhangs and fascias

# ADD THE RAKE RAFTERS

Move-copy an **end** rafter to add a rake and trim to fit the ridge, fascia, and supports.

EastRake

GuideAsRail

Add a **guide** line for rake **overhang**

Scale the ridge to **support** the rake overhang

Scale the **fascia** to the length of the rafters

Edit the rafter group to **copy** out a rake rafter

Right-click to **edit** and Push/Pull to **trim** rafters*

Make the rake rafter **unique** and Right-click to edit

Add component and rotate to **match** roof slope

Push/Pull

Cut with the **Line** tool and Push/Pull to **erase**

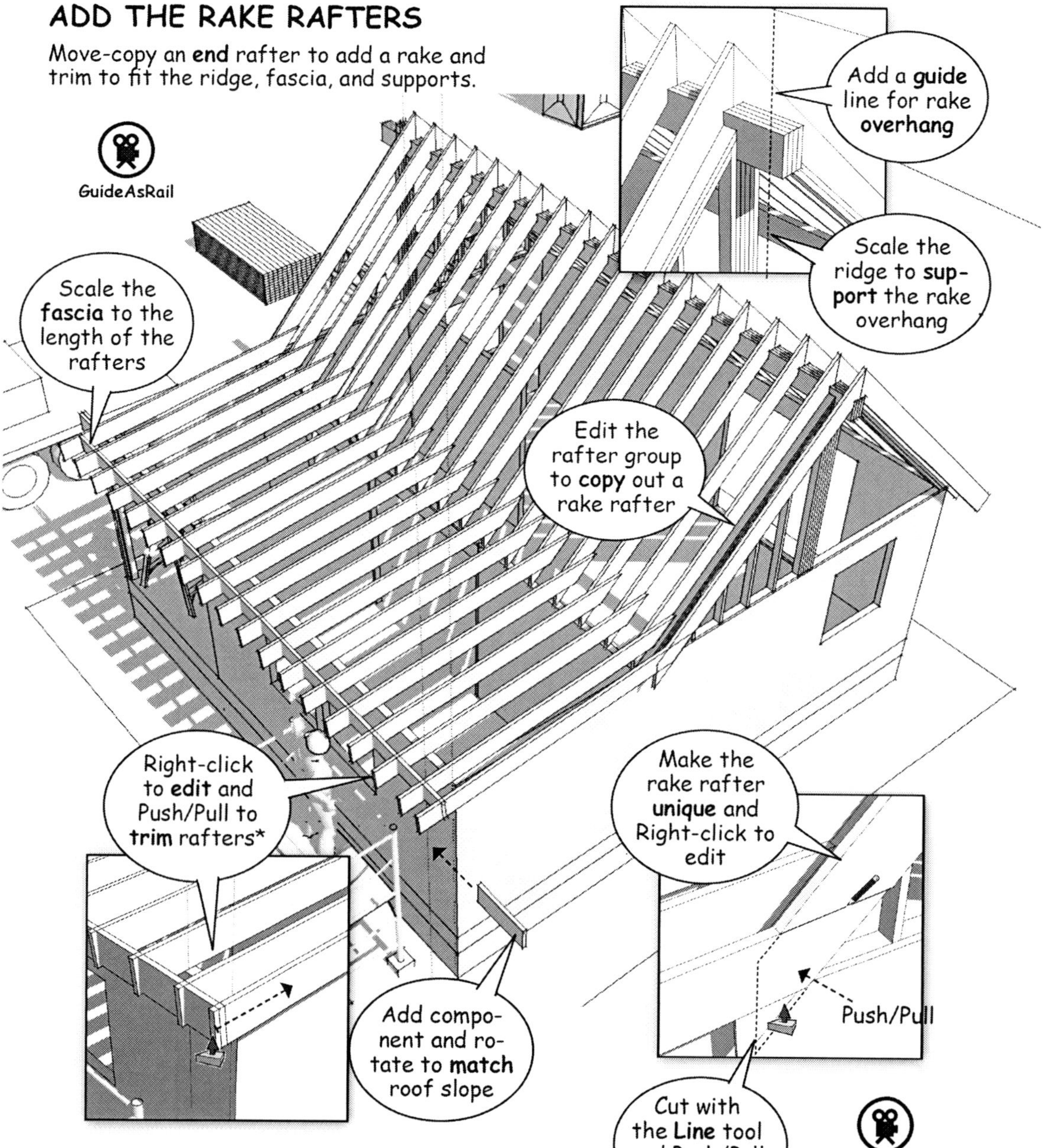

FastFabrication

*Right-click or Double-click to edit the rafter component and all similar components are changed

Ridge&Blocking

## Outlooks and blocking detail the framing

### BLOCKING AND NAILERS

Roof frame is **detailed** with solid blocking at the ridge, outlooks, and **mid-spans** of rafter.

Add a component as **nailer** and scale to **fit** rafters

Add **nailer** and array-copy **along** the ridge

Array-copy the blocking **along** the ridge

Add a **component** for blocking and **scale** to fit

Group the **blocking** and Rotate-copy to **mid-spans**

Array-copy the **nailers** along the **slope** change

Add a **component** nailer and scale to fit rafters

Rotate and Move-copy for **outlook** blocking

LockUnlock

Group and **name** the pieces so they are nested into a larger subassembly

125

**Add rakes and blocking to detail the framing**

WestRake

## MOVE AND ROTATE-COPY

To start, Double-click to edit the roof **framing** component, then Move and Rotate-copy the **grouped** blocking and outlooks to complete the framing on the **west** side.

- Move-**copy** rafter
- Double-click to **open** the roof component
- Move-copy and **scale** blocking
- Scale the **fascia** to fit the **rafters**
- Add a **guideline** and scale to **fit**
- Move-**copy** rafter
- Add a component and **rotate** for fascia
- Move-copy **outlook** blocking from the **east** side

These illustrations are a **visual index** of the video **explanations** on the book's CD

BlockingNorth

### COPY TO THE NORTH SIDE

1. Use the Outliner to select the **grouped** mid-span blocking and outlooks from the south slope.

2. Inside-Out scale the selected groups to **mirror** them for the rafters on the **north** side.

3. Align copies to fit and **rename** in the Outliner.

AddSheathing

Place staggered sheathing on the rafters

## ADD STAGGERED SHEATHING

Remember to use Zoom, Orbit, and Pan tools to **quickly** move around to scale and **fit** sheathing to the rafters.

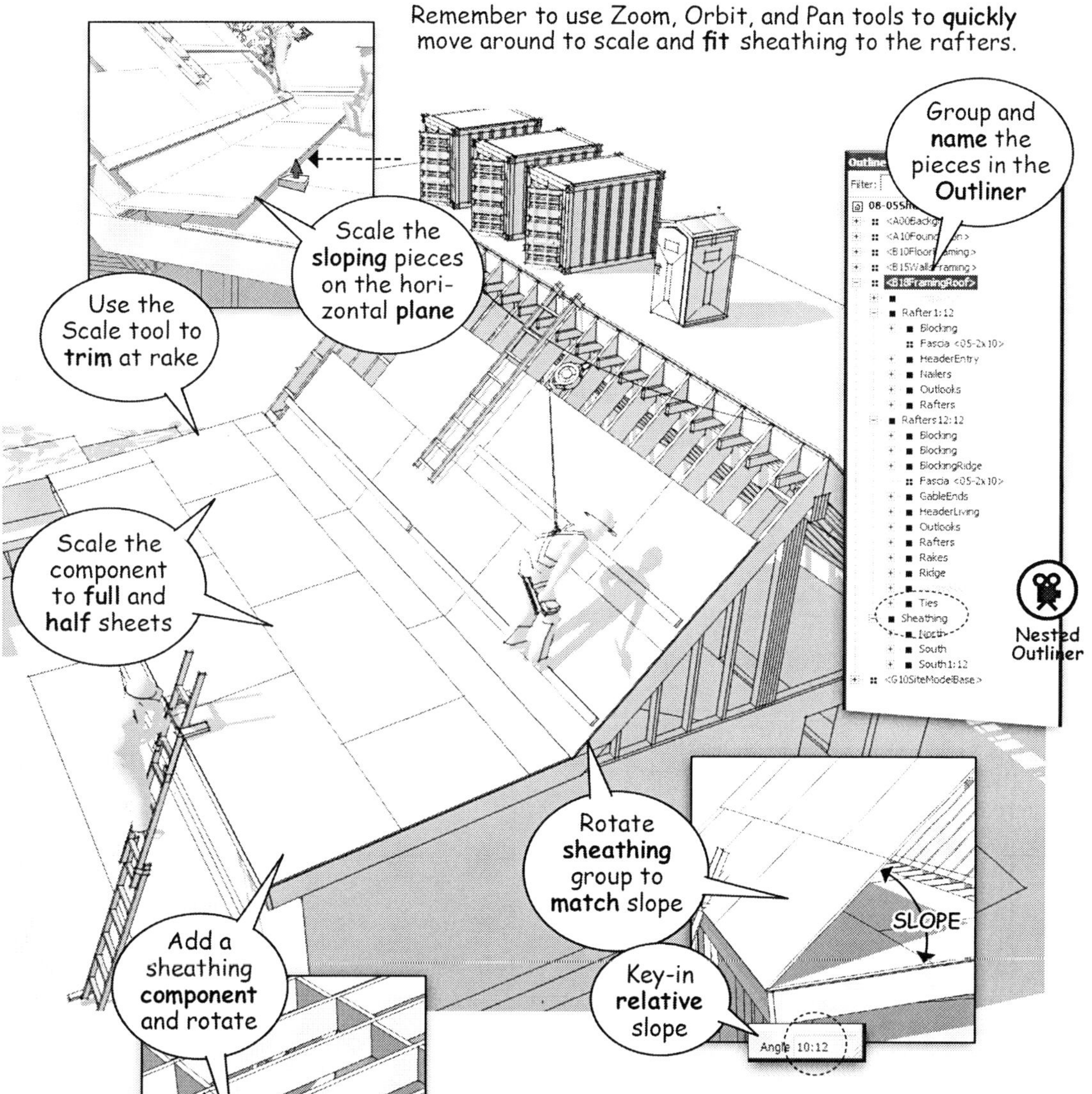

- Group and **name** the pieces in the Outliner
- Scale the **sloping** pieces on the horizontal **plane**
- Use the Scale tool to **trim** at rake
- Scale the component to **full** and **half** sheets
- Nested Outliner
- Rotate **sheathing** group to **match** slope
- Key-in **relative** slope
- Add a sheathing **component** and rotate
- Key-in **slope** of rafters

## COPY TO THE NORTH SIDE

1. Use the Outliner to select the **grouped** sheathing on the upper roof.

2. Rotate the sheathing **180 degrees** to the **north** side of the framing.

3. Align the rotated copy to fit the rafters and **rename** in the Outliner.

127

Reshape the roof dummy to fit framing
RoofDummy

## ROOF DUMMY
**Unhide** the roof dummy and edit the groups to Push/Pull the **surfaces** to fit the roof framing and **support** structure.

- Double-click the **dummy** groups to **edit**
- Use a **transparent** color to see the **framing**
- **Unhide** the roof framing **dummy** in the Outliner
- Push/Pull the **dummy** to tilt the framing
- Push/Pull to the **face** of **rafters** and rakes
- Hide the framing when **dummy** is finished

Double ClickEdit

## CROSS REFERENCES

When the framing components are complete, **Right-click** each phase component in the Outliner and **Save As** to a separate **library** folder.

Each component in the **library** is then a completely separate file referenced from the **same workpoint**.

This means pieces and assemblies can be cut or copied and **pasted-in-place** from one file to another to refine or isolate the details of any one of the foundation or framing models. **Different** versions of the **same model** are then possible for different purposes.*

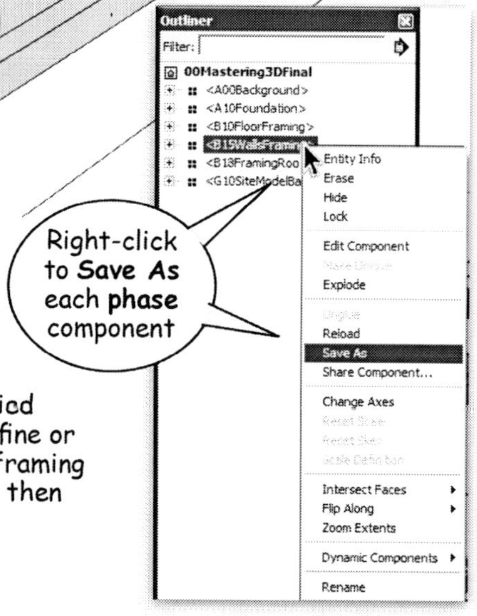

Right-click to **Save As** each **phase** component

*Files are not linked so changes made in one version of the model are not automatically updated in the other file

SectionCut

# The construction model illustrates a process

## CONTROL THE DISPLAY

The completed model can be **displayed** with different pieces or assemblies **visible** in order to visually explain specific details or **sequences** in the construction process.

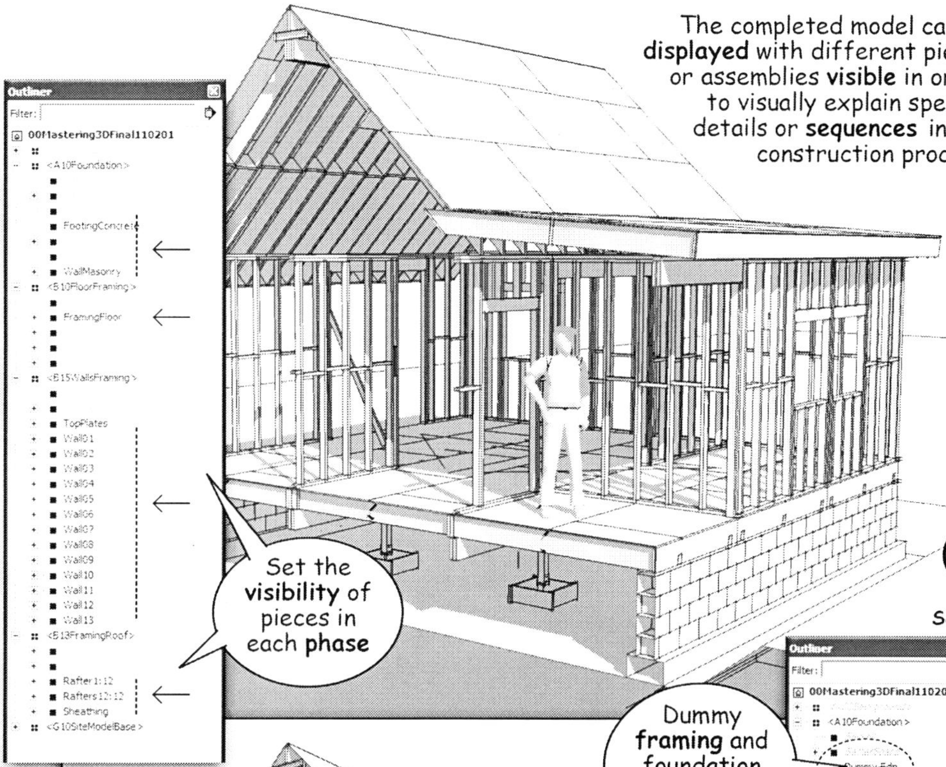

Set the **visibility** of pieces in each **phase**

Setup Sequence

Export Illustrations

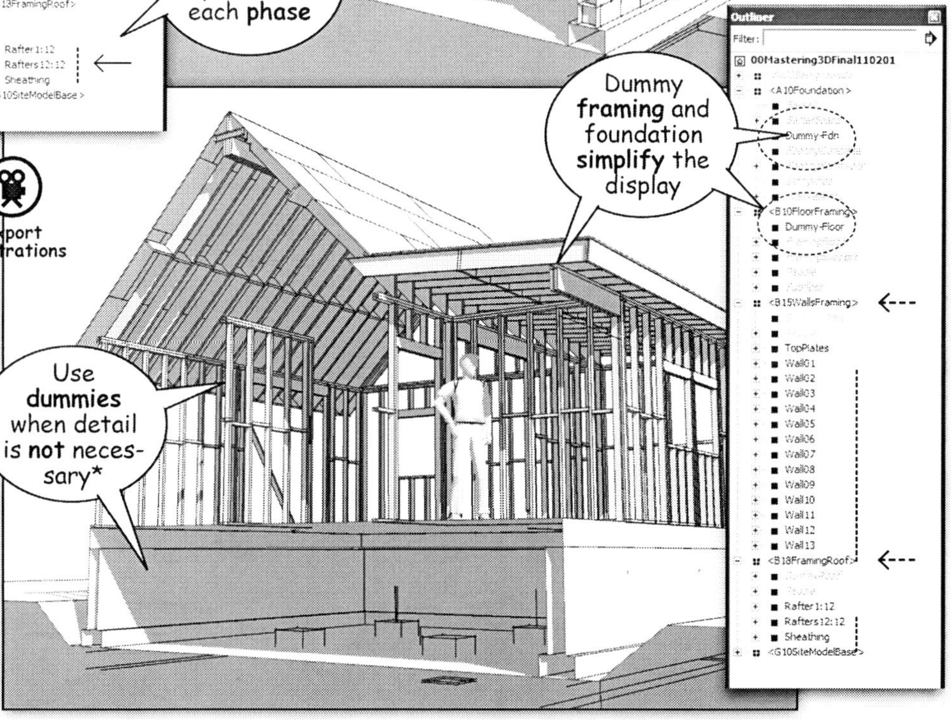

Dummy **framing** and foundation **simplify** the display

Use **dummies** when detail is **not** necessary*

*Use the Outliner, Layer visibility, and Scenes to set up and organize the model for detailed displays

# CHAPTER 8 CHECKLISTS - ROOF FRAMING

RoofFraming Checklist

*Use gable frame for **clerestory** and walls*

## A. FRAMING THE GABLES
Edit the phase dummy and frame the gable ends to support the ridge beam, rafters, and sheathing.

- ☐ Draw a template at the gable
- ☐ Rotate template as guidelines
- ☐ Add components and Explode
- ☐ Rotate and Move-copy to frame
- ☐ Cut and Push/Pull ends to trim
- ☐ Move-copy gable onto the wall
- ☐ Add studs to copy and move
- ☐ Move-copy gables to east side

*Move-copy header from **interior** bearing wall*

## B. ADDING SUPPORTS
Add structural headers along the interior bearing wall and outside entry wall to support the rafter framing.

- ☐ Add header and post components
- ☐ Assemble interior double header
- ☐ Position the header and posts
- ☐ Scale the pieces to fit the opening
- ☐ Move-copy the header to the entry
- ☐ Add a post component to the corner
- ☐ Resize the entry header to fit

*Scale jambs to **form** the ridge beam **pocket***

## C. SET THE RIDGE BEAM
Use the gable template on the subfloor to lay out the ridge and rafters. Mark height of the ridge with a handle.

- ☐ Assemble ridge beam components
- ☐ Lay out ridge and rafter block
- ☐ Draw a handle down to the plate
- ☐ Move ridge/handle to the gable
- ☐ Rotate both and resize ridge
- ☐ Lower handle to set ridge height
- ☐ Adjust gables for beam pockets
- ☐ Scale the ridge to length

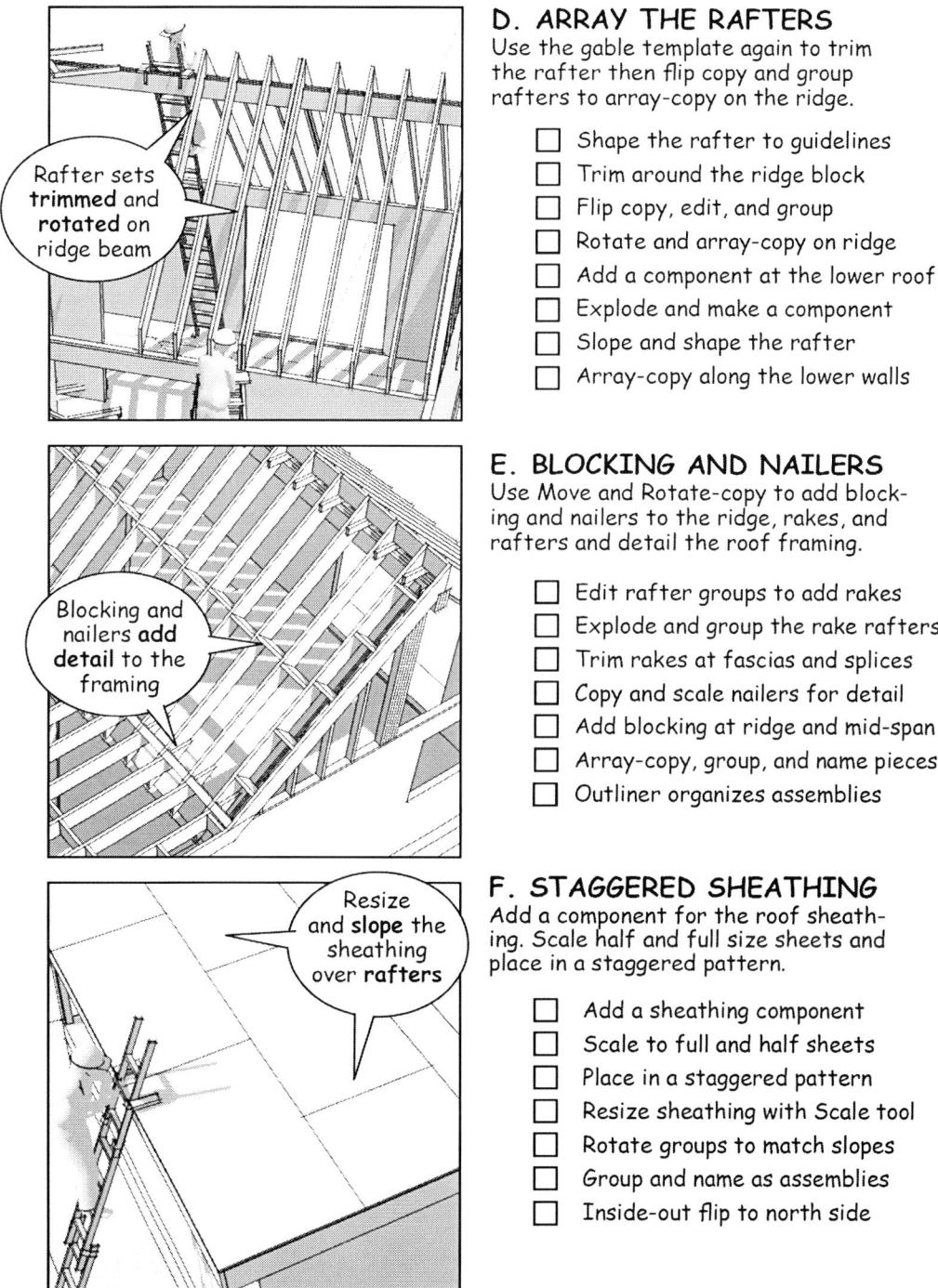

### D. ARRAY THE RAFTERS
Use the gable template again to trim the rafter then flip copy and group rafters to array-copy on the ridge.

- ☐ Shape the rafter to guidelines
- ☐ Trim around the ridge block
- ☐ Flip copy, edit, and group
- ☐ Rotate and array-copy on ridge
- ☐ Add a component at the lower roof
- ☐ Explode and make a component
- ☐ Slope and shape the rafter
- ☐ Array-copy along the lower walls

### E. BLOCKING AND NAILERS
Use Move and Rotate-copy to add blocking and nailers to the ridge, rakes, and rafters and detail the roof framing.

- ☐ Edit rafter groups to add rakes
- ☐ Explode and group the rake rafters
- ☐ Trim rakes at fascias and splices
- ☐ Copy and scale nailers for detail
- ☐ Add blocking at ridge and mid-span
- ☐ Array-copy, group, and name pieces
- ☐ Outliner organizes assemblies

### F. STAGGERED SHEATHING
Add a component for the roof sheathing. Scale half and full size sheets and place in a staggered pattern.

- ☐ Add a sheathing component
- ☐ Scale to full and half sheets
- ☐ Place in a staggered pattern
- ☐ Resize sheathing with Scale tool
- ☐ Rotate groups to match slopes
- ☐ Group and name as assemblies
- ☐ Inside-out flip to north side

Resources for construction modeling

**NOTES:**

Resources for construction modeling

## SKETCHUP LINKS

Download SketchUp (Free)
SketchUcation Forums
SketchUcation Tutorials
Google SketchUp Website
SketchUp Quick Reference Card (Mac / PC)

## LINKS FROM THE CD

Google Maps                Bonnie Roskes's Website
Google Earth               Aidan Chopra's Books
PickPic: Screen Capture    Form Font (Components)
Faststone: Image Editor    GoToSchool
                           SketchUp Wiki

## FILES ON THE CD

Insitebuilders Template file
Insitebuilders Shortcuts file
2D Drawing for the construction model
Plat Map Sample from public records
Satellite Aerial from Google Earth
Insitebuilders Components Library
Insitebuilders Shortcuts Index
Insitebuilders Buzzwords Index
Insitebuilders Tips and Tricks Index
Chapter Checklists (1, 2, 3, 4, 5, 6, 7, 8)
Construction models

    Completed Model
    Phase-Dummies Model
    Floor Framing Model
    Roof Framing Model
    Connectors file

### HELP HELP

Email **anytime** you have a question or problem with the book or CD. We're happy to **help**.

babs@insitebuilders.com

Resources for construction modeling

ShortcutIndex

# SHORTCUT KEYS

## TOOL COMMANDS

- Select (Space)
- Line (w)
- Rectangle (r)
- Circle (c)
- Arc (a)
- Offset (v)

- Orbit (Ctrl-Shift q)
- Pan (Ctrl-Shift s)
- Zoom (Ctrl-Shift z)
- Zoom Window (Ctrl-Shift w)
- Zoom Extents (Ctrl-Shift e)
- Zoom Previous (Shift z)

- Move (b)
- Rotate (Alt r)
- Scale (s)
- Push/Pull (t)

- Tape Measure (f)
- Dimensions (d)
- Protractor (p)
- Components (Ctrl-Shift c)

- Follow Me (Alt t)
- Eraser (e)
- Paint Bucket (Alt p)

*You can change any of the short-cut keys with Preferences in the Windows Menu\**

## MENU COMMANDS

| | |
|---:|---|
| Undo | Ctrl z |
| Redo | Ctrl y |
| Cut | Ctrl x |
| Copy | Ctrl c |
| Paste | Ctrl v |
| PasteInPlace | Ctrl-Shift v |
| Group | g |
| Hide | h |
| UnhideLast | Shift h |
| UnhideAll | Ctrl-Shift h |
| EraseGuides | Alt e |
| HideRest | Alt c |
| Section | Alt s |
| New | Ctrl n |
| Save | Ctrl s |
| All | Ctrl a |
| LookAround | Ctrl q |
| Explode | Alt x |
| Axis | Alt a |
| Text | Alt w |
| Text3D | Alt 3 |

## DIALOG BOXES

| | |
|---:|---|
| ModelInfo | Shift i |
| Entity | Shift e |
| Materials | Shift x |
| Components | Shift c |
| Styles | Shift d |
| Layers | Shift w |
| Outliner | Shift q |
| Scenes | Shift r |
| Shadows | Shift s |

\*You may have noticed that the shortcut keys are all on the left side of the keyboard, using a right-hand mouse,

# BUZZWORD INDEX

**Array-copy**: copy out a line of multiple copies
**Assembly**: a collection of components or groups
**Axis**: red, green, blue directions in 3D space
**Bitmap**: raster image like a JPEG, PNG or TIFF
**Camera**: view point of observer in 3D space
**Colors**: edited material painted on objects
**Component**: a remotely saved SketchUp file
**Ctrl key**: generally use this key to leave a copy
**Ctrl-scale**: resize objects from the center
**Divide-copy**: divide out a line of spaced copies
**Double-click**: to open a group or select 2D surface
**Download**: resource file linked to the book's CD
**Drag**: cursor move with mouse button down
**Dummy**: acts as a low poly substitute for details
**Edges**: the lines that define the edges of an object
**Edit-group**: Right or Double-click to edit group
**Embed**: dummy object or group within a group
**Entity**: an object as a piece of a collective assembly
**Explode**: breakdown a group or component
**Extrude**: 2D to 3D with the Push/Pull tool
**Face style**: different displays of the model
**Flip-copy**: Right-click to flip a copy along an axis
**Follow Me**: extrudes an object along a path
**Group**: a named collection of pieces or assemblies

**Guidelines**: temporary construction chalk lines
**Handle**: bones or the wireframe of an entity
**Hide**: temporarily conceal an object to work behind
**Inferences**: built-in guides and snap points
**Inside-Out**: Scale tool used to mirror copy
**Key-in**: input values while a tool is still active
**Layers**: distinct blocks or subassemblies
**Library**: a proprietary collection of components
**Make Unique**: a new copy of a component for editing
**Model base**: 3D box under the model to be excavated
**Model Info**: settings for the current model
**Modeling method**: 2D+3D+Group&Name
**Move-copy**: toggle the Ctrl key with Move tool
**Nested**: a piece or group in a group in the Outliner
**Object**: an entity or piece of an assembly in 3D space
**Offset**: move or copy with an isolated cursor
**Origin**: the zero point for the 3 axes of 3D space
**Outliner**: organizes the pieces and assemblies
**Phase dummy**: used to simplify level of detail
**Pieces**: entities or objects ready for assembly
**Plumb&Level**: parallel to an axis or flat on a plane
**Poly count**: number of edges and surfaces in an object
**Preferences**: settings for all future models
**Real-world**: technically accurate, scaled to full size

**Reshape**: edit a component with Push/Pull tool
**Resize**: stretch component with Scale tool
**Rotate-copy**: toggle Ctrl key with Rotate tool
**Reshape**: edit a component with Push/Pull tool
**Resize**: stretch component with Scale tool
**Rotate-copy**: toggle Ctrl key with Rotate tool
**Scale**: resize objects without editing using Scale tool
**Screenshot**: captured image for an illustration
**Shape**: edit a group or object to trim distinct objects
**Sequence**: series of Scenes to illustrate a process
**Shift key**: generally constrains or locks to an axis
**Shift-scale**: constrained resize with Scale tool
**Shortie**: a short video explanation or tutorial
**Snaps**: object inference points for assembly
**Staging**: set up the model for a screenshot
**Surface**: the skin or plane between edges
**Styles**: settings change look and feel of the display
**Surface**: the skin or plane between edges
**Template**: common settings saved as a startup file
**Transparent color**: edit any color for transparency
**Triple-click**: selects connected surfaces/edges
**Unhide**: make a hidden object visible again
**Visibility**: selection control in Layers Dialog box
**Visual scale**: components to simulate process
**Workpoint**: point of reference set to Origin

Resources for construction modeling

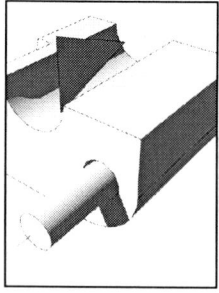

# TIPS & TRICKS INDEX

As your models become more and more **complex**, remember to use components with **dummy** substitutes or stand-ins to **turn off** levels of **detail** or keep components simple until details are added later as the model **evolves**.

CHAPTER 1
01TypicalAssembly - Assemble with inferences, snaps, rotate
02SimplifyColors – Simplify colors and textures to focus on the construction
03HandlesHelp – Add handles to align and guide the assembly
04AlignHandles- Use component and group handles to align the pieces
05OutlinerOverview - Use the Outliner to organize your materials
06GuidelinesGuide - Use guidelines to lay out the construction
07HidingPieces - Hide pieces to edit the model
08ObjectInferences - Object inferences speed assembly
09ScenesSpeed – Use Scenes to speed construction modeling

CHAPTER 2
01EraserTool - The Eraser tool deletes, hides, and smoothes
02FaceStyles - Change Face Styles during construction
03GoogleMap - Use Google Maps, aerials, and Google Earth in 3D
04PrintSend - Print a map or send a link location via email
05EmbedMaps - Embed the map on a website or a html email
06Screenshots - Use screenshots to capture images
07ScaleStar - Use the Scale tool to make a star
08LineScale - Scale a line with a temporary line

CHAPTER 3
01Import&Crop- Import and crop an image in the model
02ImageStretch- Stretch an imported image to fit the site
03StayOrganized - Use the Outliner to name and organize the pieces
04ToggleOrbit - Use the Shift key to toggle between Orbit and Pan
05CheckPlumb&Level - Regularly check for plumb and level
06Dock&Undock - Dock and undock toolbars to customize your workspace
07ComponentLibrary - Build a custom component library
08GoogleWarehouse - Avoid the bloated models in the Google Warehouse

# Resources for construction modeling

## TIPS & TRICKS INDEX

Large and complex models also benefit from computers that have graphics cards with built-in memory. When the computer is set to 100% OpenGL, all 3D calculations are handled by the graphics card, leaving the computer's memory and processor free to run other program activities.

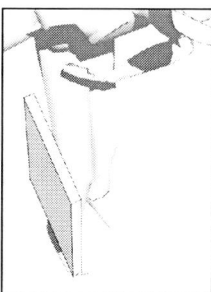

**CHAPTER 4**
01OutlineExcavation - Review the Outliner to organize the excavation phase
02LayerControls - Review visibility controls to hide pieces of the model
03ZoomField - Change the field of view for the Zoom tool
04ZoomPrevious - Zoom Previous to go back to recent viewpoints
05InsideOutFlip - Reverse scaling and mirror flips to copy or edit assemblies
06MoveLock - Left, right, and up arrow keys lock moves and lines to an axis
07TypicalInferences - Use SketchUp inferences to speed the construction
08EquipmentOperation - Use handles as pivots to operate equipment

**CHAPTER 5**
01CopyArrays - Make quickly spaced copies in two ways
02MaintainComponents - Save and update component changes to your library
03FoundationOrganized - Organize the foundation pieces in the Outliner
04DividedAssemblies - Divide assemblies with the line and protractor
05OffsetMove - In tight spaces, move objects using off-set references
06Scale2Fit - Add a component and scale to resize and fit
07HideSplice - Hide edges to form a seamless splice
08PumperOperation - Stage equipment and personnel for screenshots

**CHAPTER 6**
01RotateCopies - Make array and divided copies for fast modeling
02ReviewComponents - Add framing components and scale to fit
03PasteInPlace - Cut objects to a new file with Paste-In-Place for editing
04StayOrganized - Organize the pieces of the floor framing model

**CHAPTER 7**
01WallTypeComponent - Add and modify walls from a library of wall types
02NestedGroups - Access and modify nested groups within groups

**CHAPTER 8**
01LockUnlock - Lock objects to keep them in place while editing
02GuideAsRails - Use guidelines to move and edit objects in space
03DoubleClickEdit - Double-click in the Outliner to edit a piece or group
04NestedOutliner - Use the Outliner again to organize and nest the pieces
05SetUpSequence - Set up a Scene animation for the phases
06ExportIllustrations - Export views and animations as separate files
07FastFabrication - Use Group or Make Unique to edit a single component

## OUR BOOKS

All our books are graphic narratives with detailed illustrations, short tutorials, checklists, resource links, and SketchUp models.

Step-by-step instructions for a model of a wood frame house using trial copy of SketchUp V4

Guide on how to plan, permit, and pay for the construction of a home of your own

Every step in the construction of a wood frame house and its mechanical systems

Every step in the construction of the shell for a mid-rise commercial building

Models and illustration of the building systems in a mid-rise commercial building

Plans and details of 20 traditional and unconventional small houses and the lessons they give